Carl —— Solo I.

Position — on floor — "Sister"
Beat of shoulders —
use of arms
rise into Bali attitude on knees
turn and fall on hip
Repeat beat of shoulders
come into 4th Sit 2nd on
knees to Jason —
Rise — face front —

Warrior stance } 2 X
knee vibrations
to front

Back fall on shoulders
facing Jason —

Come to 4th —
wide turn with rise.

3 Darts to R.
" " " L
{ Beat R. leg across body
{ Beat L. foot in profile
3 X
into small turn —

Lifted L. leg in profile
banking upstage to
Jason —

Pull skirt in profile
3 X to snake

Jump 2 X
Circle around to face snake
Back shoulder fall
Recover to original
position —
Beats of shoulder
Bali attitude
Turn into lean back
on both knees —
Sit —
Hip circles — 11
walking with leg high

Spring —
Seated on porch — face upstage
1) Run into st. center with semi —
knees — use arms —
3 x
2) Turns upstage — with lift of
hands —
3) Kneel to preacher — to straight — to reach —
Bow to girls — to preacher
4) little walk in a left front
hands lightly resting
at shoulders, r - l - etc
5) ½ turns in place — clapping
hands — silently — 4 x

The Notebooks of Martha Graham

The Notebooks of MARTHA GRAHAM

WITH AN INTRODUCTION BY

Nancy Wilson Ross

Harcourt Brace Jovanovich, Inc., New York

Excerpts from these Notebooks first appeared in *The American Scholar*.

To
Lila Acheson Wallace
an expression of gratitude
for
her recognition of
"Divine Turbulence"
as manifested in Man's notebooks
whether they be in
stone or in dance

Contents

The Notebooks

Introduction

To embark on a journey through the working notebooks
kept by Martha Graham for many years of her active creative
life as a dancer, dramatist, designer, choreographer is—
to borrow one of her own inspired titles—an Errand into the
Maze. The casual, almost domestic, word "errand" is not intended
to imply a facile undertaking any more than it did when Miss
Graham attached it to her interpretation of the Ariadne and
Theseus legend. This journey, for Martha Graham, the artist
who embarked on it and indicated the signposts along the way,
represents a lifetime's search for meanings and fulfillments.
For the receptive reader the journey, though at first it may
appear impossibly labyrinthine, can well become high and
rewarding adventure, the nature and degree of his participation
depending on his own private Ariadne's thread, that is to say,
his own intellectual and intuitional development, tastes,
background and education. If this hypothetical reader is
attracted to and even enlightened by symbolism and classical
mythology, by legends from all lands and times, by the poetic
extravagances of the Celts, the passionate dramas of the
Bible, the mysteries of the "Great Within" of Asian sages,
the theories, thoughts, insights of Carl Jung, Heinrich Zimmer,
Joseph Campbell, James Joyce, St. John Perse, T. S. Eliot,
Dante, Rilke—to name only a few of the many well-springs from
which Miss Graham has drunk so deeply—then this is his book.

If he is a dancer or actor he may marvel more than general
readers at the uses to which Miss Graham was able to put this
tenuous record of "mind-stuff," its subtle employment in those
remarkable dramatic projections—through bodies in movement on
stripped stages—which have brought her world fame. Yet it is
not necessary to be a dancer, or even a dance aficionado to
respond to these notebooks. Much of the material could well
belong in a private compilation of mankind's collective wisdom
similar to Huxley's *The Perennial Philosophy*. Although Miss
Graham's admitted "piracies" reach us here winnowed through
one woman's intellect and imagination, the result is a vast

universal storehouse of myths and illuminations, many of them long-buried and only now brought to light because of shifts and changes in contemporary cultural attitudes. In the creative interpretation and use of such neglected subjective material, in the activation of those mythic symbols that can, in Campbell's words, "evoke and direct psychological energy" Martha Graham has been for decades, in her world of dance-drama, the unquestioned forerunner.

Paul Valéry, in a famous essay on Leonardo da Vinci (who also kept prodigious notebooks), observed that few great artists ever had the courage to say how they produced their works. Courage is a very strong word. Is it perhaps not so much lack of courage as over-concern with the end-products of their gifts that disinclines most artists to leave us more than the vaguest hints of how, in the secret recesses of creativity, tentative shapes moved toward realization? Or is it genuinely beyond their powers to practice Graham's special kind of attentive inattention, at once precise and unfocused and as delicately precarious as that difficult exercise of holding on to the swiftly vanishing images of a dream?

Whatever the explanation of Miss Graham's rare achievement we must remain eternally in her debt for these records which permit us to see how creative events transpired within her and how trusted reliance on the processes of free association, linked with a truly Faustian will, enabled her to summon forces whose later assimilation and externalization were to demand almost the whole of a many-sided nature.

In firm ink strokes, or swift pencillings, she has covered uncounted (literally) pages with private clues to her working methods. As spectators we are invited to accompany her as she searches, probes, reads, ruminates, questions, rejects, accepts diverse compelling gleams and ghosts, signs and symbols from the "holy jungle" of mankind's imagination, including, of course, her own. At last we have been allowed to enter the magical alchemical workshops from which emerged such evocative archetypes as Medea, Clytemnestra, Phaedra, Jocasta, Judith, the Witch of Endor, Mary Queen of Scots, Emily Dickinson, the Brontë sisters, Héloïse, Joan of Arc—and their attendant partners, protagonists, lovers and victims.

Here also are the first tentative outlines of notable choreographic stencils employed later, in whole or in part, to guide her and her dance company in expressions of what might be considered essentially inexpressible truths about life and death: that heady Graham mixture of love, hate, greed,

lust, tenderness, ambition, deceit, grief, rage, remorse set
forth in theatrical terms with an original kinetic vocabulary
and in a manner at one and the same time explicit and abstract.

Miss Graham is quite willing, even one might say eager,
to admit her debt to the many literary and philosophical spirits
who have, in their special way, helped to effect that mysterious
metamorphosis whereby poetic abstractions assume for her living
dramatic shapes. In one of the very rare passages where the
pronoun "I" appears she cries out:

"I am a thief—and I am not ashamed. I steal from the
best wherever it happens to me—Plato, Picasso, Bertram Ross."
And then, as if warning her own troupe, she suggests that no
member of her company show her anything unless they expect her
to "steal" it:

"I am a thief—and I glory in it—

"I steal from the present and from the glorious past—
and I stand in the dark of the future as a glorying and joyous
thief—There are so many wonderful things of the imagination
to pilfer—so I stand accused—I am a thief—but with this
reservation—I think I know the value of that I steal & I
treasure it for all time—not as a possession but as a heritage & as legacy."

One is reminded here of an often-quoted line from Emerson,
"The greatest genius is the most indebted man," a line on
which R. H. Blyth, whose comparative studies of Japanese haiku
and English literature must have also received Miss Graham's
far-ranging attention, comments dryly, "and it is not *what* is
borrowed that matters." Miss Graham would agree with Blyth's
dictum. Not the borrowing but the uses to which it is put—
there is the crux of the matter!

By her engaging candor about borrowing or even stealing,
Miss Graham effectively frees us to trace the many influences—
both subtle and direct—that have played on her imagination
during her long, distinguished career, and to which she has
so creatively responded. To the various theatres of the Far
East she brought an immediate appreciation, an acute perception.
There are a number of references to Asian theatre arts. We
find notations suggesting movement that is "Balinese" or
"Javanese" woven into the measures of her own special dance
techniques, and anyone who has made the most cursory study of
the ancient classic Noh drama of Japan can readily find com-
parisons between it and the Graham repertoire. In the Noh, as
in Graham, the audience faces an almost bare stage on which
stage properties have been reduced (or elevated) to symbols.

Stylized movement is required to express passionate emotional states and violent crises of the spirit. Frequently a single dancer-actor may serve as a detached observer of the action taking place before him. The emphasis in the "story" often falls on ghosts, on a past that is, nonetheless, still vitally alive in the present.

Miss Graham did not copy her theatrical conventions from the Japanese theatre, although the Noh probably strengthened and affirmed many of her own visions. The truth is that in the Graham world the sense of time is not linear or Western but cyclic and "Oriental"—if one may be permitted the use of this rather indefinite, but readily comprehensible, term. Her time-sense must account, at least in part, for her ability to dramatize given moments in the life of a character and, with no loss of theatrical vigor—in truth with the most forceful imme-diacy—to require that her audience accept as a unity an inescapable, inextricable commingling of past, present, future caught together in the illusory net of the Now.

Miss Graham has, it would seem plain, always understood fate in a special way. It is no more surprising to come on the once alien word "karma" used in suggestive context than it is to find Eliot's line from the *Four Quartets:* "In my beginning is my end."

Clytemnestra, the creation generally accepted as the high point of her work as an artist, offers perhaps the best illus-tration of her particular approach to time, plot and character. When the curtain rises on Clytemnestra the audience finds her already in the Underworld; she has come to "that most deep and subterranean end of wandering." Yet even in Hell, Clytemnestra remains true to the exigencies of her fiery nature and we see her, in the first act, defying the very king of Hades himself. Why, she demands to know—by movement, not words, of course—is she being so terribly punished when she has, in fact, done nothing worse than any of the other participants in the fateful drama that began—or did it?—when her beautiful sister, Helen, was abducted by Paris and thus started the tragic Trojan War?

It has been stated that there was never a written script for Graham's *Clytemnestra.* If this is true one hazards the guess that it is because a script was not needed, Martha had immersed herself to the saturation point in the lives of the fateful participants in this classic myth from that ancient Greek repository on which she has drawn for years with incomparable brilliance.

Although there is no working script for *Clytemnestra*

there are in these notebooks many pages headed *Studies for Clytemnestra*, and scattered elsewhere a number of passages suggesting costumes, properties, stage decor, music and the exact dance language required for telling this particular tragedy in Graham terms. These *Clytemnestra* pages contain many significant clues to Graham's working methods, as when she suggests to herself, "The use of moveable scenery—curtains—a torch—a tent—a litter—all to be carried on—or contrived—from a cape, a coat, a cloak." The word "contrived" is a key word. It indicates one major difference between Graham's use of symbolic stage properties and the Noh. The latter does not permit improvisation; Graham's theatricality, on the contrary, has remained singularly fluid. She has never been excelled in investing simple stage properties with symbolic and dramatic meaning. The cape in *Clytemnestra* is a supreme example of inspired, non-literal use of an object to heighten drama and advance the plot. The extravagant length of cloth used by Clytemnestra as a magnificent queenly robe serves also as a curtain for a doorway opening on doom; she herself offers it as "the royal purple" for Agamemnon, the arrogant returning hero, to tread underfoot; and lastly it becomes the funeral drapery of the cart which carries away the victims of her vengeful rage.

Some of the pleasure to be had in reading these notebooks, if one is familiar with the Graham repertoire, is searching for first glimpses of certain remembered stage properties that conveyed the deeper meaning of a given drama: the ominous earth-stabbing staff by which blind Tiresias announced his arrival; the rope by which Jocasta eventually killed herself; the weaving of the net that inexorably bound together Clytemnestra, Iphigenia, Orestes, Helen, Agamemnon; the Zen-like flower so tellingly thrust through the axle-hole of the wheel Hercules must lift in his heroic labors. But whether these, or other particular symbols, were noted down or not, or for that matter noted down and then never used, does not lessen their visual impact either in memory or in Graham's descriptive shorthand. Near the middle of the book one comes on an unforgettable image of a wheel (a frequently recurring Graham symbol), here designed to be used as a part of Clytemnestra's make-up. The queen is already in the Underworld, a ghost. There is a "tragic cry of recognition"—(a silent cry of course): "The Wheel." At this point the Graham imagination takes a characteristic leap: "A tracery of gold to fit over face—when she is ghost she wears it—when she is alive she is without it."

Graham very seldom used words to accompany her dance-dramas. (*Letter to the World* is the outstanding exception.) Yet her fascination with language, its power to stimulate and evoke images, is undeniable. "In the beginning was the Word, and the Word was with God, and the Word was God" she reminds herself and gives us the exact Biblical reference: John 1:1. There is no mystery about her fascination with verbal language as one among many kinds of language. Words are a means of communication and it is communication that concerns her no matter on what level of the conscious, the unconscious, or the preconscious it may take place. Why does she make a special note of the title of Dr. John C. Lilly's *Man and Dolphin*? She tells us herself. Because it is a book "concerning the attempts to communicate with other species." After repeating the word dolphin, as though to fix its image better in her mind, she writes the name of Shakespeare and then the names of Antony and Cleopatra and here the onflowing stream of free association brings her the specific image for which her kinetic sense has perhaps been groping; an image that may just possibly prove useful at some later time. She quotes from Act V Scene 2 of *Antony and Cleopatra:*

> His delights
> Were dolphin-like, they showed his back above
> The element they lived in.

Although we have said that time for Graham does not stretch out in a straight progression from a present "here" to a future, or past "there," her notebooks indicate, as already mentioned, an interest—also paradoxical—in "beginnings." She even goes so far, in one of the very rare personal passages in many years of note-taking, to speak of actual beginnings in relation to herself:

"People say—
How did you begin?
Well—that is the question
And who knows—
Not I—
How does it all begin?
I suppose it never begins, it just continues—"

And then, after some further thought in the same vein, we find these words of almost Puritan resignation: "But one takes up . . . the necessity of one's heritage and in time it may become one's 'calling', one's 'destiny', one's 'fame', one's 'immortality'."

Since no artist has ever more fiercely guarded her own private life, her own personal myth, it is not surprising in reading this map of a mind's journeyings to come on so few references of an intimate nature. If one does appear it can be wrenchingly abrupt, as when she suddenly speaks of the "lonely terrifying gifts" life has thrust upon her. Then for a moment or two she may ruminate: Why does she dance, why does she, for that matter, keep these notebooks; why, strangest of all— under affectionate firm pressure from outside herself—has she agreed to perhaps, maybe, sometime, allow a book to be made of these subjective jottings. "Is it a need to affirm a faith?" she wonders.

Certain tenuous fragments of her own legend are known to close friends. One is the story of how, when she was a child, she told a lie to her doctor-father and to her amazement he knew she was lying. When she asked him how he knew he told her that her body had given her away. This is the origin, perhaps, of Graham's often-quoted dictum: "Movement never lies." "At 4 or 5" (her age at the time) she remarks rather wryly, "that was an admonition—'Lie' in a Presbyterian household was and still is a clanging word."

Although she does not speak here directly of the episode with her father, to which, in later years, certain threads of creative connection have been woven, she is kind enough to give us one swift sketch of this same "small person of 4 or 5." Not listening, though "of course she was," she overheard adult members of her family describing a certain grown-up young lady who "carried her head in a strange way." When this same young lady came to the house to call one day "the small person of 4 or 5" (no "I" even here, one notes) began to circle around the visitor, "looking, wondering, pondering, imitating— experimenting—grotesquely, lavishly, intensively—" until after mystification, amusement, and at last discomfiture, a member of what is referred to as "a small assembly" was able to per- suade "the young person of 4 or 5" to go to "Lilywhite's Party— which it took time to fathom meant 'bed'—nothing more."

It is only human to snatch greedily at such small crumbs of anecdote. In these pages they are never of the dimension of a "revelation." An eager psychologist might, of course, seize on "Presbyterian household" and build from it a thesis of creative opposites: tension and counter-tension, attraction and repul- sion, hidden guilts and frank erotica that weave in and out of Graham dance structures, but her own writings will give him precious little help in his work for she can spring straight from the pale Calvinistic shadows, the accepted proprieties of a conventional upbringing, into a far wider landscape of vaster heights and deeper chasms. She extends "movement never lies" into "God is pure act," quoting from the noted scholar of Hinduism, Ananda Coomaraswamy, and then she proceeds to find visual extension for a thought of such a lofty nature in Zimmer's words on Indian mudras (those stylized gestures by which devout Hindus have for centuries given praise to the All Highest): "expressions and supports of spiritual resolve."

Impossible as it is to describe or accurately assess the vital impact of these notebooks, one could, if pressed, list some of the swiftly changing moods they engender with their often surreal, mystifying, tantalizing, yet continuously stimulating manner of expression. Certainly among responses one will find regret: regret for the fact that her notes on the dance-drama *Pocahontas* never came to choreographic form, that the outline of a brilliant film script on *The Scarlet Letter* never grew beyond its outline. Although there has been little in these pages that could be called intimately personal they have succeeded in conveying a vivid awareness of the personality behind them, along with a feeling of having shared something of the yearnings, gropings, failures, the realizations, triumphs and fulfillments of an artist's nature. One leaves them with a clearer sense of how great gifts, and the hard-won necessary supports for these gifts, can be transformed and even shared with others less richly blessed, or cursed, with a creator's vision and temperament.

"This is an ecstatic voyage," Martha Graham tells us just before she warns, "Please do not embark with me unless you know the destination, an arrivement at a port of call (the self) where the cargo is demanded." And then teasingly, tantalizingly, slyly the words, "It is 5 minutes to 12. . . . Tchelicheff."

These are not the words with which Miss Graham closes the notebooks she has chosen to share with us. They can, however, serve as well as any others to remind us once more of what is probably her most significant contribution to the dance-drama of the world: her ability to bring into intense physical expression a private vision of the transient beauty and awesome compulsion, the fateful interweaving of past and future in any single moment of the forever Now.

Nancy Wilson Ross

Beggar Prophet
A Provocative Fragment

Drawing by Mark Tobey, from the collection of Nancy Wilson Ross

The Beggar —
The Prophet
The Poet
The Dancer
The Acrobat
The Seer
The Warrior
The Victor
The fool —
The Jester —
The Rogue —

aflame
Mass as speaker
Wiesgal —
I —
Chapter 1 —
Episode 1
"My private madness" — (34)

    — "Do come nearer"
"If he is strange it is because he is possessed of a strange memory" —
   4 —
"The game is rigged" 8 — Wesel
"Sorry, friend, it isn't you" — 9
"I — I played with children" (11)
"a name — a secret" — (11)
"Laughter can provoke morals" (33)
"If man be a messenger of man why should a madman be a messenger
   of God?" (37)

Errand into the Maze
Studies

Miscellaneous notes

Tobit —
Tobias & the angel —
  (see Fable of the Grateful Dead
     Apocrypha (185)

The aged one — Death
  Sphinx —
      M.G —
Satan as instrument of God
     Cohan
Dreamer — Victim — Poet
   St. Anthony Bert —
He dragon
She dragon

Fish
deer with horns

"Hammer of witches"
  Bosch Skira — (18)

"The temptation of the Hermit"
  Bosch — (11)
"Brotherhood of Our Lady"
  (Bosch)
"Terrible frivolities of Hell"

"St. Anthony — Temptation"
    (Bert?)

---

7 Deadly Sins —
 Anger
 Vanity

The Hay Wagon
  (Bosch)
1) An Episode of the Struggle for life
2) Of Dragons

Adoration of the Magi
  (Clive)   Black
            Mass —
            Clive
Skira (46)

A Time of Anguish
"A laugh was laughed
The earth was split
The sun is up
A red rift in the sky"
  Johannes R. Becher
(Bosch — Skira) — (53)
"No, 'not always shall we dally in these yellow lands, today's delight'."

  at beginning —
? Fight ————
      Magi ———— Clive
      Satan ————Bob Cohan

Perhaps —
      Sybil
as Magdalene
      from beginning
Clive —
      King of the East
Bob —
      Satan
Dudley —
      Dragon —

"The Road of Trials"
      (1000 faces — 97)
"The Ultimate Adventure"
      (1000 faces — 109)

Magdalene — { Bellini?
              Florence
              Donatello?
  The various ways —
        — not good — obscene

The neophyte to God — dedicated
The Aphrodite — the dream of men —
              Lady of the Labyrinth
The Sibyl — ancient one —
The Young One —
        (The Virgin —)
The Moon Goddess —
The Hippie —
The Provocateur –
The Taboo figure
The Mother (Jocasta)
The Queen of Heaven —
    ("Jeremiah — 7")
cakes to the Queen of Heaven —

Lady of the Labyrinth
    (a jar of honey)

Priest of the Rites —
        Youth — Powell? —
        Young, cruel — lonely.

Perhaps each man kisses her mouth (Lady of the Labyrinth) —
The humble arrogant one who washes the feet of the unseen god (Jesus)
with her hair (Phyllis?)
God is not seen — just the image of feet —
The Sound from the Earth
The Dawning of Light —

The invocation of the $\begin{cases} \text{poet} \\ \text{man} \end{cases}$

    Bert —
    Bob

The negation of the Lord of Death
                    (Devil) —
Battle between poet & death
The demand from the men
The Emergence of the Lady of the Labyrinth with her various aspects

The removal of the grime & the emergence of the hair — gold as in
statue in Florence
        the forgotten beauty —
Magdalene thru the ages —
always available —
never possessed —
The Sibyl
    at the mercy of the Voice of life —
    the commanded —

The Prophetess
The Dancer
The Creator
The Young
The Beloved
The Goddess
The Courtesan

Thus the woman is the original seeress, the lady of the wisdom-bringing
waters of the depths, of the murmuring springs and fountains, for the
'original utterance of seerdom is the language of water'. But the woman
also understands the rustling of the trees & all the signs of nature,
with whose life she is so closely bound up.

Scene opens —
    sound —
    light, slowly
    woman with long gold hair walks to the back & disappears — fades —
                                                                 pales?

The Poet enters
Dance to the Hair —
At end of dance she turns — Her face is a mask of the Gorgon
He falls —
Men summon her presence as goddess
She appears with her court of aspects
        Sibyl —
Her dance as Sibyl
Men make her what they want — lift her — lift legs, lift arms —
She does a mad dance of prophecy — what the world demands of
a goddess — a Magdalene —
                        _____

Then she sits enthroned while her aspects dance —
                        _____

See
    Cicero — Ecologues — IV
(Masks of Occ. God, Campbell — 325)
Cicero's "dream of Africanus, the Younger"

The Sound
The Light
Sybil walks to back —
    long golden (?) hair —

The Questioner (Orpheus)
Dance of supplication
        (use of lyre or bow?)
Sibyl turns
The mask of the Gorgon is on her face – It is large – she holds it.
Questioner — suppliant — falls.
Perhaps Sibyl advances & takes masque & hair & covers suppliant
   (Orpheus)
She dances —
She ceases —
Men enter & invoke her in dance — Orpheus still prone —
Sibyl dances again — as tho' going into trance — Each man kisses her —
Men manipulate her legs, arms, body, as tho she is in a state
of hypnosis — a puppet of the Gods —
She ceases —
Women enter as priestesses,
                (prostitutes?)
semi-mad —
(Take mask from Orpheus?)
Bring Orpheus to life again
He is dazed —
Sibyl dances in real madness.
?mask could become curtain thru which he passes?

Labyrinth —
   sound
   light
   architect

"The lore of Dreams"
"Net Imagery"
(Burning Fountain. 245)
_____

Dance
1)   Darkness
2)   Serpents & women —
_____

Net Making —

Frontier: photograph by Barbara Morgan

Imaginary Gardens
Some of these notes are the inspiration for
One Other Gaudy Night,
a rarely performed work

"Imaginary Gardens"

not?

. . . "till the poets among us can be
        'literalists of
    the imagination' — above
            insolence & triviality & can present
for inspection, 'imaginary gardens with
            real toads in them',
        shall we have
it. In the meantime, if you demand on the one hand,
the raw material of poetry in
    all its rawness and
that which is on the other hand
genuine, you are interested in poetry"
                    M.M. Poetry 41

~~~~~~

A Pavilion — or summer house
            or
bird cage in the Chinese manner — like Hongkong (later)
What is an "imaginary garden"?

It is a place more wondrous than any actually beheld garden —

There are no limits to the flowers or trees grown there
            or
the possibilities of behavior there.

This concept and the idea of "Love Letter" could combine.
It is sinister — terrifying — beautiful — joyous —

"For love that will gaze an eagle blind"
        Trollope — Barchester Towers
        (see M.M. notes 163)

Letter from the moon
            the arctic —
        extrasensory perception —

Beloved —
    I love you — I desire you —
    I miss you — I am well —
    I am doing my job —
    I shall communicate with you at 10 P.M. (Time)

in the summer house
    our   "   "
    our pavilion —
    Please be there —

From a station in outer space
    from
a pioneer
an explorer

a man's voice as she enters the summer house —
    Hello, darling —
    You are wearing my dress —
    Remember —

It is his voice which pushes the walls aside — opens the barriers —
"I keep an ottoman in my heart exclusively for you."   208
                Life & Letters of E. D.
                    (Bianchi)

                Fugue
In the over all there are 3 sections
                _____

                Section I
Has 3 statements of theme
Each statement followed by its own episode —
    The episode is rhapsodic
                1st Statement
6 measures of statement
6   "   " episode
                2nd Statement
in nature of a trio
    2 women — 1 man —
8 measures — statement
        2 women (man enters on 8)
3 measures — Episode — all 3 —

Section I

                Third Statement

    4 measures –
        man begins
        2 women enter

6 measures — 1st episode
7   "   2nd   "
10   "   3rd   "
                 (5 + 5)

                              End of Section I

        "One other gaudy night"
        Antony & Cleopatra —
A. . . . but now I'll set my teeth,
    And send to darkness all that stop me.
                    Come,
    Let's have one other gaudy night — "

C — "It is my birthday:
    I had tho't to have held it poor; but since my lord
    Is Antony again, I will be Cleopatra"

Eno — Now he'll outstare the lightning . . .
        . . .
                I will seek
    Some way to leave him. . . .
                    Act 3 — Scene 11 —

Guitar — 6 pieces for lute —
                ⎧ guitar player
characters ⎨ Fortune Teller (Oracle)
                ⎩ man

            Dancers —
                Bert
                Helen
                Ethel
                Paul?
                Akiko
                Linda
                Dick

Lines — "Art of Wisdom" Gracian
        (spoken at ends of pieces — guitar tuning —
        etc — during lines)

Life Studies –
   suggested by Rob't Lowell —
       or
Life Study —
   The technic   joy
   The barre   anger
   Duets   passion
   Solos   love
                             play

(Possible? 6 pieces for lute — guitar)

Pandora Gifted —
   Flaxman drawing — p. 95
     (Pandora's Box)
         Panofsky

"Miseria honorato"
   (honor-covered misery)
     — Panofsky — p. 67 —

"Works & Days" — <u>Hesiod</u>

". . . Hesiod, rather than founding a school, might have come relatively late into a living tradition"
   (Hesiod — Lattimore — 4)

"The Works & Days"
  (from Hesiod)
(". . . the outline of a useful farmer's life addressed to this scapegrace Perses . . ."
(use of technic — barre — etc)
The catalogue of Women
Pandora — "the beautiful mischief"
"The divine graces & queenly persuasion put necklaces of gold upon her, & the rich haired Hours crowned her head with spring flowers.
And Pallas Athene bedecked her form with all manner of finery. Also the Guide, the slayer of Argus, contrived within her lies and crafty words and a deceitful nature at the will of lord thundering Zeus & the Herald of the gods put speech in her. And he called this woman Pandora, because all they who dwelt on Olympus gave each a gift, a plague to men who eat bread."

Satire

                    (a la Circus)
"I'm only a bird in gilded cage,
a beautiful sight to see" —
                    1890 —

a woman dancing, moving, attitudinizing
        swing (like bird perch)
        hammock
        love seat
        tete à tete chair —
        croquet —
            (each object flies in and out)

Duet with one man
            (Prince Albert)

                                Rondo form?

        canticle —
                        "Imaginary Gardens"

Sun
Moon
Water Witch
Poet
Clown
Night
Earth   curve
                                    door
                                    window
                                    bridge

                    Bert   Helen
                    Paul   Ethel
                    Glen   Linda
                    Dick   Mary
                    David   Akiko
                                Yuriko
                Matt
                Carol
                Ellen
                Bette
                Lois

Psalm Nineteen —
Theme & Variations

Raptures —
(a series)
Praises

Memento (MEMENTO)
Teresa de Avila
Castle   159
("the space of a Credo or an Ave Maria")
(memento — the short interruption at the Mass, when the priest makes
a memento of those for whom he intends to pray)

"Such ecstasy, then, is an exalted form of contemplation"
Mysticism 36

"caught up to God"
(caught up to their vision)

"The ravishing of sinners for their correction" Dante — Mysticism 369

"I know it by experience"
St. Teresa (Mysticism 371)
(This?)   _____
"Saving madness" Plato
Mysticism 372
_____

"Festival of the cars" —
(Corpus Christi)

Age cannot wither —
She enters alone —
Nor custom stale
Dance with 3 or 4 men
Her infinite variety
duet —

The poet — Shakespeare reads the lines —
Joe —

He of the many guests
Wrestler
Prize of the Wrestler
Day of the Strange Procession

Gk. Tradition
Alcestis — Thomson — 115
"Valley of Dry Bones"
a ceremony in which
The Passing
The Return
of Alcestis is enacted

could this be spring after winter?

"The resurrection of a Divine woman
literally being dug or hacked out of
the ground by . . . Satyrs"

Prize of the Wrestling —

He of the Many Guests
        Hades — the husband —
(the same?)   Admetus
"mythically expresses the temporary obscuration of the Light-god
or Sun-god . . ." 118

(The moment in one's life when there is darkness, inactivity, negativity,
death of desire) —

"Helios is only the bright side of Hades" — 119

"It was to Admetus in his shining aspect — as it were the Sun-God
himself — that Alcestis was married on the day of the strange
procession — In his other aspect she is the bride of Death.

"The Reveling Procession"
(120)   (Komos)

"typical victor"   Heracles

. . . "victory . . . was incomplete without celebration . . ."   (123)

"the muses a singing & dancing company"

Heracles . . . "Leader of the Muses"

Komos — a marriage-pomp in which the Leader played the part
of the bridegroom.

Heracles — a marriage-god
written over the door of a newly married man —
"The Son of Zeus, Heracles the Victor, dwells here.
Let nothing evil enter"   (124)

"Apollo, Admetus, Heracles, are varying names for one divine being,
a Power of light & life —
And since in primitive religions the Power of light & life is at the
same time the Power of darkness & death, Thanatos or Death, who seems
in the play the enemy of all three, is in reality their double"   (127)

Ekstasis: photograph by Soichi Sunami

Techniques of Ecstasy

Techniques of Ecstasy —
   (sub-title — Shamanism — Eliade)

The Plain of Prayer —
                     Lhassa —

What are the aspects of ecstasy —
   Prayer   union with gods
   Love   union with Mother
   Divination
   Hate
   Faith

The Dark Door —

"Prophecy which Plato called 'the noblest of the arts' . . . which is a
special gift of heaven, & the source of the chiefest blessing among men."
"For prophecy is madness, & the prophetess at Delphi & the priestesses
of Dodona, when out of their senses have conferred great benefits on
Hellas, both in public & private life, but when in their senses few
or none."
                                                      Socrates

   p. 18   Story of Prophecy —

Cassandra
"She is the . . . symbol of the prophet. For so skeptical is man, that
 . . . unless he credits everything, he credits nothing"
                     (Prophecy — 8)

"The Enemy Joy"   Ben Belitt

"The nocturnal sun"
   passing thru the underworld
p. 246 The Mysteries
                     Eranos 2

The Gorgon's head

". . . the figures in our bowl represent a community of mystery
worshipers who have risen to the supercelestial realm at the climax of
their cult rite. Here the godhead appears to them in the form of a great
serpent, whom they salute in the attitudes of servants to the god, the
women expecting to conceive by the god, the men praying for them.
. . . the mystai drew a snake between their thighs in order to consum-
mate a mystical union with the god."   Eranos 2 — 245

Techniques of Ecstasy / 25

The Valley of Vision —

"If the sun and moon should doubt,
They'd immediately go out"
        Blake —
        (Symmetry 64)

"Man is all imagination. God is man & exists in us & we in him"   (31)

"Blake says 'that he was born with a different face.' But he did not
want to be; he . . . had what no real artist can be without — an intense
desire to communicate"   (4)

Plain of Prayer — Lester

Valley of Vision   Starer —

To whom it was shown
                spoken
      (The spirit of the ancestors)

spirit of the ancestors —
appearance of the evoked one —

She who is entranced by vision —

The summons (Voices? sounds?)

The declarement of vision —
        (prophecy)

The enactment —

(1)
The summons
The Entrance — (The Dark Door)
    The one spoken to — enters —
    To whom it was shown   (M.G.)
    Voices — no words —
    sounds — no words —
    She who is entranced by Vision
    Blinded by light
    Vision — light used in a wonderful way —

The entrance
    after light appears —
    (Lanterns of Isamu)
    Entrance alone —

(perhaps percussive summons — like feet)
    Dance — as in trance
    Man's vision —
? The ancestral strength of men —
                or
? Woman's vision of man's ancestral strength —
? Man's vision of women's lonely strength —
    (all separate, not in duet)

In Dance of Trance
people on outskirts who direct action — move arms — legs — direct
action design —

Dance of Trance
    animal figures — etc.
    used as puppet
    subjected to light
    driven by it
    intoxicated by it
    blinded by it —

Women's Dance
                }Enducing madness
Men's Dance —

madness — M. G.

consummation — revelation
    men & women

Plain of Prayer
    scene — banners as prayer banners thru which they move —
                        Jean Rosenthal —

Valley of Vision
    sets move in as banners go —
    or else intermission after   Noguchi
Plain of Prayer
    banners flying —

"Universe of discourse"
re — poetry — Rexroth —

"arranging his memories"
    Abelard — Waddell

Sibylline Oracles —   (368)
"The peculiar authority exercised by this oracle from pagan, Jewish, Christian thought alike. . . ."

The Sibyl —
"The name Sibyl first attracts attention. It is maintained by some scholars . . . that the word is not a proper name but implies a sound, issuing from a subterranean oracle, conveyed by the rustling of the wind as in the case of the Oaks of Dodona, or by the splash of water."   (368)

Pseudepigrapha   (p. 361)

Sibyl of Cumae . . .
". . . Ovid relates that being offered by Apollo any boon she chose, she took up a handful of sand & asked that she might live as many years as there were grains in it."   (369)

Heraclitis . . . preserved in Plutarch
"The poems contained many gloomy matters, and specified 'many revolutions and upheavals of Greek cities, many appearances of barbarous hordes, and murders of rulers.' "   (369)

The Jewish Sibyline Verses —   (370)

                    (361)
Vision — of Naphali —
"Further, I will tell you the vision I saw when I was pasturing the flock. I saw, & lo my 12 brothers were pasturing with me in the field; and lo, our father came & said to us, 'My children, run & seize ye, each before me, what comes to his portion.' We answered & said unto him, 'What shall we seize?, lo, we see nothing but the sun, moon, & the stars.' He said unto them (take hold of them).
When Levi heard it he seized a staff in his hand & jumped upon the sun & rode thereon. And when Judah saw it he did likewise; he seized a staff & sprang upon the moon, and rode thereon. So did all the tribes; each rode upon his star & his planet in the heavens; & Joseph only remained alone upon the earth. Jacob, his father, said unto him, 'My son, why has thy not done as thy brothers?'
He said unto him, 'My Father, what have they that are born of women to do in the heavens, as in the end they must stand upon the earth?' "

continue (361)

"To the Lady of the Labyrinth, a jar of honey"
  (Occidental Mythology
      Campbell — 47)

"Consort of the bull"
      Campbell

The Labyrinth is a symbol of life — when an offering is made to
"The Lady of the Labyrinth" such as a "jar of honey," it is made to
life itself in all its glory and pain —

Perhaps the dance is an ecstatic offering on all levels of experience
to the act of life —
"The Dark Door" —

One enters & is swept into a highly stepped-up experience of living —

"The Sibylline oracles . . . pieced together by Jewish editors; . . . in
which the sibyl is made a witness to the coming life & work of Jesus
Christ"   (Webster Dict.)

Before prophecy — the mating with an animal —
all in semi-darkness — so very little is visible.

"The main object of the Jewish Sibyllists is to maintain the unity &
sovereignty of God. God is one Being, invisible, self-sprung,
without beginning or end."   Pseudepigrapha (374)

Prophecys —
      Disaster
      War
      Love
      Crowning happiness

            ⎧ why
            ⎨ whence
            ⎩ wherefor

The Sibyl —
Perhaps Emily Dickinson as she was possessed by the Sibyl — the
Muse —
The entry into the Sibyl area — the ancient time — as Emily — a
Victorian figure —

The Dark Door —
      The Poet
            (Emily Dickinson in period dress)
(Letter to the World II)

The Sibyl —
      like ancestral figure

"Magic Prison" —
   Emily Dickinson —
"Gratitude is the timid wreath of those who know nothing. Of our
greatest acts we are ignorant"
                              Dickinson —
see Sat. Review Oct 28 '67 — (21)

Orpheus & Eurydice —
One enters thru the Dark Door and emerges into a Valley of Vision,
incandescent with light —
"Poetry is a form of power. It fell to early thought to make that
power visible & human, & the story of Orpheus is that of vision
& mortality"   Orphic Voice (2)
One does not look back — If so the maenads tear one to pieces —
"The myth of Orpheus is statement, question, & method"

                                            Orphic Voice (4)

See Occidental Mythology
     Campbell — (p. 326)
about sound of spheres

"Forbidden object
the One Forbidden Time
(sacred day, magical hour.) . . . The Orpheus taboo not to look back
is related"   Occid. Myth. 110

The sound
The light
The emergence
   "To the Lady of the Labyrinth a jar of honey" (Sibyl)

"Lucian is of the opinion that Orpheus had already prescribed that
anyone introduced to the wisdom of the mysteries should be received
with dancing"
(Sewell   Orphic Voice (21)

"For he who recollects or remembers, thinks; he who imagines, thinks;
he who reasons thinks; and in a word the spirit of man, whether prompted
by sense or left to itself, whether in the functions of the intellect,
or of the will and affections, dances to the tune of the tho'ts"
     (BACON)   Orphic Voice (26)

The lyre — poet
The bow — archer

The Sound
The Light
 a bare stage —
 dancers emerge from shadows
 Song of Orpheus — poet-dancer
(with lyre?) solo — Bert —
 Dance of men —
  like summons to the Sun Goddess of Japan —

  Emergence of the Sibyl —
  Dance of Women —

A timeless, placeless invocation — demand for vision, for love,
understanding, good & evil — for participation.

Alcestis

Dance with the veil —
sitting on piece —
exit girls —

———

1 hand gesture — r
2 " " — l
3 both hands — rise

———

Twist r — in veil
 "   l   "   "
move forward —

———

high kicks to r — 4 X
turn — run to st L. & fall

———

pushing away 3 X
from L to r —

———

Kneel with poses
veil over head — design
melting —
3 contractions
 between poses —

———

rise —
  2 cave turns
  step draw

————

go to Hercules
bend over him to sit
He does not reply —

————

runs st. r to piece
sits on bed —

————————————————————

Satyrs enter

    Beginning of Alcestis —
1) Exit girls & men —
2) Piece lifts —
3) Alcestis falls — wide 2nd — turns on floor into kneel ripple to r
4) piece turning —
5) On little melody Alcestis darts to bed over Admetus —
6) Alcestis pushes Bert away —
7) Admetus moves on bed to where head is high —
8) Alcestis goes on bed to hover over Admetus
9) Bert comes & pulls me up
   and begins to turn bed
10) Alcestis takes Admetus' place on bed, Bert continues to turn bed —
11) After bed is turned Alcestis slides off — faces bed, turns it
    until it is flat on floor — she lies on it to l. with only head &
    shoulders on it —
12) Admetus solo — He finishes it leaning over Alcestis — and Bert
    pulls bed, leaving Admetus — Alcestis lies on bed.
13) Bert lifts Alcestis & they do hesitating pulling steps to piece —
    Bert holds her hand. He is unseen — she leans out to Admetus —
14) Admetus exits —
    Bert pulls her behind piece —

1) Heracles rolls stone — st. C.
   solo with stone —
   finish st. L. lying on piece facing up. st.
2) Admetus enters st. r.
   satyrs enter st L.
   conversation between Heracles & Admetus —
   while satyrs lift stone —
   2 men walk under it —

& lie on it as at table —
Admetus leaves & is carried out by satyrs — st. R.

1) Bert & Alcestis come out, she standing on his feet
   Takes her to sit on bed — kisses her — arranges her hands —
   gets flower from piece & places it in her hand —
2) Bert's solo —
   finishes it over her on bed —
3) She slides under, places flower on piece & goes behind piece
4) She comes to front — he pins her to piece, his r. leg lifted —
   She catches it & pitches him off —
   Starts to run to st. L.
   He catches her
   little walk to L.
5) Leg lifts —
   mine L
   Bert R
   (as in tilt)
6) Slow wide 2nd fall (Alcestis)
   She turns on back —
   lift on her knees —
7) They sit back to back
   He lifts her into hesitating walk St. R.
8) He draws her in, makes her place her hands on his face
   He lifts her —
   she breaks away in running arabesque as he tries to catch her
   (high kicks) 3 X —
9) He catches her, lifts her & turns with her — places her on feet —
10) Pony walk lift to bed. He places her on it —

"Biting Winter is the time for that"
Hamlet loved plays —
The fencing match
The ghost
      (conscience)
Ophelia
Gertrude
   Her sins —
"The mysterious affair"
Form & Meaning in Drama   Kitto — (246)

Pocahontas
Notes for a dance never choreographed

American Provincials: photograph by Barbara Morgan

Pocahontas —

Seen first as court lady in London — Her entrance — a dancing scene

(Sarabande, Gavotte — Dance of period) As she appears dancing ceases & she is seated to watch dancers —

The women of the court eye her — She watches the men & gradually the court men are replaced in her eyes by very elegant Indian warriors in ritual dances. The women of the court eye her & seem to strip her of her court clothes & she becomes the beautiful savage again —

(These could be as dance forms — old dance forms, but with drums beneath) (In her eyes she enacts the saving of John Smith)

(note — John Rolfe — his letter about marriage — His fear of damnation in marrying a strange woman — P. 128)

The Eye of Anguish
Alcestis
Notes for a Study of Lear
The Scarlet Letter

"The 'mystery' of their trade, as it was customary to call it, they
passed on to their sons or to apprentices"   Puritan Oligarchy — 49

"A solemn day of humiliation" —   "   "   59

"exquisitely calculated unintelligibility of Gertrude Stein"

                                              Mona Lisa 223

"Hear the words of Lachesis, the daughter of Necessity. Mortal soul,
behold a new cycle of life & mortality. Your genius will not be allotted
to you, but you will choose your genius; & let him who draws the first
lot have the first choice, & the life which he chooses shall be his
destiny. Virtue is free, & as a man honors or dishonors her, he will
have more or less of her; & the responsibility is with the chooser – god
is justified."   Republic X   P. 426

                                        Behold this Dreamer
                                            de la Mare

Our Ladies of Sorrow —   De Quincey — (177)
    Our Lady of Tears   Mater — Lachrymarum
    "   "   " Sighs   Mater Suspirorum
    "   "   " Darkness —   Mater Tenebrarum —

The Theme of Night.   Theme of the Moon
    mystery   mystery —
    love   love
    terror   terror
    contemplation   contemplation
    dream   dream

Night as a Woman   Moon goddess
The Poet   The Dreamer

magic
funereal
religious

Barranca   Voices in the Tree
Black Mesa   Life of the Tree
Arroya   The bedded axle-tree.
                                    (T. S. Eliot
                                    Norton)

"circular desert"
Eliot

"quick now, here, now, always"
Eliot

disconsolate chimera

Eve! Magdalene!
or Mary, You?
Hart Crane

Destiny of movement —   Sartre
Speaking of Calder Mobiles
"A general destiny of movement is sketched for them, & then they are left
to work it out for themselves. What they may do at a given moment will
be determined by the time of day, the sun, the temperature, the wind.
The object is thus always between the servility of a statue & the
independence of natural events; each of its evolutions is the inspiration
of the moment."
. . . Mobiles do not seek to imitate anything because they do not "seek"
any end whatever, unless it be to create scales & chords of hitherto
unknown movements —

"A mobile, one might say, is a little private celebration, an object
defined by its movement & having no other existence."

Theme & Variations —
a Rondo form —

statement — affirmation
     clear, brilliant, deep breathing —
     long stretches of the body in space

El Pontal

In the sun   The pines
Early evening   The cliff
Moment of shadow
Time of Day
Private celebration
Instant of lightening
There was a sign
Moment of light

"the poet seeks an earth in   The rock
himself."   Greenberg   "Below all that, holding
                                     all that, the foundation stuff
                                     of this world, lies the rock.

                                     . . .

                                     To understand the Everglades
                                     one must first understand
                                     the rock."
                                          Everglades — 25

                                     . . .

                                     There was a sign

                                     . . .

                                     The fires began

                                     "Edenic memories"
                                          Speaking of animals — 31
                                     Eden — dream

"an everlasting re-iteration of unchanging principles & events takes
place both in space & in time, in large as in small"   Grimms — 861
"to reveal through mortal things the brilliance of eternal forms"
                                                          Ibid. — 866
"the quality of their work was not a naturalistical but a spiritual
precision, & their power 'Instructive Wonder' "   866
"not simply to fill a vacant hour, but to fill it with symbolic fare"   866

"The clown has had to learn how to banish hope & exist solely
in his performance."   Wallace Fowlie
                                          Chimera Autumn 1943   (7)

Euripides . . .

Alcestis —

    Chaucer makes of this heroine the noble lady of a May Day procession,
       the gracious queen of all women . . .
       For the translator of the 'Romance of the Rose' . . . Alcestis was
       above all the example of perfect love.
. . . Plato . . . who spurns the whining Orpheus of legend but places
       Alcestis highest in the rank of human loves, a strong-hearted
       woman, fully the equal of masculine lovers.

. . .

    Milton . . . quite naturally identified the beloved wife who died in
    childbirth with the Greek Alcestis, womanly symbol of the
    Resurrection.

    Euripides . . . His grotesque Hercules, both glutton & ribald, in
    whom superhuman strength & power suddenly becomes manifest,
    is a distant prototype of the clowns of the Idiot & The Possessed,
    who are subject to divine visitation.

"The Bacchantes of Euripides foreshadow the Magdalenes of Calvary, but
each of these two phenomena of tears & ecstasy would cease to be unique
if their differences did not outweigh their resemblances".

"We shall never know whether Euripides realized that his drama of death
& redemption revolves not only about the problem of conjugal love, but
about charity which is the essence of love.

Alcestis . . . a fugue built on a succession of sacrifices:
    Alcestis sacrifices her life for the man she loves. Admetus
    sacrifices his ritual of mourning for these tributes of hospitality
    (love one's neighbor as oneself) Hercules sacrifices his grosser
    pleasures for the salvation of an unknown woman
    The father is low simply because he makes no sacrifice.

    winged & bearded Thanatos

. . . this meditation of the philosopher facing the end of self, this slow
    descent toward nothingness, that the modern poet has to portray . . .
    where Euripides had only to call to mind the fight between Thanatos
    & Hercules.
    A contemporary play on Alcestis must make clear, also, in this single
    miraculous story, both the commonplace & the mysterious circum-
    stances of the last hours of life, showing that the drama of Hercules'
    struggle, or Admetus' resignation, takes place at the bedside of every
    beloved one.

A 20th century treatment of Alcestis can logically present a group of 3 characters, a variation on the eternal triangle, here composed of husband, wife & rescuer, a 3-dimensional group as complicated in its combination of realism & lyricism as an Alexandrian marble, a Laocoön or a Niobe.

From a certain point of view, this Alcestis can be considered as a tragedy invaded by a perpetual ballet of Moliere's Facheux Nuisances intruding on the romantic reverie of Admetus mourning.
These grotesque equivalents of a satyric chorus —

Trio —
fight between Herakles & Thanatos with the eloquent, almost inanimate, certainly passive — Alcestis.

Alcestis as in a semi-transparent silk tube — (Lamentation)
"Semi-transparent envelop which is life" — V. Woolf
Use of a ghost —

Alcestis?

Triple Muse ↓   white goddess
                                          of inspiration — Poetry
                               worshiped as

white raiser —   new moon   white goddess of re-birth — growth
red reaper —   full moon   red   "   " love & battle
dark winnower — old   "   black   "   " death & divination

(action idea — entering & crossing stage —
            in white
            in red
            in black cloak —
while chorus moves during absences like priestesses)
            ritual to moon —
    1 birth
    2 life
    3 death (re-birth — artist)

For description of White Goddess — see "White Goddess" — P. 54
(Golden Ass)

"First she had a great abundance of hair, flowing & curling, dispersed & scattered about her divine neck. On the crown of her head she bore many garlands interlaced with flowers; & in the middle of her forehead was a plain circlet in fashion of a mirror, or rather resembling the moon by the light it gave forth;"

The Origins of Attic Comedy —
   F. M. Cornford —
   See — Roland M. Smith   The Lion & the Fox
King Lear & the Merlin Tradition   Wyndham Lewis
   MLQ VII — (1946) — 153–174   Hudson?
7 Types of ambiguity — Empson
The fool — Miss Enid Welsford
   His Social & Literary History
         London 1936

Lear   great stage.
"and take upon's the mystery of things . . .
When we are born we cry that we are come   Stage of Fools
To this great stage of fools."   Storm

Disorder in nature   (violence of the storm)

The coming together of different   nakedness
kinds of real or apparent mental   storm   (24)
disorder —   blindness
    the Fool's wit & irreverence   madness
    Edgar's assumed idiocy
    Lear's real madness —

What is man's nature?   (26)   nature of man
What is nature?   relationship of man & nature (28)
What in the nature of things may   nature of nature.
        man depend upon?

"Lear is a play about ways of looking at & assessing world
of human experience"

Shrewd sharp worldly   vs.   apparently helpless incompetents
    Regan   Edgar
    Goneril   the Fool
    Edmund   Lear

Lear —
   "the mad Lear is in one sense the
   man of letters: his imagination is
   wholly alert, & whatever the disorders
   present, he has the searching &
   synthesizing insight of a poet.
   He may not seem quite safe.
   But the good poet never is.
   And the entirely safe man is
   never the good poet."   29.

"Shakespeare concerned with
Evil . . . as private inner reality &
as public force . . . uncompromising
in his record of its destructiveness
to those whom it possesses, in whole
or in part, & even to innocent bystanders"

"dramatic definition of a
specific kind of evil."   29

"that he can ultimately learn thru
representative suffering, is one
of the fundamental intimations
of the patterns of Lear"   30

"Tragedy records victory
rather than defeat"
Suffering in tragedy not
an end — but a product
& a means —
       thru it comes wisdom
       & if not redemption,
       a renewed grasp
       upon the laws of
       redemption.   (32)

(in Cady's garden —
3 men in tree — crucifixion of 3)

Subject of play = Lear's mind —

"movingly inclusive dramatization
of man's liability to error."

Lear imposes on
world.

"Lear puts into power the daughters"
"We see good & evil in conflict in
the world, but by the structure we
are reminded that the conflict is an
emanation of that in the individual
soul. Lear must recognize evil,
resolve his conflict, a conflict
externalized by his attitude to
Goneril & Regan & Cordelia.

                           (33)
"To be the father of Goneril
is to create an evil brought
forth from oneself."

                           (34)
"In investing Goneril & Regan
with power, Lear gives rein to
a part of himself — . . . the
spirit of calculation.
. . . Cordelia is the side of Lear
capable of tenderness, love
& insight."

For Cordelia — see
   Granville Barker — "Prefaces"
   Coleridge's Shakespearean
   criticism

                           (35)
Cordelia's situation analogous
to Antigone's.

also notes 32–33–34 (p 300–301)

"some little faulty
mixture of pride & sullenness"

what happens to Cordelia not central
effect of play — we see her always in
her impact on him —

Cordelia — tragic actor not
pathetic victim

The Fool — his social & literary history —
   Enid Welsford — London 1935

Lear — study in relationships   see daughters as animals
   unnaturalness   tigers, wolves,
                                                           vultures, serpents

"the monstrous chaos & destruction into
which man's unassisted nature will lead him."

"It is the discovery that Cordelia is
alive, that life is the reality under
appearance, that the reality is good —
it is this that breaks his heart at last . . .
It seems almost beyond
question that any actor is false to the
text who does not attempt to express as
Lear's last accents & gestures & look,
an unbearable joy." —   Shakespeare & the Nature of Man   152
                                             Spencer

Great Stage

Edgar's nakedness —
   symbol of that defenselessness
   in the world —
         unprotected by worldliness
         in a world swept by the storms of
         ambition & other uncontrolled
         emotions.

            . . .

(70)   nakedness a defense . . . against ultimate corruption.
         The naked wretches may
         ultimately have a better
         protection than those who are
         proudly arrayed in what the world
         values. To strip oneself may
         be folly; but nakedness may
         be an aid to understanding.

Lear —

   He seeks to undress — first — to   Lear must pass from simple
      "divest us both of rule   blame of villains to an awareness
      Interest of territory, cares   of his own responsibility for
      of state".   disaster.

(71) He would retain prerogatives
without responsibility of
king, immunity without
safeguards, warmth without
clothes.
He forgets there are no naked
kings
Lear reduces himself to the
status of a child —
when he runs in storm his un-
protectedness is more than
physical

"Lear is living in a melodrama;
he must learn to live in a
tragedy"   309 — (8)

Theme of bareheadedness –

(73) the storm beats about Lear's
head in the same way in which
emotional & intellectual
storms batter at his mind

"Ha! here's three on's are

(76) sophisticated! Thou art the
thing itself; unaccommodated
man is no one but such a poor
bare, forked, animal as thou art."
The Lear who is naked wants to be
clothed in fact.

divesting of lands etc
    hope of quiet old age —
divesting of clothes
    bitter disillusionment

(78)

Cordelia describes Lear —
    Crowned with rank fumiter & furrow weeds,
    With burdocks, hemlock, nettles, cuckoo flowers,
    Darnel, & all the idle weeds that grow
    In our sustaining corn (IV — iv — 3–6)

plants long identified as "bitter,
biting, poisonous, pungent,
livid & distrolling"

"emblematic of
madness"

parody of kingship

act   I — Lear took off crown
 "   III — bareheaded
 "   IV — mock crown

Lear has his crown of thorns
  symbol of the anguish which
  is the heart of the
  redemptive experience

"miniature christ"   (309)
"ritualistic conception of sacrifice"

Granville-Barker — speaks of
Lear's taking upon himself the
burden of the whole world's
sorrow — of his transition from
malediction to martyrdom —
                        309 — (11)

"In another sense Lear is on the
way to restoration of a kind, at
least such a one as he can have,
to recovery in part of mental
balance, a reunion with
Cordelia, a realization of his
spiritual potentialities."   (78)

Finnegan
  "how day, slow day, from delicate to divine, devases"   p. 598.

The quest
  The tragedy of love versus the quest for love
  The quester is a clown — partly —
  The woman searching — for awareness —
The Circular Desert —

Lear
  "his final brilliant court scene" (IV, iv, V, iii)
      a natural scene
      a crown from nature
      a king by nature

"For the poor naked wretches of the
play, the victims of the world, will
survive in spirit, the gorgeous are   men of the Bowery —
doomed. In proud array, Lear failed,
uncrowned, half-naked, he is saved."
                    (86)

"We may say in general — that upon the
quality of his seeing & upon the
quality of his dress depends man's fate

in the world. The play goes on to a subject beyond man's fate in the world — man's moral & spiritual fate. In that realm, paradoxically, blindness & nakedness may have their values, for they do not exclude the possibility, respectively, of man's having insight, & immunity to world corruption. The blind are not misled by their eyes, nor the naked by their proud array." (87)

play concerned —
   <u>not</u> with making a formal philosophic statement
        <u>but</u>
= with presenting the quality of experience
                (89)

The inquiry into the nature of man & his world finds its physical counterpart in the terrific storm of Act III.

     . . .

There are convulsions of (90) nature on two levels.
"The tempest in my mind"
    his madness is
    another convulsion of
    nature
thru purgatory

Coleridge
   "The howlings of convulsed nature would seem converted
(90)   into the voices of conscious humanity."
(312) anodyne for pain caused by conduct of daughters

   Storm & madness — tremendously real, but we are never allowed to forget the moral disorders of which they are both symbols.

Lear says—
"Rain wind thunder fire are not his daughters — they are not unkind, they owe him no allegiance."—   (90)

"Storm & animal imagery gives picture of moral failure of man"

if
   play as a whole asserts man's ability to achieve salvation
      experiences of Lear & Gloucester
         purgatorial

The tragic world is a kind of chaos; the disorder within the soul is projected into the larger world . . .

The paradox of tragedy is that order comes out of a world wracked by disorder —   (91)

human nature — _ambivalent_
  operates — 2 levels
    1 — its proper order
    2 action on other level
      clashes —

recourse to animality —
"animality is what they observe
behind the surface, behind the
coverings & the disguises. In
the same way the play makes
use of the facts & the imagery of
sex to show the descent of man,
who has high spiritual
potentialities into animal will
& appetite."   (92)

"man may regard himself
in two ways: as moving by
discipline toward spirit,
or by undisciplined desire
toward the animal."   (92)

"animal often takes over in
man who has extraordinary
intelligence, that is, gifted in
a particular human way."
There is a paradoxical union
of generically opposed qualities.
The combination is fertile,
productive; it generates immense
force; like a storm it is a wrench
in the order of things"

The clear-seeing are
blind ultimately —

animals — the 2 sisters
  "I am tied to the stake & I
  must stand the course"
(a bear tied to stake, attacked by
  relay of dogs)   95

"you she-foxes" —
"those pelican daughters"
  "most serpent-like"
  "sea-monster"
  "detested kite"
  "wolfish image"

The gallantry
      against
The fight

too much age

Death —

"tigers not daughters"
"Be-monster not thy feature"
"This gilded serpent"
"each jealous of the other
as the Sting
Are of the adder"   (96)

(Goneril)

"Women will all turn monsters"

(97)   sting
Her mind so venomously 'that burning shame
Detains him from Cordelia.' IV.iii — 47–49

sting — venomously — burning shame   something of the
    describe Lear's past deeds as tho   animal, the
    they were serpents   monster, in Lear, too

        It is not for nothing that Lear is father to Goneril
        man in his sins is animal-like
        immediate function of animal imagery to make evil concrete

    women
    "Down from the waist they are centaurs
    Tho women all above;
    But to the girdle do the gods inherit;
    Beneath is all the fiends.

Hide thee, thou similar man of virtue
that art incestuous"   (103)
                            Fortune, that arrant whore

Knight — man is turned back to nature   "wellness is the state
(317)   in his purgatorial experience   of nature"
        "movement from civilization"

Storm is symbol of emotional stresses
to which Lear is subject —
"unnatural & bemuddling sorrow."   without reference to
                    (118)   goodness or badness

"Impulse, desire, appetite — if
these be the sole reality, they
lead man to the animal, but by
the acceptance of order as the
final reality, man becomes human.
That is his ripeness".   (128)

Edgar
    the worst is not
    So long as we can say
    "this is the worst." IV–1, 27, 28.
    "Ripeness is all" — V, ii, 11   maturity —

"In earning his humanity, man gives
up his pride, & thus gains sight of
final truths"   (130)   animal theme —

"if man is unwilling to deal or incapable of dealing with experience imaginatively & substitutes rationalistic procedures where they cannot be successfully used, he will get into trouble: rational man is in the greatest danger of rationalizing essential values out of existence."
(177)

animal imagery used — to emphasize another complication in humanity — its capacity for adjuring its especial characteristics & taking on the rapacity & ruthlessness of the beast . . . further in figurative use of sex . . .

~~~~~~~~~~~~~~~~~~~~~~~~~~~~~~~~~~~~

use of storm —
    animal figures in darkness   —   2 sisters & bastard
        pursuit of Lear   (use of three — other 3 —)
        " Cordelia   evil   good
       beautiful, frantic at times   — symbol of harassed soul
Fool as King — at times —   the pure —
Feeling of purgatory

~~~~~~~~~~~~~~~~~~~~~~~~~~~~~~~~~~~~

"Play does not attempt answers to problems; it is primarily bent upon evoking a sense of their magnitude & of the well-nigh intolerable burden which they place upon the human mind." (178)

Lear's passion in re-developing his intellect
    "Lear's whirling tumult & anarchy of thought which until imagination has time to work, chokes down his utterance."
    "Then comes the inward tugging conflict deep as life, which gradually works up his imaginative forces, & kindles them to a preternatural resplendence." —
    . . .
    "Thus his terrible energy of tho't & speech as soon as imagination rallies to his aid grows naturally from the struggle of his feelings." (325)

abnormality — types — see
    Roland M. Smith
King Lear & Merlin's Tradition
MLQ — VII–1946–153–174

"It was Coleridge's opinion (reported by Crabbe Robinson) that the Fool of Shakespeare supplied the place of the ancient chorus . . .
The ancient wisdom, disguised as laughter, dances like the light of a summer sea."
E. Sitwell — notebook on Shakespeare
(12)

The Fool has the imaginative power
which the mad Lear achieves . . .
that is, the ability to read image
& symbol, to leap from the concrete
manifestation to the meaning, to
the values implied. — 182

                 of Lear & the Fool
"In view of the evidence to be considered . . . we might almost treat
King Lear as a dramatic presentation
of the fate of the imaginative grasp of
truth in a wholly practical world."

    "Lear's own imagination failed in
    Act I rest of time his really
    powerful imagination is
    contrasted with rationalistic
    spirit . . ."   (152)

Fool's education of Lear is in part
a re-education of his imagination, an
implied attack upon the calculating
rationalism by which Lear had
inaugurated all his troubles (177)

Lear's imagination is recovering
        he understands Fool's poetry
        he is learning to grasp symbolic
          meaning of action
(187) he is moving toward imaginative
          synthesis which he will
          make in his madness
        closer he comes to madness more
        he exercises gifts of Fool.

      Storm —
          more than storm

Fool outside world of normal
order & logic — so that his
imaginative insight into the
meaning of phenomena is
always free to find immediate
expression.
  . . . He forgoes prerogative
& is free of responsibilities
of normal everyday world.
"known by term of contempt
lives at mercy of others
hardly taken seriously no
conventions restrain him"
      (182)

Fool   "conscience of Lear inner
voice externalized which will
not cease in its condemnation
of error."
At another level tutor —
intellectual master of world
who lessons Lear in way of
world.

Lear falls to folly
Fool rises to wisdom

    Fool becomes King
      see things in per-
      spective usually
      belonging to royalty.
    Love for Lear —

Fool = man of imagination —
    grasps values cannot
    be demonstrated
    rationally
    speech — poetry.

also "rainy day"

Fool parodies cynical unfoolishness   worldliness is Folly
        of Goneril, Regan —   un-worldliness
"Folly is to mistake the short range for the long distance"

"Fool starts Lear off on imaginative
restoration by which he shall grasp
again permanent values"   (191)

        Lear's — career —
            record of mistake & consequences
            of mistake
            folly — his mistake
            madness — the consequence —   re-union with Cordelia (206)
                                            psychological & spiritual
                                            recovery

        Lear loses his imaginative grasp
        of truth, & tries to express truth
        in wrong way —
        horror of world his folly creates
        drives him to madness —
        In madness a powerful lucidity
(193)   a tremendous exercising of
        imagination that failed him before.

                                            Cordelia
                                                adult
        "Stage of Fools"   not naive or stupid
            world of fumbling humanity   integrated
            Fool —

            man of insight.   In dance her observation of
                                            Lear & his acts — her under-
                                            standing & awareness — her
                                            helplessness — her tragic
        "Spiritually Lear rises thru the   acceptance — patience —
        course of his anguish to a   (perhaps seeing it as
        wisdom which he has never before   from another plane)
        approached, including a   altho' she loses all world she
        sympathetic appreciation of   saves everything essential.
        suffering among the world's   kind of devotion required to
        unfortunates & full realization realize her humanity.   (217)
        of Cordelia's love."   (327)

    Lear's imagination restored,
        otherwise mad scenes would
        be pathetic, grotesque, sardonic   3 wise men   (221)

lunacy of demeanor can co-exist
with a most penetrating insight.
"Reason in madness" (Edgar)

madness presented not merely
psychologically "realistic",
madness presented as having value

Cordelia (& Kent)   (225)
"thought is act"
rarely see thinking
process as such

"The sanity of the men is that they
can understand eternal truths"   (255)

(259)   "Edgar's pretended madness takes,
in large part, the form of
religious mania."

description by Edgar of diabolical
"thing" who was with him on top
of cliff.
. . . "It was some fiend" — that is,
an infernal temptation to suicide.
The episode is very strongly
reminiscent of the temptation of
Christ (just as Lear who enters 10
lines later with his crown of
nettles & weeds is reminiscent
of Christ in another way).   260

Play — King Lear —
Lear marks old order
    confusions & destructions
        arrogance
        hasty, indiscriminate
        action
        self-aggrandizement
marks turning point of
old order to new
the overwhelming problems
which beset both the
individual & the age at the
historical crisis —

Lear says to Cordelia after he has
awaked from curative sleep —
Thou art a soul in bliss; but I am
bound upon a wheel of fire"
IV — vii — 46–47 — (270)

"The ultimate failure to find
order in the world is madness,
& the madness theme in the play
is the most profound indication
of the world in convulsions.

"Love-trial" — Charlton
(192)

(283)   a mad world drives man to madness
either as a pathological state or
as a consciously sought refuge
imposing humiliation that
only desperation could accept.
But if madness is asylum
it is also, paradoxically,

"man may achieve ripeness. —
that fulfillment of his humanity
by which he may come to inner
security."   (291)

"Shakespeare's Satire"
  — Campbell   163–4

". . . finds the current of his being
dammed up . . . the resulting
starvation of his inner life produces
in him the familiar state of exaspera-
tion . . . He stands for a man, a mere
'unaccommodated man', who is
embarked on the frantic search
for his soul. In his mad desire to
divest himself of all unessential
trappings he tears the very clothes
from his body . . . nature has no
peace or security to bestow upon
the human spirit. Only when he is
united with Cordelia, does he
discover the secret of happiness
which he has been seeking with
utter desperation. Love, unselfish
love of one human soul for
another, is the solvent of all
unhappiness. Upon the
sacrifice to love of all the world
has to offer 'the gods themselves
throw incense.' Lear's death at
the moment of his great discovery
thus becomes a transfiguration."

the beginning of illumination;
the feigned madman, who is
part the victim of his own
inertness & gullibility . . .
gains a new practical & moral
insight . . . the Fool, who gained
immunity by means of dis-
cordances & irrelevancies
which appeared to the unknow-
ing to represent the innocuousness
of essential disorganization,
outlines the way of the world
with relentless insight —

Lear finds in his mania a kind
of order, an imaginative grasp
of a disintegrating universe —

John Gielgud feels —
Cordelia & Fool played
by same boy — that
explains Fool's death
                Edith Sitwell (67)

"Pray you undo this button
thank you, sir"   V — 3

Lear asks to be relieved
of his outworn life —
from his lendings . . .
So little a thing now is
Death to him — only
undoing a button, then,
casting off of the rags of
mortality.
                Sitwell 68

Cry of the Fury
I'll beat the Drum — II — 4

"Extremitie of the skies"   The Night of Lear
Scene on the heath.   Turn thy wheel
Tyranny of the night   Veil of the temple
Wanderers of dark   Lake of Darkness
                                            III — 6
"Autumn's Dust"   IV — 6   "hero is an angler in the lake
"Darkness of Revelation"   of Darkness" — Edgar

Swinburne

3 sisters in tube of material   (like Lamentation)
        conflict —
        stillness & purity of Cordelia
        reptilian quality of other two —
    (Lear as spectator)

Tree is throne —
   "   " crucifix —

Lear enters alone into storm area —
    Tree stands sharp (painted with luminous paint?)
    Dance of wandering —   flowers —
    Enter Fool & Edgar —
        Three have dance together —

                                    like Morris dance

3 women in tube at foot of tree — unseen —
Lear's cloak falls & they seem to rise from beneath it & he sees them as
ghosts —
        Cordelia escapes —
                perhaps 2 dances —
                one like sarabande — a dedication
                other — dance of grief — a dirge —
Distorted dance of 2 with the Bastard —
    crawling around him — over him — between legs —

1) Lear's entrance — solo of desperation — being driven into storm —
2) seeing 3 sisters — like ghosts
                    like laughing
3) Cordelia's escape —
4) ceremonial — like dance (or her despair here) of dedication — exits
5) Lear's grief — seeking her — as his soul —
6) Two men enter —

                                    Calvary
        dance of 3 mad figures in the storm — demonic joy?
7) Changes into trial scene —
        women like animals —

Perhaps
  St. George & the Dragon —
   Bastard as Dragon —
 Cordelia's anguish & despair —
Use of large fish net to hold Lear — as caught fish held by 2 daughters —

"Divine Combat" (Exorcism) Possession — 7

Motion Picture Project.

 <u>Cave of the Heart</u>

To make objective all those moods of action which demand in stage presentation the devices of repetition, immobility, development rather than pure statement alone of intention.
  example — May part —
  could some staging device be used — a return to a nature symbol of some kind, for instance —

Is there some way of stating in other terms — camera eye — the relationships?
Medea as a sorceress —
     perhaps —
Jason as an Argonaut
Or of making objective the ancient dark world from which Medea is.

The malignancy of corresponding plants?
The relentlessness of the stages of a storm — or catastrophe —
A chorus?
 Muses
 Fates
Tides of sea —

What could happen on walk in with Yuriko?
 What is happening under cloak to Yuriko
       to me
       to Erick
       to May
 (The tide of the sea coming in — engulfing the beach until it overflows in a crash against rocks)

Perhaps the figure of Medea very large on screen — until it is her breast or heart — & part of face — & then the action taking place superimposed on her breast

Motion Picture Project

  Scarlet Letter —

wash of waves on rock as in Plymouth —
fading into figure of Hester on trial in courtyard — doorway
  reminiscent of Venus rising from waves —
symbol of rose-bush — at prison door —
  perhaps seeing it first & door thru it as it opens on Hester — rose
  covering child & symbol on her breast — Her face seen thru rose-bush
  — concentrated on rose on her breast which becomes letter **A.**

The walk to the market place —
  2 realms of action —
    against the slow walk — naturalistic almost — is a dance of
    terror — shame — anguish — the movement of a trapped
    animal —

As Dimmesdale sees her there —
  Perhaps thru rose bush — from beyond Prison door —
  or from behind her — as seen from above where he is —

Perhaps first solo — as she stands on scaffolding
  "she felt at moments, as if she needs must shriek out with the full
  power of her lungs, & cast herself from the scaffolding down upon
  the ground, or else go mad at once."
  rocking from wall to wall — tilting — running —

The fall from scaffolding into dimension of dance —
           shame — terror — anguish

As Dimmesdale sees her — his dance of remorse — fear — guilt.
As their eyes cross —   Duet of their love —

The women as chorus —
  May as leader.
  What goes through minds of women as she stands there.
    May-Pole
    Dance of wildness —
    One woman — several men —
    Perhaps May as figure incarnate of May pole —

The Lilith of their imaginations —
    wound in ribbons — revealed by unwinding —
    The man is a demon — beautiful — but the Devil —

The Sermon on Sin.

Hallucinations
    witches dance
    The Devil —
        The bar of judgement
        The altar of marriage

The child —
    beauty
    fantasy of dress
    wildness
    inhuman qualities
    perhaps synonymous with May as May queen —
    like a princess —
    an allegorical figure of sin —
        beautiful — decayed — almost mysterious — oriental

The attack of her
    by children — climbing all over her.
                engulfing her.
    by men —   sensually
    by women —   in torture
        as witches
            tearing at her etc.

moments of idyllic bliss —
  crossing the path of Dimmesdale
    This should be like the re-iterated ode which is calm, beautiful,
    passionate as well —
    & should break the rigid terror of the other scenes —
        It sustained her —
        was the lyric relief —
        Garden of Eden
        Paola & Francesca

Glowing of Letter in the dark —
    as the women of that time felt it to glow —

Seeing in Pearl's eyes — Dimmesdales —
    The unrest of time
    The love moment again
    like a dream each time but always ending by being broken rudely
    off (the devil — a witch)

Scene in governor's house —
    Restoration of **A** in convex mirror —
    Pearl's desire for rose
        (like first rose bush)
    Governor called her
        "children of Lord of Misrule".

Pearl is the Scarlet Letter
           opening scene — perhaps of her dancing —
           waves
           Pearl's hair —
           rose-bush —
           Letter

Remorse of Dimmesdale —   Black Veil
    Night-mare —
        flagellation of himself
        night trip to scaffold —
           meteor fall — Hester & Pearl —

Sermon of Dimmesdale —
    Dimmesdale as seen
      by young girls —
      " old people   — angel
      " Doctor   — crucified one
      " Hester   as her beloved

Doctor —
    Alchemist
    Sorcerer
    Devil

Fall of meteor
    We impute it, therefore, solely to the disease in his own eye & heart,
    that the minister, looking upward to the zenith, beheld there the
    appearance of an immense letter, — the letter **A** — marked out in lines
    of dull red light

Hester's majesty of despair —

a kind of stately dance — Sarabande
    minister   Pearl
    Chuzzleworth   Hester
Fatalic — unending — interlocked
terrifying — beautiful — tragic

Sometime a dress covered with **A**'s or eyes —

The 1000 eyes —
    first as she stood on scaffold
    later on Festival Day in Market Place —

Procession after Election sermon —
    How he sees himself —
    music
        procession in another size & area from him —
        girls with flowers —
        Instead of solemn clothes he has crown of thorns —
        People with branches
            (like Christ's entry into Jerusalem — Palm Sunday.)

Hester as the Magdalen at foot of scaffold.

cries of — no — from multitude ending in Prayer whispered in silence
of discovery — by one voice —

Seeing her standing with dresses blown by wind — child appears in back
of skirt as it is whipped aside by wind —
(or cloak)

In dance dimension scenes
    It is as though one fell into a pit, into an abyss — such as the
    Puritans dreamed of Hell — It is like a vacuum. There seems to be no
    space sense — All the walls & floor black — At times it is like looking
    into a well —
    In each scene there should be some thing — some object — to indicate
    a place in the mind — a mood —

In opening scene —
    Dimmesdale sees her thru rose bush.
    The doors of prison should move like great shadows & as they press
    open they keep turning on a pivot until the light flashing on them
    seems to make him see the gateway into the garden of Eden with the
    flaming sword.
    The doors should be like flaming whirling swords.

Try to reconstruct the Garden of Eden & the Fall as seen thru the mind
of the preacher.

Narrator —
    a woman
    The figure of Maya —
        The world's illusions —
        Kali
        "The everlasting Divine Drunkenness of Dream"

She of the Rock —
The woman of the rock sculpture in the West —
"Underneath all is the rock"
It is as tho' the Rock spoke —
    (Plymouth Rock —
        The feet stepping upon it.)
Primordial spirit of the land —
    central figure in the May Pole —
Like a George Grosz painting of the coast & sea —
like Louis' painting —
It becomes the woman who speaks —

Figure of Bull
Bull's head becomes like primeval letter **A** and that becomes
Scarlet letter **A.**
All different forms of letter **A** as it has developed from bull's skull —
fertility symbol —

Perhaps use of color in figure of narrator & black & white for other parts,
the main sections of picture —

Man narrator also?
    Figure of God as man —
    Symbolic figure — Roof of Church which becomes a broad Puritan
    hat & then a man —
    It is as tho' he were above stretching over all — a dark cloud hiding
    the sun —
She was the earth beneath him —
        Her hair the grass & weeds —
        Her arms the river —
        Her breast the bay line —
        The burning bush —
            The rose bush
                Hester

A legend of first sin —
A legend of man's fall —
A legend of desire —

moment of torment when she is conscious of the letter **A.** Flashes of
letter **A** in all its different forms — beginning with the head of the bull &
continuing on down to the letter on her dress —

opening — The eyes of a man in which appear very small the indistinct
    outlines of a sea coast — with grass — the rock —
    It slowly becomes to his eyes a beautiful supine figure of a woman —

as tho' waiting to receive him —
The breast becomes the rock —
The step of Puritan buckled shoes upon the rock — breast — one
after one —
Body of woman is like a map of a landscape.
The landscape becomes the body of a woman & back into landscape —

The Square —   New England Legend
    4 sides —   Footsteps on the Rock
        The judges — 1   Ancestral Footsteps
        The people — 2
        The Scaffolding — 3
        The Prison — 4

characters —
   Hester
   Dimmesdale
   The Devil
      (as a gallant)?
   witch
   girls who see themselves as brides —
   Populace —
      no faces are seen —   or feet
        hats for men
        bonnets for women — or skirts

women see her with the Demon Lover while she is walking —
   What is happening — the walk
   What is imagined — the dance with Demon.

A man's hands in agony & in prayer —

Could there be some way of camera encircling rose bush with man one
side, woman other side —   ??

Elements —
   The statement of theme —
      Either
        hands
        rosebush
      Storm with meteor into letter **A** —
        man & woman very small, widely apart on screen —

Legend of a Fall
Legend of Sin
   crucifixion of the spirit

by intolerance
" superstition
" dread
" sense of guilt
" cowardice —

Banishment
Torment
Return

Flashes of lightning on a dark screen —
Sound of rain on roof —
                or
surge of sea —
    monotonous
    repetitive —
It becomes the slow steady beating of a man beating his own body in a
dark encircled room — He is naked from the waist up. —

The surge of the sea becomes the monotonous swish of the lash
on his back —

The lightning becomes the throw of a woman's loosened hair as she
throws her head from side to side in a frenzy of anguish — It is like a
trail of light across the sky —
                until
It bursts in a crash in the orchestra into music & the lightning is
like a meteor trailing across the sky revealing small & separated &
remote the figure of a man & woman — poles apart — each on a
separate hill — like the cross — on a hill —
    One a woman — skirts & hair blown in the wind —
    One a man — rain beating on his breast & running from him
    like tears —

The light becomes like a vivid letter **A**, then into a burning bush —
then into a rose bush —
    Through which a vast door is opening
    It is morning —
    Thru the rose bush in the shadows can be seen the woman approaching

She is now calm, quietly walking — fully dressed —
there is no more wind —
You see her first thru the rose bush then what seemed roses on the
breast of her gown become, as she advances, a fantastic & beautiful
& bold letter **A** — embroidered with all the elegance of a medieval
manuscript letter **A**.

(Thru sound of sea or surge of storm everything becomes
interwoven — interlocked
   The surge of the sea
      The movement of a woman's hair in an anguished
      tossing of the hair —
      The tossing becomes a lash which in turn is
      the whip in the man's hand.
      It is as tho' the sea surge at night became to him her hair
      with which he beat himself — to her it was the sound of that beat
      & her own low moaning — perhaps even the walking of buckled
      shoes that cross the rock of Plymouth striking sparks with the
      heels —
      The stone becomes her breast
      The sparks the lightning with the letter **A**
      which becomes burning bush —
      which narrows until it becomes a door slowly opening to
      admit light into darkness revealing rose bush —
(All something like scene in Lear)

Perhaps camera could be behind her — as tho it were her eye
looking out into light into rose bush which suddenly seems to have
only thorns on it & she turns suddenly away — with terror
stricken eyes peering back into darkness of the prison
    perhaps she might be confronted there with a lovely evil
    smiling face of the Demon — for an instant —

Shuddering she turns & we see her from the eyes outside the door —
Dimmesdale's — thru the rose bush — with roses on her breast —
but as she moves forward it is seen to hide the letter **A** on
her dress —

As she walks to scaffold she looks at ground seeing only the
buckled shoes of the men — so very many — & the moving skirts
of the women's dresses —
(Perhaps scene of rock & feet striking it as they cross — Rock becomes
                                 her breast)

As she mounts the scaffold the bonnets appear — then the hats —
finally Dimmesdale's eyes high above her on the balcony —
She feels she is walking into his very eyes —
For an instant she walks into his & he into hers — They fuse —
They seem to enter some quiet place — idyllic — where the rose tree
makes vivid the place — It has no walls — no ceiling — no floor —
It has no space —

her own foot steps sound so lonely & become feet
on the rock which is her breast & the letter **A** —

A duet of love takes place —
tender, passionate & wildly sweet —
He has on no coat — his ruffled shirt is open —
Her hair is loose — her gown partly open at the throat —

It finishes when she becomes aware of his eyes again — & then there
seem to be millions of eyes swarming in a haze of heat & sunlight —
Her dress seems covered with eyes — The **A** seems as she looks at it

*also development of letter **A** from bull's head*

becomes the scaffold on which she stands & from which in wave of vertigo
she seems to fall into an abyss of darkness & stillness & no space —

There follows a dance of anguish, terror, wild despair —
again there is the smiling demon — who finally strikes her with a whip —
but his whip strokes seem to be outside herself & become the strokes of
the old judge's staff which bring her back to consciousness —
(toll of bell like dirge of funeral — hers —)
(or else it could be the devil's finger pointing at her which becomes the
accusing finger of the judge above her)
The judge seems to be the embodiment of God — a wrathful diety —
She cannot see his face — only the shadow cast by his hat which becomes
larger & larger, stretching as he seems to appear above her — cutting
out the light of the sky until it becomes like a storm cloud — pointing
at her as he seems about to engulf her
She thrusts her hand forward to avoid being smothered — Her hand is
caught in the darkness by the Demon's hand — The scene resolves itself
into the aspects of puritan sermon —
> the condemnation of sinners
> the descent into hell which is like the ascent of the scaffold,
> only downwards instead of up into sun —

As the demon catches her hand he draws her into a scene reminiscent of
the image of Hell in the Puritan sermons —
Some of this might be reminiscent of Dante's Inferno — It is like the
Cave of Sleep with the figures of nightmare —
There are dances of lamentation and dances of demonic torment —
> The women are made to dance by & with the demons there —
> There is one woman there in whom she sees herself —
> There are Paola & Francesca forever joined
The end of the sermon is marked again by the bell tolling —
She turns to leave the scaffold & starts to descend — It seems that she
descends a long way — down, down into the very earth itself — until she

reaches the ground — The doors open for her & she disappears — As they close behind her to Dimmesdale's eyes they seem to keep revolving until they appear like the flaming sword which guards the entrance to Paradise when Adam & Eve are thrust out —

As they revolve faster & faster & the light streaks & shines & becomes black in turn he has a vision of the banishment from Paradise —

There is the Rose Bush & the flaming sword —

"And He placed at the east of the garden of Eden Cherubims, and a flaming sword which turned every way, to keep the way of the tree of Life"   Genesis 5

It is Dimmesdale who begins to descend the steps from the balcony & as he does it seems to extend forever — deep into the very earth itself — and when he reaches the bottom he falls to the ground in an anguish of shame —

There is a dance here for the man — a lone dance — of a man tormented — There could come into it symbols — such as roses & thorns — strange sounds such as whirring noises increasing to unbearable volume — until it becomes the surge of the sea as in the beginning — It becomes the tossing of a woman's hair as he retreats as before a flood — until again he is flagellating himself as before with a whip that seems to be her hair & becomes her hair as she is standing in a windy place as before braiding or brushing her hair — or else her skirts are wide in the wind & they fill the screen — but are brushed aside to reveal behind them a young girl whose hair she is brushing —

The difference in the 2 scenes of the storm is that this leads into a lyric play between the 2 — the woman & the child —

Instead of a black place of no space this should be a white place of space limits — like a white sand on a beach — with no limits of sky or earth line — Only 2 lines of footprints crossing the sand — the woman's & the girls —

first walking in shoes — then faster then barefoot — then running — on the part of the child until it becomes a demonic, wild, untamed dance — a figure almost animal-like in its movements — in the utter innocence which is the state before dread enters the human beings life — It is the true innocence of life — before the sense of sin enters —

As the child dances she catches strands like sea weed, throwing them into the air, adorning herself with, twisting into them until the woman sees the May Pole begin to form from the assembled strands of sea weed —

In this May Pole Dance of Spring led by the child she seems to see something which might happen between couples — gayety, pleasure, loving ways & innocent grace — a wealth of love & sun & joy — herself a part of it with Dimmesdale — It could be almost an instant of prophetic vision on her part — Cassandra-like episode —

The May Pole becomes the child again, the ribbons become sea-weed &
the dancers seem to fill the beach-like place — bodies moving in the
utter freedom of the present day boys & girls on a beach — The child
as one of them
One of two balls are thrown — one strikes against her dress as she is
standing as first seen — She looks at the ball & realizes it is a stone —
she stoops or kneels — & a shadow falls across her —
It becomes darker — The sky is blacked out — She looks up at a woman
standing above her — their great skirts blowing like ominous clouds on
the wings of great birds — & deep within the bonnets are just shadows
of faces — In all they do they move as one — the three — It is like a
crowd unanimous —   She is back in her daily world —

There is a short dance for these three
The 3 women stand still —
She falls into a dance dimension again & the 3 women's skirts blowing
resolve into the wings of great birds — creatures half women — half
birds — like the Harpies — It is this 3 who dance with her — lifting her
— sweeping her off her feet with their dresses — They turn her — until
they thrust her backwards falling, falling into the arms of the Demon —
The 3 women then fall backwards in a paroxysm of delight & sit —
clapping out rhythms with their hands — striking the earth as a drum —
even singing a perverted hymn tune —
To this she dances with the Demon — She has become a witch in their
eyes & her lover a Demon & the child an oriental-like figure of evil
beauty — with jewels instead of sea weed — & dressed barbarically —
The music for the dance is the beat of the hands & a strange singing &
the tambourine the child carries
The stone in her hand has become a gourd rattle —
In the midst of this strange pagan demonic scene the Demon kisses her
on the breast —
She feels herself falling into blackness with the meteor-like flash of the
many **A**s in their origins about her like fireworks until they settle
into the form of the scaffold under which shadow she is standing with
the child —
The 3 women looking at her as part of a crowd — spreading until there is
a crowd of skirts — like a vast tent or billowing sea —

The rattle becomes a military drum & the perverted singing the
recognized hymn tune from which it stemmed —
From behind the billowing skirts come buckled shoes & legs of men —
Then a man alone — Dimmesdale — It is a procession of honor to him
reminiscent of Christ's entry into Jerusalem — the many buckled shoes

are like flowers around his feet — the billowing skirts like the waving of palms —
It is thru his eyes that we see her beneath the scaffold —
She looks like a Pieta — The Mother — with the child asleep, partly across her knees —

In the scene with the Demon, the child, the woman — the child runs wildly after the Demon who dances away seeming to be escaping from her, or after the gourd thrown by the Demon — It seems to be a ball. It strikes the woman on the breast & becomes a stone — becomes a rock — Plymouth Rock — The beating of hands becomes the military drum — the beat of feet the walk of shoes on stone — the singing — the real hymn —
It resolves into a procession of honor with Dimmesdale in the center — It is like the entry into Jerusalem — as seen thru the eyes of the 3 women — As each one sees him she sees herself as his bride — There is the effect of a 3 pointed bridal — 3 brides — 1 groom —
Dimmesdale feels himself as in a trap — He walks in the procession — but in his eyes the 3 women becomes Gorgons dressed as brides — He as the one who kills them

He tears off coat — Shirt thin — letter **A** shows   they become themselves again
on his breast.   (Perseus?)

The child places a wreath of flowers on   next scene is thru
              Hester's head —   their eyes —

He sees Hester as the Mother — the deep Mother — across her knees lies the child asleep — like Pieta (Cloisters —) see note later — the **A** on her breast becomes larger — higher — until it becomes the scaffold — The shoes, the hats, the skirts, the bonnets show as in first scene
It has grown very dark — as tho' a veil were over the sun — an eclipse — The veil of the temple appears to rend —

   (Dance of remorse),
He sees Hester with the child's head near the letter **A** on her breast — He stands behind her until her head reaches the **A** on his breast —
There is a small dance of the 3 — seen in a sea of a million eyes again — The military drum again becomes the Demon beating a little drum — The shadow of the scaffold becomes the skull of a bull — of death — they mount it — until it becomes the scaffold again —
It grows dark — with only the **A** luminous as Dimmesdale lies across her knees with the letter illuminating the scene of the 3 — as the sea surge begins as in the beginning — & he seems to float away in a sea of her hair — washed by it as by the sea —

It continues as it is dark until in the early light you see the woman &
child walking along the sands — making foot-prints into the distance —
Perhaps group on beach as in vision scene —

In last scene when Dimmesdale sees Hester at foot of scaffold with
child — Think of Madonna in Cloisters — the Pieta — Perhaps short
plastic interlude of child across her knees — then playing with wreath —
crowning Hester — etc. Like play of Cosmic Child —
This is what makes Dimmesdale confess —

For isolation —
    All women are brushing each other's hair — like Campagli — It is a
gossip scene — Women linked by deep bond of femaleness — Hester
stands alone — or dances alone outside this group —
    The many in Tradition against the one —

In first scene — the doors whirling like swords — a little fantasy of a
Garden of Eden scene — with creatures about — like a primitive
painting — The Peaceful Kingdom — but animals only seem as masks —
It should be like Rousseau jungle — man & woman dancing —

At the moment of Dimmesdale's redemption, his confession — as he
walks along — there is an instant when he becomes Jacob wrestling with
the angel — It is from this instant he confesses — Scene reminiscent of
Gauguin's Jacob & the Angel

Idea of Intolerance today —
Person in present time — asleep — running on beach as in a night-mare
Pursued by all manner of symbols of conscience from the old New
England point of view. Windows of lavender glass — criss-crossed in
the sun — winking in the sunlight —

Scene around a long table — family conference —
on possible marriage — rejecting it —
dream of Scarlet Letter —
broken by flashes in present time —
    running in streets
      windows winking —
To marry a foreigner — an outsider — The Father — becomes the
Judge — the Preacher — the Devil's Advocate,
asking questions —
Thru corridors of sleep —
    whaling museum as in Salem —
      identifying herself with figureheads of sailing ships — etc —
        in night gown

minister at times wears black veil over face —
All this to pass thru in one night — The night she is to make decision
to marry —
Dream begins as she goes up thru attic in her night-gown — all filled
with old things —
    from Hawthorne —
      House of 7 Gables — etc —

Minister in black veil —

Group of ghosts descending stairs —
Kind of melange of Hawthorne's tales in the consciousness of the
woman —

Ancestral footsteps —

Scene in garden —
    clipped hedges — like birds
                    dogs etc —
    all coming alive —
"Hear the words of Lachesis, goddess of necessity . . ."
Some decision to make after graduation that day —
Family wants her to stay & to marry —
She wants to be — a dancer
             a singer
             an actress
             a painter
             a musician

Graduation exercises in an old New England church with square pews —
as in Bennington —

Outside graveyard with its ancient stones, at some other moment — one
can tower over her — such as   Mrs. Mindwell Hopkins
                             amiable consort of
                             Elijah Hopkins — etc.
                             died in the 20th year
                             of her age — 1793

Graduation address —
    words from Plato — Republic — about Lachesis — daughter of
    necessity — "You will choose your genius —"
Young graduates (all girls) seated — a whispering obligato begins —
heard beneath the words of the speaker — each girl saying her choice —
speaking her dreams — each type carefully represented from any New
England town. (all earlier in time than now?)   1880 (?)
                       or now?

Obligato of voices swell in sound because each family adds its words —
its hopes — Mary must —
        Susan shall —
        I hope Emily can —
as the girl mounts steps to get diploma   (It will be reminiscent of
                                    scaffolding in **A** sequence)

She goes up one side & down the other (as in B. church)
Receives diploma — descends
Diploma suddenly unfurls into great curtains with her name etc
painted on it —
It may be it could fall as in theatre from 2 sides & her name is on it —
to thundering applause — It parts again — reveals her bowing — &
name on curtain becomes electric lights on theatre — which blind
everything until nothing can be seen —
She passes thru light — & is seen emerging from church door into
blinding sunlight where family awaits her —

            or else —
all this could be about love & marriage — to a foreigner,
                 a divorced man —   ?
                 (southerner)

prejudice — nationalism —
         isolationism —
         provincialism —

If it is marriage — the diploma could swirl into a wedding veil & the
name into a coronet of orange blossoms —
as she comes down steps she sees into man's eyes — (as Hester will see
into Dimmesdale's —)
as she comes out of church-door it will be like Hester coming out of
prison door — Picture taken in graveyard near Mindwell's grave stone

That night at dinner —   (she thinks of it later)
                    (like preacher later)
    Grandfather
                    she drops her diploma on grave —
    Father —   as she stoops to pick it up —
    Mother   she sees gravestone — 19th year —
    3 Aunts   (She is 19 — The day is the same —
                    200 years before)
    3 Uncles —   She leaves her flowers there

    (These form a chorus who will speak all thru film)

Grandfather is preacher who made Graduation address — He will be
preacher in Scarlet Letter episode —

Argument at dinner about her future — her marriage — The denunciation
of her grandfather saying it will be original sin —

Later —
    Sitting on porch — on stoop — in evening —
    She is silent — or talking to "boy next door" — while family
    whispers in obligato — under all that is said —
    Boy says Good-night —
                I'll see you tomorrow?
    She answers — I suppose so —
She is beaten — all the strings are tight —
She goes upstairs to bed —
a four-poster —an old room —
She sleeps —
She dreams —
She climbs to the attic —
It will be the attic of an old house — filled with ghosts — old dresses —
chairs where ghosts sit — etc —
Or else as she sleeps — or dreams — The door of her room swings
back — inward & she sees it is the tombstone of Mindwell Hopkins —
whose shadow is on it —
"Thank you for the flowers — "
She is holding little bouquet —
They go for walk — up thru attic — at time she drops diploma she
might whisper —
    Was it worth it, Mindwell?
And the whisper — yes —
Someone — you look as tho you had seen a ghost —

The idea of the inheritance which is an American girl's — The women
behind her to support & encourage her — even to face today with its
fears.
The diagram of a girl's heart —

_____

A rehearsal for graduation exercises next day — In the old church —
Evening — It finishes in a seriousness —
conversation — the world news
                the atomic energy
                the future —
Perhaps it could take place in a diner someplace — music — some
dancing — boy & girl talking together in a booth over sodas.
Boy — fearful, a little, puzzled as to what next.
She listens — says one has to go on, etc —
They go home —

Walk past church where graduation is to take place — picket fence in front of old graveyard —

She drops something — it rolls under fence. They go inside to get it — either with flash or lighting matches.

It has rolled to gravestone of Mrs. Mindwell Hopkins — amiable consort of Capt. Jedadiah Hopkins — died 19th year of age — 1748 — "just 200 years tomorrow" — girl says — "I wonder, was it worth it? Things were so simple then."

She goes to bed — her gown should be like a dress so she can wear it thru out dream —

The moon strikes her door — & it becomes the headstone of Mindwell's grave & it opens — Mindwell comes in —

"Yes it was worth it — but it was not simple".

(Mindwell — her great great great aunt?)

The type ancestress comes to her — takes her into various periods —

Hester   Indian girl?

Frontier

(Mindwell — clipper ship — figure head on her husband's ship —)

Perhaps it is late afternoon — when rehearsal finishes — & they have a soda —

Perhaps he gives her his ring or pin to wear —

On the way home it drops & rolls into churchyard — or as he gives it to her it drops —

It rolls onto Mindwell's grave & they read her headstone —

Perhaps boy is going into Navy — or career?

It means waiting.   (Annapolis)

After graduation (H.S.) next day he asks her to have a soda — She places her bouquet on Mindwell's grave — "Thank you"

Mindwell?

Sermon — graduation —

   Text from Plato — each chooses his own life —

            "virtue is free" etc —

Voices of Desire
Phaedra

Phaedra: photograph by Martha Swope

Phaedra —
   Phantasmagoria of Desire —

Rather than do in dance form the play Phaedra, I would like to show the
incidents which led to the play as story —

There are 2 times in the 24 hours we call a day when terrors walk and
we are under the spell of the uncontrollable forces — one being desire —
These times are in (1) the mid-afternoon heat — what is called the time
of siesta — (2) in the dark crucial hours of the night — early morning
really — when in extreme illness the crisis occurs & often, when the
energy is too low — that death occurs — this is between 2 & 3 A.M.

I feel with Phaedra that it is not a night scene, but the heat of
afternoon — like the terrible time before the monsoon — before the
rains come —

This time of day is for sleeping in tropical places or desert places —
Even while one endeavors to sleep, or to lie down, the restless
imaginings of the heart pace & toss —

It is as tho' at this time a small insistent throb of heart-disturbing
melody or faint maddening beat of water upon water as in a fountain, or
the insistent dryness of a drum, is heard. I think of those records of
jungle sounds — There are 2 — one, the dry season, one, the wet
season —
The sounds of the animals & insects & birds are so changed, so altered
by the demands of Nature, as the supreme Dictator of Life —

It is the time of the drought with Phaedra —
It is the time of the search of the blood for a kindred pulse —
It is the desperate time when the need is for renewal, the blessed rain
& the feeling of fertility again

I feel it is also the desire to contact youth, to be rejuvenated again,
made virgin by the
experience with
appearance of youth —
It is tragic & eternal.

The stage I can only imagine dimly. It could be hung with many shafts of
thin narrow silk which seem to impede Phaedra's pacing, seem to catch
her in their ghost-like tentacles — in which also she might veil
herself at times —

I had thought also of a suspended bed — where she lies at times & can see the stage area itself beneath her peopled by the beings of her imagination — She descends from it and enters the action, she retreats to it climbing wearily a small stair to her lonely bed. I have not as yet spoken to a designer. I am not certain who it will be.

As you suggested I am not putting the incidents in sequence — It seems better to allow them a little more freedom to fall into place —

The characters involved are —

Phaedra
Hippolytus
Theseus —
Artemis
Aphrodite
Aricia
   (child-like)
Persephone
Chorus of 3 couples
Pasiphae

The action involves —
   Phaedra —

      with her theme or characterization there is a constant recurrence.
      I do not suggest this to you as a musical form but it has a certain
      quality of a rondo. It constantly returns in new forms & images
      but centered around the main expressive instant of obsession by
      desire — over which there is no control or ease until death —

The spectacle before Theseus when he first went to Crete & Phaedra saw him —

Should it be Phaedra or Pasiphae — ??
    The ancient one —
          Pasiphae
        or
    The young one —
          Phaedra —
Gide — words   ??

2 parts in one —   ?
    Phaedra
    Pasiphae

Ariadne — ?   viewing

The arena —
   The acrobats — etc —
   Group —
Daedalus ?
Labyrinth ?
       see Gide 76

". . . induce a delicious intoxication, rich in flattering delusions,
& provoke the mind, filled as this is with voluptuous images, to a
certain pointless inactivity; 'pointless,' I say, because it has merely
an imaginary outcome in visions & speculations without order, logic, or
substance. The effect of the gases is not the same for all those who
breathe them; each is led on by the complexities implicit in his own
mind to lose himself, if I may so put it, in a labyrinth of his own
devising." . . . 76

". . . these perfumes is that when one has inhaled them for a certain
time, they are already indispensable; the body & mind have formed a
taste for this malicious insobriety; outside of it reality seems charmless &
one no longer has a wish to return to it. And that — that above all — is
what keeps one inside the labyrinth —"   (Theseus — Gide 77)

My sister —   Ariadne
My brother —   Minotaur
Myself —   Phaedra
My mother —   Pasiphae
My husband — Theseus
My Desired —   Hippolytus

It happened
   once upon a time —
It happens —
   Every day —

Is there a possibility of using a man's voice as Theseus — from
the Gide text — ?

"The voices of desire"
     Gide — Theseus — 93

The Rites of the day
   lamentation   (father)
         &
   songs of joy   (Theseus)

Beginning —
    Phaedra (arms locked)
    Theseus (locked)
Backing away —

Spectator's seat — (high)
Phaedra on the exploits of Theseus —
Phaedra — the victim — the one who is sacrificed

Struggle   (toward youth)
1)   Phaedra —
       longing — anguish —
       visions — of the bed —
       symbol of desire —
       (solo)

2)   Visions —
       The Labyrinth —
          Theseus
          Ariadne
          Pasiphae

3)

1)   Anguish of desire —
2)   Labyrinth of desire
3)   Ashes of desire —

Tragedy of enactment

Anguish of Phaedra (Desire)
Labyrinth of Desire
Tragedy of enactment (Desire)

"It is written"
    in Arabic "Mektoub"

Observations on Deaths and Entrances
and notes for a film never realized

Deaths and Entrances: photograph by Barbara Morgan

Feb 18 — 1950

Tonight in Deaths & Entrances while standing I suddenly knew what witchcraft is — in microcosm — It is the being within each of us — sometimes the witch, sometimes the real being of good — of creative energy — no matter in what area or direction of activity. The witches' sabbath is the anger we know at times. The sacrament is taken but the wine of life is the blood of death — It is the abomination which is partaken of rather than the essence of life — when I lose my temper it is like a witches' sabbath — the Black Mass — the world is given over to the powers of darkness & the rule of the blood — It is Kali in her terrible aspect — It is Shiva the destroyer — It is Lucifer — "as proud as Lucifer" — the obverse of God —
This, too, is what D & E. is about — only I did not know enough to quite see it through —

All the repentance is of no avail. It is "giving for" one mood the other state of consciousness — doing it quite consciously — in face of all temptation to do otherwise & to "ride the broom-stick." Strength comes from a use of the muscles — The athletes of God wrestled & grew strong. They chose, & they acted.
What I do must be done in full sunlight of awareness — I must learn a means of changing the mood — the state of consciousness — without double-mindedness or tho't of gain.

Notes for a something — not a dance —

The last few hours of the last day of month —
The driving thru the streets to the lecture —
The man who had lost himself —
The car Jerry — his publisher — had made him buy as an attribute of success —
wrote book on Love — best seller   Psychologist —
                                     inveigled into lecture tour
                                     by publisher —

Degradation of Love —   Love in Literature
    Literature   "   " 20th C. Literature
    movies —

The Cult of Love

Psychologists Notebook on Love
Serious book but lecture
tour not serious. It had become a
kind of cult with women to read &
discuss book.

He had been a small serious professor of psychology in a midwestern
college —

Diagnosis of a nation's health by attitude toward Love —

gypsy —
    You have lost something —
    no — I think not —
    You have lost something —
    You come in mockery to
    spite your friend but I
    will see for you —

gypsy —
    You come in mockery to spite
    the man with you —
    That is bad — but I will tell
    what I see — because
    You are in danger —
    You have lost something —

sometime within these next 4 weeks
adventure will present itself to you
If you listen to the voice you
will find what you have lost
which is yourself — $5.00 please

will find what you have lost —
which is yourself —
$5.00 please

Psychological analysis of Love —

The element of the probable & the wonderful —

It was here — the last day —
The last few hours of the last day of the month allotted to him by the
gypsy — were here — made him think of Caesar
"The Ides of March have come
                but the soothsayer's reply had been
Aye, Caesar, but not gone"
It was small comfort — but it was some comfort.   He suddenly realized
how intensely he had lived this month, counting on that fortune teller's
words. He, who had never been to a fortune teller of any kind — had
tea leaves or palms read or fooled with cards — he a respectable professor
of psychology — Just because by some curious twist he had written a
serious work on Love which had become by some fluke a best seller —
here he was driving to his lecture — just one of many — in an expensive
car no professor's salary ever bought. It had been on account of the car
he had gone to the fortune-teller in the first place — simply & deliber-

& a gypsy at that

The Notebooks of Martha Graham / 88

ately to annoy Jerry — Jerry Darrow was a good publisher — but a hard & often corrupt man. It had been due to Jerry's ideas of publicity that he had been persuaded to buy this expensive, vulgar car in the first place. He had done everything Jerry wanted. Somehow he found himself on a merry-go-round & it never stopped — (nice image, that merry-go-round — because he felt he had ridden the swans, the lions, the tigers, the horses, everything a merry-go-round has, on this infernal tour). But on that day a month back something snapped — On just such a sunny day as this they were driving thru a poor section of some city — Jerry in his usual obnoxious way was pressing the point of another book — Cato was driving — Suddenly on impulse — he really never yielded to impulses — he stopped when he saw the fortune teller's place — saying he would ask her advice — leaving Jerry helpless in a swarm of children —

He entered & the curtain dropped behind him. He could barely see after the sunlight but a woman was sitting quite quietly & serenely —
she spoke
"You have lost something"
It was a statement — not a question.
Cato said no — he tho't not.
She continued —
"You come in mockery — you will not leave so.
I will see for you
You have lost something. It is yourself. Within the month adventure will come to you
If you will receive it believe in it you will find what you have lost —
Precisely & exactly in one month it must happen or you have missed it —
That is all — $5.00 please."
And here he was driving thru a small town after his lecture — on the last afternoon of the last day of this marked month — He realized how secretly — denying it even to himself, he had counted on this month — How carefully he had dressed himself today — groomed himself physically, spiritually almost — for this day — how all month he had looked at everything with open eyes, seeking & ready — It had been a nice month. Take today for example — He had ended his lecture on an impulsive improvised statement — somthing he had never done before —
   "Drink deep of the waters of the intuition"

———

He was as startled & delighted as any one of the listeners —
the applause etc — . . .

Witchcraft —

The Mysterious Woman — Hecate
    The matriarch —
	(who secretly directs activity) —
	    She is the real witch —

The Instruments	Three girls —
The Victim	She who is accused a witch — It is the same woman but variously accused —
The Tall Man — The Tempter Judges	Lucifer —

I Salute My Love
Some of these notes are the inspiration for Ardent Song

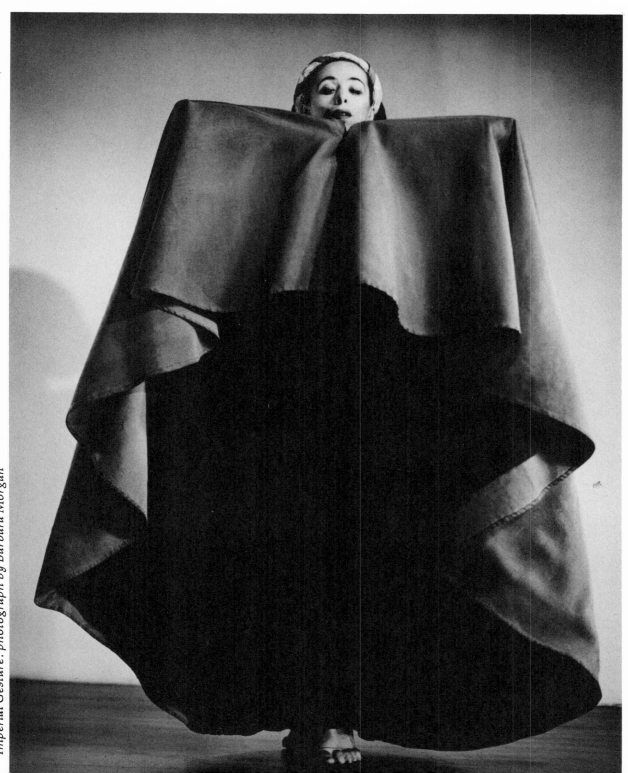

I Salute my Love —

Twilight —
Perhaps — Scene as in cafe —
      Dancer on small platform — as gipsy —
      4 men as matadors — or angels — about table —
      4 points of compass —
          4 experiences of love —
          4 Angels — guiding angels — possessive spirits —
      Formalized — compulsive dance — antiphonal with men —
      leading in sarabande —

Memory speaks —
  The Ghost enters & speaks —
  Movement is arrested — men retreat —
        perhaps great Giacometti puppets enter sideways —
  Costume changed by ghost as she hands garments to dancer —
            or
perhaps puppets appear as she dances — like audience —
      contemplation of Images —
          Life
          Death
          Love
          God
          Pride?

farewell —	Night fall	Late evening	1
		Moon rise	
		Moon high	2
Remembrance —		moon set	
Tragic loss —		deep dark	3
New life —	Day break	early dawn	
Hope			
faith			

What does it mean   —   I salute my love —

To love is to see clear —   all the elements of being —
          The four arch-angels —
The Images do not come uninvited — they can be shut out and the door
closed — This does not mean that they are desired guests — They are
dreaded — but they are invited, nonetheless —

Freedom — will it come when the door is shut and the fires lighted — and the Images shut out by the sleep? Freedom from the dread of the strange Guests?

If — and when — they are invited they must be met and entertained with honor & precise courtesy — always it is one who is loved best — but the all consuming love of that one makes known the others — All four are not loved equally. It is the Beloved who invites the others and reveals them —

> The Father
> The Brother
> The Husband
> The Lover —

The Dancer —
 as a gypsy?

The Ghost
 who has been this way before
 who introduces her to the images?   Yuriko?
 who is the eternal woman

The 4 Warriors
  Matadors?   or 2 Matadors?
   or   Silent One — dark — night — death
  Angels ?   Vast Singer — light — day — life

      —
    — or —
      —

ghost returns
 Relives her past
 Salutes her love
  <u>as</u>
play within a play —

〰〰〰〰〰〰〰〰〰〰〰〰〰〰〰〰〰〰〰〰〰〰〰〰〰〰〰〰〰〰〰〰〰〰〰〰〰〰〰

 Group — 3 couples — or 4 couples
     re-curring in joyous love dances
 interludes

〰〰〰〰〰〰〰〰〰〰〰〰〰〰〰〰〰〰〰〰〰〰〰〰〰〰〰〰〰〰〰〰〰〰〰〰〰〰〰

"For we wrestle not against flesh & blood, but against principalities, against powers, against the rulers of the darkness of this world, against spiritual wickedness in high places" Eph 6 — 12

"And be renewed in the spirit of your mind" Eph 4 — 23

"Keep thy heart with all diligence because out of it are the issues of life" ?

"The Great images by which people live are this kind:
God, love, the soul, space, time, the sense of death, the awareness
of life.
They do not grow as plants grow
Everyman's thought subtly changes them & all experience, & every
voyage made by every man, & every shock of grief or love makes its
minute accretion to the theme."   Wanton Nymph — Payne — 70 —
". . . these are the dangerous images by which we live
and all the history we can ever know is the history of these images. ↑
. . . these images are constantly changing . . .
. . . the images themselves possess a kind of magical instinct for change."

        Love   opens the eyes to light — see
                        "   " hand to touch   receive
                        "   " lips " speak   accept
                        "   " heart " act
                                    (remember?)

"Morning without clouds"   II Sam — 23–4

idea —
   a motion picture projection on enormous screen —
   a hand seen drawing as in sand the great images,
   one at a time —
   Just the hand, using driftwood — a stick —
       placing a stone perhaps —
       The great drawing hovers in the dark air —
       of the stage —

The Angels
   The Romantic one —   Lucifer
   The idealist
   The practical one —

              (Invitation)   Invocation at sunset
                              muezzin —
Night fall   The dedication — (call to prayer)

Moon rise ⎫
Moon high ⎬   The temptation
moon set ⎭

Deep dark   The agony

Day break   The resurrection —
(morning without clouds)

The Gypsy
    Lighter of new fires

She who has been here before
She who is here now
They
The Four
The Three
The One   ?

Three Women —
        (de Quincy)
She who sighs
  "   "   weeps
  "   "   makes men mad

She who has been here before
She who is here now
They
    (the Images)
Four (the angels)
Outside the arena   )
Without the arena   )

Three —
    3 girls — graces   ?
                Fates
    as interludes —
        (scales in various modes)
One —   ?   (Lover)
    Daybreak?

angels —
    messenger: messengers of God.
    Thought of the Lord — Luke 1 — 11

    "Our angels are our spiritual perceptive
    faculties, which ever dwell in the presence of the Father."
        (Matt 13:49)

    "Our angels do always behold the face of my Father who is in
    heaven."   (Matt 18:10)
    These angels of our childlike, spiritual
    tho'ts, "these little ones", are the
    tho'ts that understand spiritual
    principles. The office of the angels
    is to guard & guide & direct the
    natural forces of mind & body,
    which have in them the future of the
    whole man.

    The "two angels in white sitting
    one at the head, & one at the feet;
    Where the body of Jesus had lain"
    are affirmation & denial. It is
    by the use of these messengers

of the I am that the body is
taken out & away from the
tomb of matter & flesh. (John 20:12)

The Angel mentioned in Exodus
3:2 symbolizes a messenger; it is
the projection into consciousness
of a spiritual idea direct from
the fountainhead, Jehovah.

Gabriel — (Heb) mighty man of God; hero of God, man of God;
God is my strength —
The Angel who appeared to Daniel to interpret his vision to him
(Dan. 8:16).
This angel also appeared to Zacharias to tell him of the coming
birth of John the Baptist (Luke 1:19) & to Mary concerning the
birth of Jesus — Luke 1:26.
To Zacharias this Angel said:
"I am Gabriel that stand in the presence of God."

Gabriel signifies man in realization & demonstration of his I Am power
& might, unified with his inner faculties, & elevated to conscious &
manifest oneness with God.
This man will rule the universe.

The name Gabriel, & the gibborim,
mighty men of renown, the offspring
of the sons of God, & the daughters
of men, of Genesis 6:4, are very
closely allied.

In the latter, however, the consciousness of I Am power & might (sons
of God) unified with the inner soul
faculties (daughters of men)
does not hold to God the good,
is not conscious of God, & so
brings about great evil,
which culminates in the flood.

Gabriel could also be said to
refer to the masculine or
wisdom phase of the divine in man.

Metaphysical Dictionary (219)

The masculine contacts the
love (feminine, soul, Mary)
phase of man's spiritual nature,
& causes man to become conscious
of the Christ in himself, to the
end that the individual may
bring this Christ into expression
& manifestation.

Michael — (Heb)
who is like unto God?
who is like God;
who is assimilated of God:
who is like expanding power.

The "Archangel" (Jude 9)
or one of the chief princes who
came to help Daniel (Dan 10:13)

He is mentioned in Rev. 12:7
as the leader of the heavenly
army that wars against the
dragon.

There are several Israelites
by this name mentioned in the
Bible:
Num. 13:13
I Chron. 5:13, 6:40, 7:3, 8:16;
12:20, 27:18

Divine inspiration, and a
realization of the all-conquering
power of God; also Godlike,
or perfect state of being.

Satan — (Heb)
lies in wait
an adversary
an enemy
hater
accuser
opposer
contradictor —

Metaphysical Dictionary 448

The same as the Devil, the adversary,
the Evil one, & the like.   Job 1 — 6 — 12
                            Matt 4:10

The deceiving phase of mind in man
that has fixed ideas in opposition
to Truth.

Satan assumes various forms in
man's consciousness, among which
may be mentioned egotism, a
puffing up of the personality; &
the opposite of this, self-
depreciation, which admits
the "accuser" into consciousness
This "accuser" makes man feel
he is inherently evil.

Satan is the "Devil", a state
of mind formed by man's
personal ideas of his power
& completeness & sufficiency
apart from God.
Besides at times puffing up
the personality, this satanic
tho't often turns about, &
after having tempted one to do
evil, discourages the soul by
accusing it of sin.
Summed up, it is the state of
mind in man that believes in
its own sufficiency inde-
pendent of the creative Source.
Rebellion against God under
hard experiences is another
form of this "hater"
The personality that disbelieves
in God & acknowledges no law
save that of man is satanic.

When the seventy returned,
saying "Lord, even the demons
are subject to us under thy name"
Jesus said "I beheld Satan
fallen as lightning from heaven".
                    Luke 10 — 17:18

I Salute My Love / 99

Heaven is conscious harmony.
When this harmony is in-
vaded by a tho't adverse to the
divine law, there is Satan,
& "war in heaven."
When the Christ declares the
Truth, error tho't falls away;
that is Satan falls from
heaven as lightning.

Lightning is a force that
gathers & explodes & wastes its
energy because it is not in
harmony with the universal
equilibrium.
This well illustrates a mind that
believes itself an independent &
unrelated creation, when this
kind of tho't is allowed full
sway in a man's consciousness
he becomes so egotistical &
self-opinionated that he destroys
himself. Thus error is its own
destruction.

The Greek word that is translated
"devil" in Luke 4:1–13 means
"accuser", or the critical one.
Personality in English describes it.

Demons — (Greek)

a superior power (for good or for evil); a god; a devil.

As a rule the New Testament usage refers to an evil spirit; that is,
a ruling consciousness that dethrones the normal reason.

Demons, or evil spirits, are conditions of mind, or states of
consciousness, that have been developed because the creative
power of man has been used in an unwise or an ignorant way.

If in tho't or in word you are using your Creative power in an
ignorant way, you are bringing forth an ego or a personality
of like character. The mind builds states of consciousness
that become established in brain & body. . . .
Obsessions, dual personalities, & all mental aberrations are the

result of personal error tho'ts crystallizing around the will
of man. This crystallization must be broken up with a focalized
tho't energy of greater power, such as is found in the Christ I Am.
We are empowered by the name of Jesus Christ to "Cast out
demons"   Mark 16:17 —

To reach the place referred to as "my name," affirm your
unity with the Christ I Am; then silently, or audibly . . .
speak the word of rebuke directly to the false personality.

Devil —
(see proper names; Abaddon, Apollyon, Beelzebub, Belial, Satan)
Rev 9:11, Matt. 12:24 — II Cor. 6:15 — Luke 10:18
false accuser, calumniator, slanderer, liar.

"The devil signifies the mass of tho'ts that have been built up in
consciousness thru many generations of earthly experiences &
crystallized into what may be termed human personality or
carnal mind.

Another name for the devil is sense consciousness; all the
tho'ts in one that fight against & are adverse to Truth belong to
the state of mind that is known to metaphysicians as
the Devil.

Cherubim — (Heb.)
legion-like; augmentation; growth to infinity; grasped; held fast.

Symbolical figures used in the scriptures to represent the majesty &
ruling power of God: also His attributes. (Ex 25 — 18–22)

The cherubim of I Kings 8 — 6–8
were symbolic figures representing the attributes & majesty of God.
They stand for the unfettered
truths of Being, which must
always be present in the holy
of Holies within us.

The word "cherubim" of Genesis 3 — 24
means protection or sacred life.

Contemplation of the Images

Sunset	God — invocation —	Ritual	dedication
Moon-light	Love		annunciation
Deep dark	Death	Fear	denial
Dawn	Life		resurrection

Dictionary 171 —

Sunset — Night fall   Invocation —
      Day's end —   Evocation
                                 (Memory)

Moon Time
    Moon rise   The Meeting
       " high   The Passion
       " set   The farewell —
                            (or sleep)

Deep Dark

Day break

momento de la verdad — moment of Truth —
      The bull-fighter —

"bull fight represents the eternal drama of the triumph of the spirit over brute force."

I acknowledge

I evoke the memories

I submit to the agony

I salute the power

Pride — that by which mankind lives —
          not arrogance
          not personal pride —
              or social elevation —

                          That ripeness of experience
                          when fruits become the seed.

Muezzin —   call to prayer —
Dance at sunset —
   curtains sweep in to form tent — (or muezzin?)
     gypsy enters —
       Dance at sunset —

     curtains lifted by men — placed on poles?
                      (caught from flies?)
     Dance of men —
       she in center — still —
        〜〜〜〜〜〜〜〜〜〜〜〜〜〜〜

```
new Moon —    white goddess of   birth & growth
full moon —    red        "      "    love & battle
old      "     black      "      "    death & divination
```

```
                                    ⎛  3 Images?
Love      Battle          ?    ⎨    3 men
Death     divination           ⎝    3 girls —
Life      birth — growth
```

Invitation of the images —
what are the images?
    Life
    Love
    Death

               I Salute my Love —

     is so much to salute   are awakened by that title
There are so many things which can come under that title — love
           &&
almost everything — for love opens the eyes of those who are
blind and they see — see the ravishing beauty of the end of the day —all
of its tragic solitary majesty of departure — the clean white vertiginous
moonlight — cold, no matter, how warm the night — the light which
dresses in strangeness all it touches —

Then when the moon becomes weary and fades or disappears or
perhaps departs in a flamboyant remoteness — and deep darkness
comes — darkness so deep that it is bottomless — soft — yielding
—never ending — & when the extremity of darkness is reached
then the faint edge of a new day appears and a veil lifts from the
face of the world & it is dawn —   a beginning —
        "O, my lords,   loving kindness
I but deceived your eyes with antique gesture,
When one news straight came huddling on another
of death, & death, & death: still I danced forward.
But it struck home, & here, & in an instant.
Be such mere women, who with shrieks & outcries
Can vow a present end to all their sorrows,
Yet live to vow new pleasures, & outlive them.
They are the silent griefs which cut the heart-string.
Let me die smiling." Calantha — in   142
The Broken Heart by John Ford — Wanton Nymph

(left margin, vertical): "a grief which turns into a triumph, a solemn vow to endure & die dancing." Payne

Muezzin —   Prayer —

song /

The door-keeper   Fate
The keeper of the gate

She is the one who sings — who begins the action —
As the curtain opens she is standing gazing into an intense light
—- only her face seen —
She sings —
As she sits or sinks into darkness of the doorway the scene in the
room is lighted —
The conversation takes place —

At one point in the talk — which is only a few remarkable
sentences — a sound begins —
It is as tho' some idea in the talk caused a humming — a deep
vibration —
The woman rises slowly — the lights on the men fade — you can
hear only a word or 2 of a sentence until you hear nothing as she
advances toward the seated woman —
She seems to shed her large outer cape or dress as a cocoon —
she emerges as tho' the inner nature were revealed —
The woman takes the garment — also perhaps gives her a veil
for her head or a fan or a wreath or even small crotali
She is then like a gypsy dancer — lithe, taut, changed —
She dances a sarabande — of longing — nostalgia, dignity —
command —

Nightfall —
Muezzin —   call to the night — to prayer.
curtains open — on a large stage — dark, mysterious, except for one
brilliantly lighted area — It gives the illusion of
    a room in a Spanish-Moorish house —
        fretted marble.
        shadows of designs —
        sense of cool stillness in summer heat
        or a balcony —
            or
        a garden at night —
            a tree —
            a Fountain —
a table — ?
chairs
a meal is finished
except for wine —

1 woman
3 men

In the left margin, written diagonally: purple grapes — moon — Love — death — perhaps just words — lavish — (all with humming —)

She sits slightly apart — she is silent — & has no glass.
The men are in conversation — It is as tho' it had been in progress
for some time
    under the speech there is the sound of something like music —
       a guitar
       a flute
       the sound of water as a fountain —

The talk is philosophic — It is about life & death & that which
connects them — love —

This is the contemplation of the images — this slow debate — the
woman listens —

The conversation has been about love —
The 3 men have spoken of the "querencia"
"The querencia is the exact spot which every Spanish fighting bull
chooses to return to, between his charges, in the arena. It is his invisible
fortress or camp. It is not marked by anything but the bull's preference
for it, & it may be near the center, near the barricade, or between the
two, as the bull chooses. The nearer the bull is to his querencia or
stomping station, the more formidable he is, the more full of confidence,
& the more difficult to lure into the territory of the bull-fighters, for
their territory is wherever the bull is most vulnerable, & least sure of
himself."
                                   Lorca — Roy Campbell — 8 —

Perhaps the opening should include 3 girls also —
so all is determined & set —
If so — it could be
The muezzin — & out of the darkness after comes the sound of feet &
perhaps crotali —
When light comes up on scene with men — it is as tho they were
watching the dancing — after dinner — The dancers leave — Woman
gives each one a flower?
The dance itself is simple & quite lovely in a feminine way —
very young —
Then the talk begins — perhaps she has gone to other side of stage
with glass?
scene fades on men —
Then the woman leaves the table — or group,
gives her robe to the keeper of the gate —
& dances (passes thru a gate leaving cloak behind her
in keeper's hands)
or — she

or

during the talk & on the key line which kindles & awakens the woman's
imagination — her inner world opens —
    To her the great images hang gleaming & strange & she walks
    among them —
Then comes her dance —
    It is like the bull's dance in his querencia —

At a certain point the vast images turn & become invisible — They
become barricades behind which 3 men are standing — the prototypes of
the men at the table — the matadors —

Dance of three men —
Woman is in the center
    like gypsy dancer — singer —
                or
    the bull in the querencia —
The men never touch her —
It is like something of the bull ring —
    The parade —
    The fierce proud action —

(What would be the images as she sees them —)
     her background —
     what is Life   to her
     "   " Death " "   (crucifix?)
     "   " Love " "

At the end of the men's dance it is broken by Keeper of the Gate —
    Poem
    Song
    some special thing — guitar — drums — ?

They become barricades again —
The men disappear —
The woman receives her robe from the Keeper of the Gate — passes thru
gate — backing into robe.
    Perhaps a fan also?
Woman goes back to table — she goes onto platform & is there when
lights pick up men again — as tho' she had never gone out —
The words feed in one at a time until a sentence is detached —
    The men are smoking —
It is broken by a girl dancing alone —
            or
The 3 girls again
    one as solo figure —

Talk resumes & again a key word comes & the break up begins — The
woman goes to dancing floor —
  where one man waits for her —
The keeper of the gate takes her robe & gives her wreath of flowers —

(perhaps gate can move on & off — carried? by gate keeper)

(Perhaps all this should take place one scene following another, without
a return to the table until at the very end —) ?

(But then it blends together so much — perhaps it can be made more
dramatic in one episode — but then the words appear only at the
beginning & end —)

In second —   Moon Rise
               Moon high?
          Moon Set —
  Done with one man?   3 goddesses —
(The white goddess —   the soul of man — aspects)

In second — she could walk from table with one of men — words grow
disconnected, hard to hear — she could receive a rose from him
   or perhaps one of dancers —
   or she could receive glass — & is about to take it — when all
   fades & she passes thru gate into youth — Spring
& meets her love in the moon-light —
      or
men emerge from barricades one at a time for 3 sequences —

Keeper acts as stage manager
    arranger —
    Duenna in 1st scene — ?

In deep dark she is like
   Mary, the hair dresser
   The Magdalen —
   The lost one —

(At very end or in moon series men could leave her in formalized
leave taking — perhaps at very end — before Dawn) —
speaking lines — kissing hand
     picking up kerchief
     each one some definite thing as
     another speaks
all done in formalized exit —
what is the end? —

Some lovely dance — of some kind — alone — ?
                    or
men depart —
They have come down onto stage for first time —
When they leave she passes thru gate alone —
The Hymn to the dawn is sung —
One man returns —
        He calls to her
                Beloved, it is Dawn.
                        it is a morning without clouds —
They move together —
        Perhaps some love poem

The images by which we live —   The past
                                 The present
                                 The future —

The God
The Mother   The Father
The Saver   The Mother
                            The Beloved

The Moon
The Sun   Day
The Stars   Night

            I salute my love —
                        an act of contemplation

My Love is life —
        with its loves   a celebration of a night
            fears
            hates
            deaths
            resurrections
            battles
            acts of peace
            celebrations —
All these are the Images we contemplate.

Night brings the song to the heart which invites the Images —
                        from the mystery of life
night — the umbilical cord — the memory —
                        of memory between days —
            a contemplation of the heart's world —

Moon Rise	Time of awakening
	meeting
Moon High	Time of battle
Moon Set	Time of divination —
Deep Dark	
The woman	The Woman at the Window
The Keeper of the Gate	Singer at the Gate
Three men	Three guests
Three matadors	
Three dancers	Three dancers of the household
I salute my love —	Life is my love —

(It takes)
This is a contemplation of its images — taking place during a night —

To love is to contemplate the images —
"The Great images by which people live are this kind: God, love, the soul,
space, time, the sense of death, the awareness of life. They do not grow
as plants grow. Every man's thought subtly changes them & all experience
& every voyage made by every man, & every shock of grief or love
makes its minute accretion to the theme. . . .
These are the dangerous images by which we live and all the history we
can ever know is the history of these images . . . these images are
constantly changing . . . possess a kind of magical instinct for change."
                              Wanton Nymph — Payne — 70 —

The images do not come uninvited. This does not mean that they are
always desired guests. They are often dreaded. They are none-the-less,
guests whom Love has invited. As such they are met, honored, entertained
with precise courtesy and fed upon one's heart — nourished by the heart.
The time is one night —

curtain opens on dark stage —
sounds of water running or tinkling into fountain?
sound of bird?
Muezzin call at sunset —
(perhaps use inner draw curtain to give feeling of sunset)

Some action of Gate Keeper —
perhaps she gives feeling she has been singing — in which case it
would not be actual muezzin but very like it —
She moves about stage as dark presence — teller of fortunes — gypsy —

Lights come up on scene at table —
3 men & the dancer —

> the dancer could be a gypsy or a lady — probably lady as it will
> give reason for girl dancers —
> If she is a gypsy then they are also gypsy dancers in café —
> It is better, perhaps, to use Moorish or arabic feeling rather
> than too definitely Spanish — also because conversation is
> philosophic —
> Perhaps instead of program notes their talk could introduce
> everything —

when lights come up men are talking —
gradually she rises (with fan) & walks along as on a balcony or gallery —

If it is not too complicated the men could be high as on a balcony so that
images could come from underneath — as doors opening into an arena in
a bull ring. Words get fainter — more isolated as they fade out —

or

perhaps images could be at back if all is on stage level with small
platform for table etc — so that she backs downstage from seeing strange
images. They could be quite magical — & over-powering — They might
even be projected — as things of no shape — just moving light masses
in color. As tho' she were swimming or drowning in light & color. The
masses then would be the barricades for the men —

The 3 men — lines from Shakespeare
> Dante
> ?   religious one

X   X   X

Night brings the song to the heart which invites the images. Night, the
umbilical cord of memory. Night brings a contemplation of the heart's
world

lines from Balinese book on night —

My Love is Life
I salute my love

This is a celebration of a night —
Love opens the eyes — to the ravishing beauty of the end of day — in
the solitary majesty of farewell (departure) — to the clean white
vertiginous moonlight, the light that dresses in remoteness — strangeness
— all it touches — Then when the moon becomes weary & fades or
disappears or departs in flamboyant remoteness — the deep dark comes
— bottomless, endless, soft, terrorizing, never-ending — increasing in
darkness until the extremity of never-ending darkness is reached —
And then insidiously, implacably, gloriously the veil is lifted from the

face of night & reveals the new day — in a morning without clouds —
"Jehovah's loving kindness . . . are new every morning."
My Love is life

I salute my Love
Love is Life
with its loves, fears, hates, deaths resurrections
battles, acts of peace, celebrations —
These are the images by which we live —
To love is to contemplate these images.
Payne 70

X   X   X

"For we wrestle not against flesh & blood but against principalities,
against powers, against the rulers of the darkness of this world, against
spiritual wickedness in high places" Eph. 6 — 12

Place of the action
The action takes place in the arena of the woman's being — the woman
who is to be called The Dancer — at that point which might be called
the "querencia"
(quote about querencia)

X   X   X

the duration of one night.
The Time of the action is during one night — beginning with the
solitary majesty of a departure of ravishing beauty. It extends
Night begins when day departs in a solitary majesty
fades
The ravishing beauty of the day departs in solitary majesty —
Night begins with the entrance of the moon — dressing in strangeness
all it touches.
When departs in weariness or flamboyant remoteness

The place of action is the phantom arena of a woman's being, the time,
the duration of one night, the characters, people of two worlds, those of
day who speak, & those of night who are silent, a part of the shadowy
mystery of night itself —

~~~~~~

The action takes place on 2 levels of experience —
There is a supper scene — in a courtyard or on a balcony or in
some cool remote room of a tropical house in an imagined
country — There are 3 men who speak — & one woman who is
silent — The men speak — the lines are few but they are
philosophizing about the great images by which we live —

as she sinks to sit after this evocation of the night, the light reaches the area at the back of the stage.

at the end of this cry in song the lights come on a woman's face —

she is the Keeper of the Gate — a gypsy perhaps — symbolic of Fate —

X

A sentence — a word — releases the silent woman into the arena of the night — her inner world — never leaving the room yet she leaves it — & the gate is opened by a keeper of the gate — & she enters a phantom arena peopled by 3 matadors, equally silent, equally creatures of dream — & enacts her memories —

The piece beginning with a song to the departing day — beautiful, harsh, strange, a salutation to the mystery of approaching night where behind the world of appearances exists another, immaterial world.

The song is like the muezzin call at sunset — but will not be used as prayer in this piece —

There is no reality in this piece except the inner reality of feeling eternal in all of us but I feel the setting should be reminiscent of a balcony on a patio or a large room in an aridity like Spain still moorish today with its small fountains, birds singing at night, dancing feet — & unfamiliar songs wrung from the deep pain of being —

Seated in this room which is at the extreme back of the stage are people, 3 men & a woman — It suggests the end or progress of a meal —

There is a suggestion of a suspension in speech, in action — Three girls are dancing. This dance is Moorish — or semi oriental in a Moorish sense — It is a dance without dramatic meaning — beautiful, lyrical — suggestive of all very young girls — They suggest that they are entertaining the woman's guests after dinner —

X

The dance finishes —
The speech begins — The men speak — the woman never. — She sits silent, apart slightly — in it & yet not of it —
There will only be a few lines —
It is as tho' a conversation has been a progress — a socratic dialogue almost — concerning the great images of love etc —
Some word about the images causes the world of the woman's imagination to come into presence.

One is aware of great figures, bare outlines of figures hovering on the edge of the stage —
If possible these should be like tall elongated wire figures — suspended — almost transparent, strange & enormous —

The woman leaves her place & goes down onto the stage area which should be reminiscent of an arena — The unearthly figures are felt only by her — The men do not know she has left them in her mind — They continue with the words dropping away as she seems not to hear them —

It is here the action begins with a dance by her — a kind of sarabande possibly — a salutation to the great images of memory, imagination — she is formally & beautifully dressed in black, narrow, high in tension, ardent.

Her dance ends & as it does a change takes place on the stage — The images disappear as tho' they turned & became invisible by light — In their place stand 3 men — dancers — prototypes of the 3 men at the table — not as they are but as she sees them. They are dressed as matadors & the scene is reminiscent of a bull ring with her in the centre as the focus.

There is a dance by the 3 men — commanding, brilliant, relentless as figures of memory are relentless — but possessed of a strange, ritualistic beauty. Without saying it in words this scene should have the feeling of reminder that we are at times the victim of our images.

The 3 matadors are the images of young experience, deep experience, tragic experience on some level of memory —

She does not dance with the 3 matadors at this time but is danced to or at —

At the end of the dance she goes back to the table with the 3 men — who have not sensed she had left — & the scene is resumed there as tho' it had not been interrupted — to show however that the time is later the men may seem to be drinking wine —

At this point the 3 girls dance again — a different dance but still in the nature of an entertainment — If the dances could vary — in idea, in costume in music, each time — almost to fit the scene about to come —

The speech resumes — again the departure of the woman takes place into the other area — the area of the arenic world of her own images —

In a certain way the form of the work is like a rondo — in the sense there is recurrence — of elements —
The song
The dance of the 3 girls —
  ″   speech
  ″   woman's activity in her imagined world or memory world —

I do not yet know how often this could happen — but the line of the work is — from a nostalgia symbolized by sunset — into the world of the moon — vertiginous, strange, into the deep dark of the abyss of despair — rising again with the advent of the day into a "morning without clouds" — a new beginning —

The areas encompassed in the experience of the night are —
  Night fall —
    the awakening of the world behind the reality we call day — the
    powerful world of the memory — the images —
  Moon Rise —
    A strange newness — Spring — or first love — delicate aware-
    ness — fragile, ecstatic,
  Moon High
    The passionate height of the experience —
  Moon Set
    The embattled, bitterness — The vengeful — the rapacious —
    the loss —
  Deep Dark
    The despair — the utter aloneness on the floor of hell —
  Dawn
    The advent of a new day —

The place has a two-fold aspect —
        a patio
            or
        a room
            or
        a balcony
  where people are dining — in a semi tropical country — Spain of the
  Moors, perhaps — which lies at the extreme back of the stage —
                          and
  an arena, occupying the main area of the stage — an arena
  reminiscent of the bull ring — circular with barrier

The characters
    The woman who is The Dancer
    3 men who speak
    3 young girls who dance
    The Keeper of the Gate
        a beautiful woman who is the Fate figure
    3 men who dance
        matadors —

Graph of the action —
        1) Muezzin —   or a call to prayer
                                      or
                                a song to the departing day —
            a solo voice — a woman's — Fate

behavior world

2) Dance of 3 girls —

 sounds as of water

3) Speech of men —

 Contemplation of the Images

4) Woman rises —

 she enters the arena of private action of her memory — of
 the images.

5) Sarabande (the feminine principle)

 by the Woman (Salutation of the Images)
 Dance

6) Appearance of 3 matadors

 The 3 of her life with whom she has done battle —
 (not Spanish as such but clear, virile, elegant, formal
 to the point of ritual — The establishment of the
 masculine principle) —

dream world *night-fall*

7) Dance of 3 girls

8) Speech of the men —

9) Woman's 2nd entrance to arena —

 a) Moon-rise — young love
 b) " high — passionate love
 c) " set — dying love
 (Dances with 3 men, one after the other)

10) Dance of 3 girls —

11) Speech of men
 Exit of actors —

12) Woman's 3rd entrance to arena
 Deep dark — *aloneness* —
 a solo
 despair —

13) This marks the turn of the piece — into Dawn — I do not
 yet know what turns it — into a new day — into affirmation
 — into a beautiful gaiety & hope —

"ah! the grass & the wind!
And here among these stones
The shadow of a dream."
 (Secret Tibet 231 — Basho)

Dances to the strange dreams —

the immortal images —

I Salute My Love / 115

Dance in the midst of demons —
        (fears —)
                                I Salute my love.

Dance with 3 men —
It is different in this from the previous.
There I saluted my ideas of my love my remembrances —
In this I am the Woman —
In me each man sees his dream —
He creates of this same woman his image as he would have her be —
        The Mother
        The Beloved   madonna
        The Torment   magdalene
                            mater dolorosa

Perhaps I can wear a large skirted dress which at times becomes a great
sail or a curtain etc.
Perhaps each man gives me something by which he makes me what he
dreams —

        a wreath
        a veil
        a fan   ?
        a whip
        a dagger

Each man dreams & says
        I Salute my love.

The woman is the mystery — the Strange Woman — the Strange One —
The Night — Silence —

The Crossing —   The Bridge —
        The arrival at the place of portage —
                The decision —
        1 Exaltation
        2 Prayer
        3

Emily Brontë

"and the lot of the purple & the scarlet fell unto Mary"
Apocrypha   1251
(Bible of World)

The Trysting Tent —

"If thou hadst known how to suffer, thou wouldst have been able not to
suffer. Learn thou to suffer & thou shalt be able not to suffer. . . . I
would keep time with holy souls . . . I have leaped; but do thou
understand the whole, & having understood it, say, Glory be to thee,
Father, Amen —
Thus, my beloved, having danced with us the Lord went forth, and we as
men gone astray or dazed with sleep fled this way & that."
Apocrypha — Bible of World   1279

"King Solomon made himself a chariot of the wood of Lebanon. He made
the pillars thereof of silver, & the bottom thereof of gold, the covering of
it of purple, the midst thereof being paved with love."

"purple, a combination of red & blue — presumably denoted a conjunc-
tion of the red of Love & the blue of Truth."

(154)   Language of Symbolism

"Moses used to pitch the Tent outside the camp, at some distance from it;
he called it the Trysting Tent. Anyone who consulted the Eternal used to
go outside to the Trysting Tent, outside the camp."

(Moffatt) Exodus 33 — 7

"To him that overcometh will I give to eat of the hidden manna, & will
give him a white stone, & in the stone a new name written, which no
man knoweth save him that receiveth it."   Rev 2 — 17 —

"also I will grant him to see the Morning Star"   Rev 2 — 28

"World of pure inwardness"   (Rilke)

The purple & the scarlet —
   "And the lot of the true purple & the scarlet fell unto Mary,
   and she took them & went into her house."

"Mary took the scarlet & began to spin it."

"and took the purple & sat down upon her seat and drew out the thread."

"and she made the purple & the scarlet & brought them unto the priest"

"Red was the colour of Love & of Blood, & Blood was regarded as the essence of life & the source of all human activity."

Lost Language 355

The Savage Wood   Pageant of the Mountain —
     a Fable.

1) Wandering

2) Meeting —
    Beatrice   177   "movement thru damnation"

The image of a wood
     "a great forest with long leagues of changing green . . .
     strange episodes of high poetry take place . . .   Beatrice 107

Beatrice 108   The whole earth seems to become this one enormous forest, & our longest & most stable civilizations are only clearings in the midst of it."
     "There is, in that forest, as deep as any poet has yet penetrated towards the center, one especially wild part." . . . there is a valley, of great trees & tangled shrubs . . . " savage & rough & strong" where no path can be kept

Bright creature — leopard —   The artificer
                             beguiler —
            beguilement   whom I cannot pass —
                             who checks my way in
                             dancing bedazzling
                             confusion.

Roaring strength — Lion —

          Fear —   Death
                         fear
             Terror   age —
                         eater —
                         ravening one —

                    The Leopard   The faun
                    The Lion

        Entrance —

1)   Last in the depths of the Savage Wood —

        The encounter —
day dream — The bright spotted one — short — brilliant
            The golden one   —
            The grey one   —

                        or possessed
The tale of a woman who became a creature — a fish by some enchantment — & how she exorcised the enchantment & became human again —

The adoration or worship of something which bewitches — enchants —

Pentecost —

Fable —
    of one who has lost her way in a savage wood where she meets with
    strange creatures
    fabulous beasts

The Savage wood
The Encounter with fabulous beasts
The emergence
(Traveling in a savage wood)
Entering the savage wood
Encountering the fabulous beasts
Emerging from the wood —

Merlin —   master of the forest who entices the chosen one into the
                      field of perilous tests

King & the Corpse
182
                      "The magic forest is always full of adventures. No one
                      can enter it without losing his way. But the chosen one,
                      the elect, who survives its deadly perils is re-born &
initiation   leaves it a changed man. The forest has always been a
182   place of <u>initiation</u>; for there the demonic presences, the
                      ancestral spirits & the forces of nature reveal themselves.
                      The man meets his greater self, his totem animal" —

Merlin   magician as teacher & guide of souls.

                                  medicine man
                                  oracle
                                  spiritual leader

181 dwells in "enchanted forest"
Valley of no Return — Land of Death,
the dark aspect of the world —

"It holds dark forbidden things —
secrets, terrors, which threaten the
protected life of the ordered world of
common day. In its terrifying abyss,
full of strange forms & whispering voices,
it contains the secret of the soul's
adventure.

183 master of the entire cycle — the shape
shifter, the monstrous, benign, yet
frightening pedagogue, the summoner,
the tester & the bestower of the
ultimate boon.

193 "The forest shimmers in a lovely two-fold light . . . a realm of the
soul itself, which the soul may choose to know, to seek therein its
most intimate adventure . . .
All that is dark & tempting in the world is to be found again in the
enchanted forest, where it springs from our deepest wishes & the
soul's most ancient dreams."

"Merlin withdraws into the power that is himself."
What is the world to the forest? What is consciousness to
unconsciousness?

199 "I am the greatest fool. I love another more than I love myself, & I
taught my beloved how to bind me to herself & no one can set me
free."

201 "The heart of man is committed to two worlds. On the one hand
there is the wild forest of experience, which is without as well as
within, pathless, full of monsters & adventures, fairies &
enchantresses & of spellbound lovely beings who require to be
rescued & who then enchant their rescuers. And, on the other
hand, there is the dense-sweet-smelling whitethorn hedge; & all
longing for far places comes home to rest under its cloud of flowers,
painfully, yet blissfully stilled. The serpent coils into its last sleep.
And this is the eve of the day of creation, the dark night before the
myriad forms & events of the visible world have burst from the
sanctuary whose veil no hand has ever raised"

"Once upon a time"
>There was a princess who was bewitched by the master of
>the forest
>There was a princess lost in a savage wood — There she was
>bewitched by the Master of the Forest — from whom there was no
>>escape until by some magical means she could break his
>>spell of bewitchment —
>>>until —
>>>>she could find a means more magical than
>>>>his with which to break his spell —

>>The spell of the crown
>>>>crown of thorns —

>>master of the wood by whom she was bewitched into
>>wearing a crown terrifying & painful —

Once upon a time
>There was a lady who for her cruel arrogant ways
>was bewitched by the master of the wood
>wherein she found herself hopelessly lost.
in whose domain
>Her bewitchment took the form of being forced to wear a terrifying
>& painful crown until she could find some means by which to break
>the spell of the enchantment — or else to find a magician greater
>than the dark Master of the Wood —

The Battle of the Trees —

Once upon a time   — a fable —
>There was a lady lost in a dark forest — She was under a spell of
>enchantment
>bewitchment by the master of this dark forest — & forced to wear a
>terrifying & painful crown until she found a means by which to
>break the spell, either a rescuer, or a magician stronger, & greater
>than the Master of the dark forest in which she found herself so
>hopelessly lost —

>Lost & terrified & beset she invented a habit of dancing a dance to
>the last Sun each time she reached the depths of darkness &
>despair — & by so doing found a stronger magician to liberate her
>from her imprisonment & painful crown —

Once upon a time —
>There was a lady, who (for her cruel ways) was under an enchant-
>ment by the master of the dark forest in which she was hopelessly

lost — She was bewitched into being a kind of serpent princess
condemned to wear a terrifying & painful crown until she found
some means by which to break the spell —

Lost & desperate she devised small dances in memory of the
hidden & lost sun — & in time her small prayerful dances reached
the Sun & he penetrated the forest, breaking the spell of darkness &
freeing her from the painful enchantment —

The bewitchment of the voluptuousness of grief —
The traveling takes place thru a forest —

perhaps
        at each curve there is a part, an object, which is a creature —
        her clothes are gradually ripped from her as she passes —
                a sleeve
                The skirt —
                a wreath —   ?
                a scarf —
        There is a dance of the creatures —

at the beginning —
        she is still —
                tied by fish tail —   branches carried
        objects of the forest —   as tho' impeding
                birds   her way —
                streamers of moss
                barrier of leaves —
                snake —

        breathless meeting
        with strange beings
        The clearing   strange lights
        (2nd part)   (moving?)

lights go down at end of 1st movement
                a strange cry —
2nd movement — in clearing —
at end of 2nd movement
        laughter (perhaps)
                mad & beautiful —

perhaps there could be voices in crossed & whispered speech in
several languages at beginning — ?

Almost like Bosch — ?

At times all sinks into almost blackness & strange sound comes —

Totem — animals
Totem — ancestors
Record of Forest
word — "no" — beginning high, ending on pitch of opening music

1) The Temptation   The Thicket
    The Clearing
    The Depths
    The Emergence

God's birth celebrated before a tomb with double doors

Gate of Horn 314

Hidden manna   Rev 2 — 17
Island of the Innocent   Job 22 — 30
Remembered Valley
Imperishable wish   (M.M. — 150)
Imaginary gardens   MM 40
    (with real toads in them.)

Ceremony of   ?

                                Moon Rise
                                Moon High
                                Moon Set
                                Deep Dark
                                Dawn —
The Burning Bush
Valley of Vision   Isaiah 22 — 1

Theatre for a Voyage

See Dante's Drama of the Mind
    7-9-10   Fergusson

Scene by a beach

Lamentation: photograph by Barbara Morgan

"O thou, desire, who art about to sing. . . ."   Winds (120)
                                                       (St. John Perse)

     The sound of wind in high, dry trees —
     "For a whole century was rustling in the dry sound of its
     straw, amid strange desinences at the tips of husks of
     pods, at the tips of trembling things. . . .   (120)

     Like a great tree in its rags & remnants of last winter,
     wearing the livery of the dead year.
     Like a great tree shuddering in its rattles of dead wood, &
     its corollas of baked clay —
     Very great mendicant tree, its patrimony squandered, its
     countenance seared by love and violence whereon desire
     will sing again
     O thou, desire, who art about to sing. . . ."

House of treasure —
     memories —   world memories
       stars
       girls dancing
       a clown
       2 angels
         or men wrestling —

The Burning Bush —
    "whereon thou standest is holy ground"

       love
       fear — terror
       "Walls of Tragedy — "
         Alcestis —
       "Doors of Wonder"

a ghost —   a man —
    a dream of the desire —
       or the past

clown —

a grilled gate — door — window
    upstage R.
platform — steps —
       Shoji — screen —

someplace to return to —
    a line of a couch in the air —
    a line of steps — quite high —
       all fade when not in use —

an interior — of a house — a room —
    each object when turned becomes something different —

2 pillars —

                      rungs
    a ladder between — the steps invisible

The passage of a night into dawn — a new day —
another time —
an incident of re-birth —
           Voyage was the decision
           to make the journey —
           This follows voyage —

The passage of any night is ended by an emergence into Dawn —
a fresh beginning —

A woman's storm at sunset — anyone's storm at the end of a day —
  The rituals necessary for the re-birth of day
    The new moon —
        tender youngness
The young queen   fresh, shy,
        propitiation rites to this goddess who rules our
        lives — the acceptance of her domination —

The storm of memories —
The fear of the dark —

The battle cry of the full moon —
    love, lust, passion,
the emergence of the whole being —

The waning moon —
    The fight — the desperation — the ravenings —
    the prophecies — destruction —   *fear of the complete*
                            anonymous dark
The dark —
    a softness to the despair —
    a round dance?

Prayer at Sunset

Storm at sunset

Rituals necessary for the birth of Day —

Sunset —
    Return   togetherness
    Departure   separateness —

The emergence of the warrior in the woman —

House at Night —

Ghost in the House

The storm of memories	sunset
The battle cry	full moon
The prophecy	waning moon
The Love Song	Dawn
(Eos)	

The facing of the inner being —

    Sunset

    waxing moon —

    Full moon — Battle cry of one's
                 powers of love & lust.

    waning moon —

Sunset is departure — leave-taking — farewell —
It can be an end, or a beginning of a new time —
It can be the herald of dawn — if night is the cradle of the new,
rather than the death of the past —

There are many sunsets in our lives —

It is a time of rich color, of remembrance, *unease*
unbearable beauty and inescapable anguish — longing —
                  fear of the approaching night —
                          dark

It lasts a short space of time — like the voluptuous sunset near
Boulder Dam — all rose, all hushed, even the water in which one swam
rose, heavy in texture, slow-moving —
an instant of intense awareness, an hiatus in activity, an arrest, before
the plunge of the grey and the final dark —
                      anonymity of the dark

The ghosts who come during the strange hours we call night are the age-old memories — the race remembrances — those moments of residence in the anonymity of night when we re-assemble to be born again. "You have so little time to be born to this instant" — The ritual of the Goddess of Renewal — the crescent Moon — implicit with promise of fulfillment —

Night is the Time of the Goddess —
Day is the Time of the God —

Night is the Time one enters the regions
    of Demeter
       Persephone
       Isis
       Mary the Mother of God
       Hecate —   the prostitute —

       Death
       change —
       Renewal

The World of the Woman —
    where continuity is the dynamic

The Gods of the Greeks — Kerenyi.
. . . "Zeus stood in sacred awe of the goddess — Night"   (32)
. . . Three great goddesses play the part of Mother of the World: the sea-goddess Tethys, the goddess Night, & Mother Earth. They constitute a Trinity. . . . All thru mythology one comes across 3 goddesses. Real Trinities, sometimes almost forming a single Threefold Goddess."   (31)

"Our lunar month was divided into 3 parts, & our moon had
3 aspects: as the waxing
        "   full
        "   waning
sign of a divine presence in the sky"

Three Fates
    Spinner —   Klotho
    apportioner — Lachesis   — oldest —
    Inevitable —   Atropos (smallest — most powerful)

"When the moon shone, Artemis was present, & beasts & plants would dance"
                                            (149)

                    Voyage —
    The Sphinx —   The Challenger —
                                    demanding an answer
                                    to the riddle —

                                    The answer is the
                                    wholeness of Experience —
                                    (man as manifestation)

a woman stands at the threshold of night
a woman stands at the threshold of recognition
night is the cradle of the day —

muezzin —
    woman flat on floor — as in prayer
                            despair
                            wonder

rises —
    coat of fur   Perhaps shrouded as
    dagger —   in burnoose as she rises.

    dance of half beast
            half woman

            contrasts
gentleness   violence
elegance   beastliness —
wonder   stupidity —

Dancer in a night cafe?

Night of Vision
        Illumination —

                        Luminaries —
                            they burn at Fiesta time —

                    Dawn —
"Stella Maria Maris, hodie processit ad ortum"
Mary Star of the Sea is risen today —

Bugle of the watch announced the Dawn
                        (Suso)
"One day . . . whilst the Servitor was still at rest, he heard within
himself a gracious melody by which his heart was greatly moved. And at
the moment of the rising of the morning star, a deep sweet voice sang

within him these words: Stella Maria Maris, hodie processit ad ortum. That is to say, Mary Star of the Sea is risen today. And this song which he heard was so spiritual & so sweet, that his soul was transported by it, and he too began to sing joyously . . . and one day — it was in carnival time — the Servitor had continued his prayers until the moment when the bugle of the watch announced the dawn. Therefore, he said to himself, Rest for an instant before you salute the shining Morning Star. And whilst his senses were at rest, behold! angelic spirits began to sing the fair Respond: 'Illuminare, illuminare, Jerusalem! . . .''

Mysticism 277

The Traveller's journey to god is complete when he retains knowledge of Him — "Illumination", in the language of European mystics. The point at which this is reached is called The Tavern, the resting place along the road . . .   (131)

Image —   Voyage
    woman seated —   Bob?
        wide skirt making cavern of legs —
        man kneeling between her wide knees —
        Her feet clasp about him & he falls backward — down steps as
        she rises —   Voyage
Image —   Stuart —
        man & woman with crossed daggers —

Image —
        white silk curtain — as at window —
        lights of sunset thrown on it —
        occasionally it blows out as in a breeze —
        perhaps at the end when it is apparent sun has set — color gone —
            woman in silhouette as watching — waiting —
        —   or
        pieces of curtain come in slowly as in Picasso painting — to fit
        into design behind woman during muezzin —
        Then she dances dramatically tragically, beautifully to end of Day —
        colors fly out & night begins —
        (people could walk colors in — especially if it is carnival time)

Image —
        Woman   & man   seated
            ↑   hands joined   ↑
        carries a dagger   sword between legs
                                  rapier

        Valley of the Sphinx —

each section a vision of the race memory —

a participation in a state of "blessed madness" in the ritual of anonymity, the race memory of ritualistic things.
    The Young Moon —

The drama is in the strangeness of meetings in the midst of the rituals — the "shock of recognition —"

How one arrives at the dominion ruled by the "White Goddess" —
        she of inspiration —
        she the exciter of the Muse —
        She the Muse herself,
            who rules all expression —

The passage of sunset into night — with its moon-rise, moon high, moon set, deep dark, dawn, — as the souls rite of passage from the death of color into birth of new color — as self-examination —

Sunset
Night   Moon
    new moon   at waxing
    full moon   " full
    old moon   " waning
    Divine Dark
Dawn —

new moon —   "moons of wonder"
a fantasy —   time of ritual to woman —
    young girls
    The Goddess
    Young bulls

full moon —   time of love
                                 of battle
                                 of wildness

old moon   "Walls of Tragedy"

"O thou desire" —

This is a woman's experience as a woman not as a symbol as in Voyage —

This is her drama of return — in which she is a woman besieged by strange and terrifying powers & visions —

It is a telling of how she meets them & emerges into song again —

Muezzin —

Dance to Departure   Sarabande —
    Sunset

Plunge of night —
         as on desert —

Goddess of Night —   (Matt)   ?
    later a duel between
(gypsy figure) woman
                    &
            night —   (as Fate)
    against whom one battles at times

3 Fates —
    (3 in black tights) —
    white sheer dress — pleated
    transparent skirt — small bodice — like corset —
        night flowers —
(step — spiral of leg — body contracting & releasing — into
high extension)

Use of long cloth — connecting head pieces — 3 women — like their
skirts — perhaps —
Full Moon —
    woman with man —
         (perhaps several)
    like Spanish —
        feeling of bull-fight
    Moorish in feeling —
    Battle —

Waning Moon —
    Perhaps with 3 Fates —
        see piece I began with connecting veils or head
        pieces —   Matt
                  Mary   }   ?
                  Linda
    The woman with them as figure besieged by Fates —
    perhaps man & woman terrorized — tossed — separated — beset —
    by 3 figures

Deep Dark
    alone —
    Dance of Meditation —

so interior
so still —
almost like Lamentation —

Something of Woman alone between each section — the same dance
perhaps — or obsessional dance — until at end when she breaks it —
Perhaps Fates direct it — perhaps crotali or small drums make her
dance — unwillingly — each time —

Perhaps Moon as one section
) Waning —   vision of past
) full   — filled participation
    Directed by the 3 — women
          or   the 1 — woman (Fate)

Prayer to departing Day —
          approaching night
          setting sun —

Sarabande —
          woman's dance alone —
                    or
woman's dance alone —
          Then entrance of Goddess of Night — Duet — sarabande of the 2 of
          them & Goddess conducts her into the realm of Night — the realm
          of woman the realm of Death — the realm of the unconscious —

          Perhaps the Goddess of Night bears a cup —
          The woman drinks of it —
              Either at beginning —
                  & all is a vision —
                    or
              at the moment Moon wanes —
                        &
              she sinks into the deep dark —
                  There all is relived delicately & completely
                      as vision —
                          or
                      memory —
          And she emerges into New Day —
Symbolism of cup from which Christ drank at last supper — The Grail —
The act of acceptance —
The Grail for which the knights searched was the cup of acceptance
                    or
          The strength to perform the act of acceptance

shaped like a Golden flower — open —

Perhaps held by Goddess of Night

Refusal to accept   of cup
act of acceptance

held by woman — participant

Canticle —
    Ending —
        when Mary re-enters with flowers
          (another dress
            "   branch —
          different season —
        girls pass thru door —
            perhaps with silk scarves or handkerchiefs or small garlands —
            These could be hidden behind pieces as they move in —
            They encircle Mary & she moves among them as they whirl &
            dance over stage —
              a celebration —

Voyage —
    a voyage of the men —
          and

The woman —

Woman   prophetess
                      Goddess
                      harlot
                      3 Marys — in one
                          Virgin
                          harlot — Magdalene —
                          mother

men appear first —

The woman appears in each corner to each one as he searches as the
image of woman he holds in his heart —

She wears a different cape or color or garment — the same yet changed.
He finds what he seeks in woman —
She is all things to all men —
She is the One —

```
"Eve                    Beloved
   Mary                 Mother
      Magdalene         Prophetess
         you?"          Goddess
                        harlot
                        ancestral demon
```

"Mary talked with the risen Jesus, supposing that He was the gardener, until suddenly, as He spoke her name, there flashed into her consciousness a ray of pure intelligence, and in an instant the revelation of His identity was made to her innermost soul."

Cady — Lessons in Truth — 85

Each man takes with him into the far country of his experience an image of Woman —

She is the goddess, the ravaging one, the harlot, the Mother, the Beloved, the Sphinx —

She is the feminine aspect of himself from which he can never escape —

Each man is a clown
        saint   poet   warrior   one who kills
        devil   prophet   lover   one who makes whole
                   hunter   Priest   ?

Voyage
   The Sphinx —   The woman —

   As he draws hair pin out of her hair each man kisses her — rips part of her dress from — exits blinded with the piece he carries —

   She is left in another kind of dress —
      her legs showing in long tights or net stockings —
         strange — discovered — terrible & beautiful —

         It is this draws the men back to her — changed into their arch-types —

         her solo like an enchantment of them —

         perhaps under-dress also black but transparent with legs visible — & strange flowers —
         or — they enter with strange flowers — like ones they took from her hair —

   perhaps pieces of her dress made into burnous — or cape — or with cape for her of different colors —

Perhaps
    place flowers at her feet as at some strange goddess —
                   or
    build them around her as branches to make bower in
    arch-way?
                   or
    lift her onto arch with branches or flowers twined about
    her —
                   or
    have her stand partly — on top — wild & dissolute &
    beautiful & terrible —
                   or
    she is masked up there — mask hidden at top —
    taken off by Bert as he kisses her —
                   or
    instead of flowers crowned with wheat or some strange device —

           Each man's relationship different —   *demon*
Bob   If she is Mother   *warrior*
              she carries him across knees
                  Pieta —
Stuart   If she is Magdalene   witch?
  dagger   she rides on his back   *enchantress*
              like a horse —
Bert   If she is Beloved — wife —
?crown   he carries her —
?rose veil
    mask?

    Each kills her in his own fashion or transforms her —

    Each finds her at different place
    Encounters her —
       Barge
       cloud
        ?

Each man brings her a gift
Artemis   armour   Mother — Virgin Goddess
Aphrodite   dagger ?   *with which to destroy him?* harlot
The woman rose   *to do battle with* beloved
         veil   *him or*
         crown   *for him?*

She is   virgin warrior
                           to be fought
                witch
                     to be   ?

                enchanted
                bewitched
                imprisoned
                     to be released
                made free

at the end she returns —
    invincible — perhaps in white with flowers
       waiting to be met by next traveller?
       perhaps returns to barge —

what is her place   ?   Barge?
what is place of men?   Sail or cloud?

Perhaps this could open with her on barge — and 3 men at sail or cloud.
    (Bert with his brow against edge
    Stuart on top   ?
    Bob at side ?

On barge with her head at golden prow as a head dress — feet on upper
part — slippers bright or jeweled?
    (?design painted on her face?)

The action begins when men approach barge where she is — It progresses
in the conventional pattern as before —
They pass under cloud & emerge — & they flip her — take out her hair
pins — tear her dress from her — & leave her —

Her first solo is of the sphinx — the summoning of them again —

Whether they return after she leaves stage or not?
There is the problem of the breast plate
       whether Bob brings it & puts it on her — or whether she appears
       to him in it —
       as he seeks her alone on stage — his clothes changed to express
       his inner nature —
         To him perhaps the virgin goddess rather than the Mother —

If she has entered — she exits & he is lost — if not he must
kill her in some aspect —
       destroy the Goddess —
       rip the armour from her —
           ?

Possibility that Bob watches her first solo — which could be in the breast plate —

If Bob & Stuart are destroyed or vanquished — then Bert must not be —
    Each man's voyage is   unto   himself —
                                  into

One — sees her as a Goddess to be placated & paralleled in all things —
(Bob)

One — sees her as one to do battle with
(Stuart)

One — sees her as part of his own being
(Bert)

Each man changes into a costume denoting his aspect of mankind —
    Bob — the Youth —

    Stuart —   Don Juan
                    pirate
                    matador
                        (if so he can use cape?)

?perhaps he also has dagger — & it is a duel —

    Bert —   Orpheus?

These are not right — but may clear way.

The aspects she plays are those deep within every woman —

Perhaps with Bob & Stuart nothing is resolved — they exit with her in their respective natures — she in hers as they select it for her & themselves.

But when she enters again after each episode to meet the next one she is again an aspect of the original sphinx — or he (in each case) might find her at the barge — or claim her.

At beginning she might still enter but from stage L. — pass thru arch where men are — & proceed to barge — It is then the men join her as the Sphinx — Cape, then, is doubtful — but possible on green side —

Perhaps cape could be used each time to help make exit or entrance & be different under it each time —

Her aspect is lost each time under cape — what is beneath that mystery is different to each man —
    To Bob   dream? unknown?

Stuart	Death
Bert	Life

The cape could hang someplace where she could get it to use each time —
With Bert perhaps he does not permit her to use cape at end —

~~~~~~

"oh Thou Desire" —

~~~~~~

Perhaps something like a wind machine or hidden fan to blow her
dress —

Even "Deep Dark" alone with wind — or variations on muezzin theme
     very small & alone —
    "La noche oscura" — meditation —
If figure of Fate is used — a woman who foretells fortune — gypsy or
ancient goddess — perhaps there could be one point of conflict where
woman vanquishes this being and begins to shape her destiny in another
way —

Perhaps this is a conflict between what is Fate & what can be Destiny —
    The Voyage —   Theatre for a Voyage —

Scene: On the shore of an inland sea —

shipwrecked people

The woman in order to reach the shore must take the Voyage over
an unknown uncharted inland sea —
She endures the aspects of herself as in dream
She sees herself thru the eyes of 3 men —
finally rejecting each, she arrives at her image of herself —

The Poet —	The Muse	
	Gorgon	
	Goddess	*to be worshiped*
The Warrior		
conqueror	The harlot	*To be conquered*
hero		
The clown		
lover		*To be loved*

Phaedre —
    Phaedre
    Aphrodite   Pearl (Mary)
    Artemis   Matt
    Hippolytus   Bert

?Husband?

        chorus — women   Linda — Patsy

        chorus — men   Bob — Stuart

                                        Winds — 224
"Is not the Setting Sun the homeland, the true homeland of all men
of desire?"

Poet   — "Divinare"
Narrator   225
counsel   "counsel is that naked woman whom the
                       Enchanter establishes in a spot as
                       close as possible to the stars, . . .
                       counsel of force & of violence.
                       Recourse to the living energy under
                       the calcareous deposit."

                     Invocation
                     Winds — 228
"That cipher-writing which one meets everywhere on wings, on eggshells,
in clouds, in snow, in crystals & petrifications, inside & outside
mountains, plants, animals, & men, in the transparencies of the sky."
                                      (Novalis)

                         (225)
Invocation ("dedicated to intercourse with the Great Expanse")
Parade
Rite
Ceremonial

The Poet
The Narrator
The Woman

If this uses "Winds" then it is the song of a
land — or a woman in a land —

She stands on the edge of a desert at sunset —
alone and bereft or unfulfilled —
As the night fades all of the present fades
& she enters the violences of memory
      violent halls of memory —
She steps across an invisible barrier & enters the
past — the race past —

She is like a Pioneer Woman —
  In a way it goes on from where Frontier ends.

when we flew to Europe — we travelled constantly into the growing
light — the Dawn —
I did not know it was also — after a time — to be my Dawn — that I
was journeying into the light which was my soul —

The sounds of palm trees rustling —
hum & vibration of small winged insects in the sun —
the dry sound of those small drums of the universe —
      "conquerors of time, eternal in time,
      merged in the rhythm of the great round
a round dance —   dance which comes to us from the depths
      of the ages" — (236)
convolutions watching the stars move thru space —
      continuity —

ritualistic
formal   "This poet no more idealizes the world
barbaric   than he accepts it; he consecrates it."
            (Winds 237)
ceremonial to the universe "only that which is worthy of praise
      contains the sense & sop of the
      universe." (237)

Eulogy
"O thou, desire, who art about to sing . . ."

Sunset — departure
Moon-rise —

      "Moons of wonder" 125 —

Recovery of vision
    voice

arrival upon new shores

"Scything Glance"

"Moons of wonder"

"all to be done again. All to be told
again. And the scything glance to be
swept across all man's heritage"   (129)

3 acts
3 sections
   or 4
      seasons

Twilight   sun-set
Moon rise
moon high
moon set
deep dark
Dawn

muezzin call to prayer —

Sunset —
   muezzin

some device to show change of light —
   perhaps a curtain drawing slowly
   together at back
   perhaps all from 1 side —
   perhaps I draw it —

Sunset

Storm — at sunset
Distant storm

solo —
aloneness
beauty of the day
unrest — fear of the dark —
   the unknown
richness of departure of day —

Sarabande —
   with dagger as
   partner?

invocation to the night
with its power to enfold, reveal,
uncover all things —

The anonymity of the heart —
The day differentiates —
The night unifies,
   The time of the race memory —
   rather than the individual —

Dawn —
   Perhaps same
?   sarabande but with
   flower or partner —

Moon-Rise —

The Round Dance —
   Everyone —
curious semi light —
Dance to the moon-goddess
   The New Desire —

                    processional of girls —
                    Ritual to the Moon —
                    Rituals necessary for the
                    re-birth —
                                        of day
                                        of Being —
                                        into livingness

Aphrodite —
        or
Artemis —

(dance of girls with reeds on heads as tho' living plants)

"when the moon shone Artemis was present & the beasts & plants would
dance"   Kerenyi —

Moon-High

                            Carnival of Love —
                            Battle cry of love-lust

Moon-Set

                            ravenings —
                            the grey wolf
                            strange prophesying

Deep Dark —

                            "Walls of Tragedy"

                            Softness of despair
                            great quietness —

The Divine Dark

                            Surrender

". . . The Divine Dark, the Nothing, is not a state of non-being to
which the mystic aspires to attain: it is that undifferentiated Godhead,
that Supernatural Light whence he may, in his ecstasies, bring down fire
from heaven to light the world.
In the mystics of the West, the highest forms of Divine Union impel the
self to some sort of active, rather than of passive life. . . .
The individual learns to transfer himself from a centre of self-activity
into an organ of revelation of universal being, & to live a life of
affection for, and one-ness with, the greater life outside . . . not
spiritual marriage but divine fecundity is to be their final state."
                                172 — Mysticism — E. Underhill

Interlude with angels —

Dawn

"Moons of Wonder"

The Sphinx —
    a dagger —
    a jacket of fur or
    coat of hair —

The unknown one
    unknowable even to herself —

Voyage

She seeks to solve the riddle of
herself —

(Perhaps she becomes each of these —)
(Artemis — Aphrodite — Hecate —)
She enters an aspect of herself — as Woman

Artemis — Warrior-maid   Helen

Aphrodite —   Matt

clown — one who laughs   Bert

Death — the lover —   Bob

Arabian Desert —

The Sphinx —
    The unknown one in each of us —
    The half animal, half human —
        Time
    The Period of the Sphinx is that time in each of us when we are
    enigma to ourselves —

    at sunset this woman is a Sphinx —
        She is half animal
        dangerous
        beautiful —
        to herself she is an enigma —

During the passage of the Night —
        (The fall from the cliff)

after the solving of her riddle & the departure of Oedipus — her
son-husband — as each man is to his woman — his mate — she throws
herself from the cliff —
               from the personal to the non-personal
                   the individual
She dies — she becomes re-born —

As a woman whose lust for power is broken, she submits to
the healing of the night — the time of re-birth —

to the anonymity of anguish — (which is part of) pain —

She goes into the realm of women — the world of the moon-goddess —
in so doing the Sphinx dies but the woman is born —

In this time she submits to the yoke of her womanhood — & receives at
last her freedom

when the riddle is answered she is no longer the unknown, the enigma —
she is whole
The answer contains in it the whole Man — Humanity —
The secret she guards — 〔 humanity 〕
? 〔 Life ? 〕
〔 Death 〕
The sacrifice
The one thing she cannot kill is the dynamic — "continuity" —
The transition from personality to
individuality —

Sphinx —   in woman

        Phaedre   Lady Macbeth
        Medea
        Alcestis?

    The actress
    The one who plays a part

"Scything Glance"

        contemplation of the Images —
The gypsy —   lighter of new fires —
        Fortune Teller
        Teller of Destiny —

Muezzin —
Reading of the palm — by gypsy —
                    (like Marion Seldes)
    only unrelated words —
(some from Winds?)   music — wild humming —

perhaps dance of 3 girls — exit —
    (while woman stands blinded by her destiny)
    perhaps dagger has been given her by gypsy —
Then Woman's dance — Sarabande

This passes into   Young Moon —   ?
    memory of love
    3 girls as Nymphs?   or
    young Goddesses to the Moon —
    Spring — new life —

(perhaps gypsy's lines in
    English
    French
    Italian —
                        as echoes
all spoken by same woman in different pitch — each language (exact
repetition in each language)

gypsy almost mediumistic in her delivery —

I Salute my love
Scything Glance —
oh thou desire —

a legend of
re-birth —

If Marion —
    perhaps some ancient goddess — wearing cothurnal — high shoes —
    to make her very tall —
    slow beautiful walk across stage
    Memory
    Remembrance —
or
        Matt

                        Goddess of Night
    who is the Spectator who enters & arranges all after Sunset & remains
    until Dawn —

Muezzin —
    Woman stands with back to audience watching colors change in
    sunset —

    She turns into wide fall —
        part prayer
        part despair —
    Then rises & dances
        Sarabande —

Incantation
to Night??

How can I objectify sunset or end of day —

(162) Perse — Winds —
Thus in the abundance of the god, man himself abounding. . . . Thus
in the deprivation of the god, man himself betraying his race. . . . The
man with the beast. The man with the conch. The man with the subterranean lamp. And still there is cause for suspicion. . . . And like a
man born to the beating of wild wings on the shores, must he always be
celebrating a new uprooting?

(166)
    and a whole country overtaken before evening by the sacred fever of
the Ardent Sect, advances in Time toward the encounter of the reddening
moons. And the Year that passes by on the peaks. . . . Ah! May its aim
& its moving power be revealed to me! I hear them as they grow, bones
of a new age on earth.

Cave of the Heart: photograph by Cris Alexander

Walk — to center front
R. arm —
circle both arms to l.
tip to r —
final arm gesture —

small ronde jamb
           2X

turn — on r.
2 high kicks with l.
kneel —
Turn & fall —
shoulder contraction
rise in wide turn —
fast running to
     lower r.
     upper r.
     to chess piece —

Pick up chess piece
Back away from piece
Fankick to r — holding chess.
Turn away
Sit — & replace piece
Kneel ripple away — hand over eyes —
               into
Turn & walk upstage L
Kicks down stage to fall into arabesque on piece —

                    II

After Gene's solo —
               To Shell —
Small bourrees to shell —
½ Turn to goblet
½   ″   ″ shell
Repeat to goblet
     ″   ″ shell
run upstage to goblet
  ″ down ″ shell
~~~~~~~~~

Bali turn & arabesque
  Repeat
———————

Bourree & hold — upstage L
        3X
high kick to shell —
      kneel — wide turn
    3X
———————————————————————

crawl on knees to goblet
    hold.
———————————————————————

                                    III
wide extension in 2nd high step draw.
2X
Walk series twisting to L.
              upstage
———————

2 Darts — 1 Bali turn
wide 2nd extension with step draw — 2X
———————

Tip onto chess table — hold —
———————

contraction — rejection
back upstage to r —
jumps 4X.
———————

Turn
Walk — diag. to goblet —
Turn into running kneel —
Kiss —
walk
kneel — arms praying.
———————————————————————————————

after men's entrance   IV.
go to sit at table
Run on knees upstage to goblet —
      Take it — face back — <u>hold</u>
———————

Tight bourree to chess table
sit on upper level of piece

Turn head away —
_____

Off piece into kneel
facing r —
_____

wide arabesque turn —
running crawl to replace goblet.
_____

left on r —
epaulment —
    2X —
Downstage to chess table —
_____   hold
Back away r. stage
Use arms —
into forward fall
Twist into 4th rise
3 kicks with r — to piece & pitch onto piece for Gene's entrance   etc

_____

Exit with Gene with cape

V

Enter to Gene —
Party sequence —
Duet — with Stuart —
_____

Fight —
_____

VI.

Dance with skirt —
    3 steps forward.
    1. foot on each —

3X   shift wt. & r. up on arch.
    use contraction holding skirt — r. hand high at brow
    kneel —
    beat open with l. leg
    turn in rise
    walk upstage

with opening step to C. Turn — kneel wide arms high —

    Repeat opening 2X
    Arabesque beat 5X
    beat thighs —
    Walk to men opening step

changing order of feet
plead — turn away walk

after men's dance
VII
weight L. leg — r in attitude in back — plie with pulse —
turn to l. with beats
Repeat
weep to stage L —

_____

knee crawls to r — 1X

_____

5 wide turns diag. upstage r — (Cave) hands over eyes —

_____

hips from side to side —

_____

to Center
bourree, kneel r. in front —

_____

Arabesque turn into sit —

_____

VIII
mad dance —

Night Journey

Position —
near shaft of material — l. of bed.
Seer in shadow — walks forward — catches rope on staff — throws
it head of bed —
Jocasta — draws back into kneel — rises —

Runs forward into wide 2nd fall — turns on side as girls enter — rises —

Walks — st. l — with l — 7
       r   "   r — 7
       l   "   " — 5
       r   "   r — 3
       l   "   l — 3
       r   "   r — 6

Face bed —
Seer walks down beating bed —

Jocasta catches staff & slides along floor into fall —
Turns on side — tight position
faced to r.
Group dances —

On high note turns — on back —
lifts foot as in scream —
comes to 4th r in front on floor
Rises into stretch —
r. foot in hand — brings leg down —
Falls in wide 2nd —
Rises with 4th to back —
Beats with knee — r.
Walks to bed 6 —
staggers away — 3?

Runs with tip 3X
    l — r — l.
2 darts & turn to stage r.

---

fall?   Turn upst. — travel diag. to bed. l. leg accenting
    knee vibrations 3X — turning on 3rd — into run to seat —
    contr. kick — kneel — 2X — st. r.

Pulsing —{ hands over breasts & abdomen —
3X   { with small turn

Bourree turn to stage r.
l. hand holding r. elbow.

---

2 high contraction kicks
2 knee crawls to Seer to fall on his staff —
Rise
    Back shoulder falls
    3X —
    on 3rd one rise with wide Cave turn —
    Run to bed —
    Fall on bed

Dance with leaves —
    3 small catch steps profile to r.
    open r arm str. to shoulder level r.
    lift L   ″   overhead — plie.
    cross arms at elbow
(?) 2 dart lifts to st. r.
    bring r. foot across L. knee — plie —
    arms open —
    2 darts to Oedipus
    hold —
    Arabesque fall, place r. leaf on floor
    Sit —
    opening of knee 2X
    sit in 4th
    Rise into 2 Bali turns to Center
    Kneel front —
    Rise into Javanese foot movement with leaves 2X
    go upst. backward lifting r. knee 3X
    Arabesque — touching leaf to floor
    Rise with r. leg into high walk st. r. — 3X

2X { 2 step draws facing back.

      Little accented walk to st. L.

    Sit on chair — legs up
    repeat movement opening knee 2X
    kneel to side of chair.
    1 knee crawl to Center.
    pitched arabesque fall to st. r.

Spring —
    Seated on porch — face upstage
 1) Run into st. center with semi-kneel — use arms —
                              3X
 2) Turns upstage — with clap of hands —
 3) Kneel to preacher — to Stuart — to preacher
    Bow to girls — to preacher
 4) little walking step front
    hands lightly beating at shoulders.
                         r — l — etc
 5) ½ turns in place — clapping hands — silently — 4X
 6) Repeat little walk with hands at shoulders upstage

7) Bow to preacher
   " " girls
8) Repeat little walk front
   small ronde jamb with r in air —
   lift l. in air —
   Body leaning —
   arms making kind of circle to r   3X
9) half turns to back —
   to front   7X
10) kneel front —
    turn into Cave turn
    kneel front
    Turn into side fall r.
    Sit in 4th as curtsey
    Rise.
    2 little jumps —
11) little catch step to Stuart st L.
    holding dress
    Repeat to r.
    continuous as turn —
12) Wide lift r. leg to r —
    lift L — bent knee
        2X
13) Bow to front —
    Backing upstage a little to pause.
14) Turn to Stuart — L
    4X —
    hand on shoulder
15) Run to porch
    Take Baby
    Sit & rock
    Return baby —
    Turn — run to door
16) Kick with l. as in skip — drop to knees — Cave turn
        2X
    Go into kneel
    kissing — turning knees side to side.
17) Rise into catch step r with little skip
    Repeat L.
    Turn
18) lift r in wide lift
    lift l. bent at knee

19) { Circle skip to face r —
3X { turn to face l.
     { Walk upstage L.

11) Turn into wide arabesque lift of L
        on r knee
        Rise — turn
        Repeat lift of L
        Turn into
12) Stumble run d. r. into hold.
        Forward 2nd fall facing L —
        Kneel — facing r — prayer position
        Curtsey to Stuart facing L — L front
        Rise in full turn to r. facing front
        Turn to Stuart
        lift r. foot — circle to step — sit — look Stuart

Duet with Stuart after turning chair around & sitting on chair

———————————————

Stuart walks — places hands over her eyes — She breaks open his arms &
turns off chair
                        into
2 high lifts across stage to L.
turn to face each other
2 step draws to st. r.
her arms on Stuart's shoulders
into double turn —
2 step draws —
4 high kicks to st. r.
2 high lifts to fence —

Solo from bench —
    3 jumps r — l — r hold (3X)
        progress to r.
    { Extension wide 2nd
4X {
    { step draw
                to st. L.
Run to Center
  "   " steps
sit —
knee ripple to back of step

Sit —
Lie down
roll off
"   up
"   off
Into kneel facing L.
wide turn ending facing front
run to l.
Repeat turn & kneel
run to L
Repeat turn & kneel
Rise into 2 high kicks with L. facing front —
stepping back into kneel
holding baby —
       etc
Rise
Turn chair
sit — Swing leg.

Prayer —
    Step off with r —
    Run to center
    kneel facing front
    Bow to r with extended l. leg — hands in prayer,
    face front
    Rise with small turn
    Skip to R — 3X
    little walk upstage —
 — downstage —
    to center stage
    face front.
     " back
    hands behind back
    walk upstage
    4 side skips downstage
    kneel facing diag up st. R
    sway back on knees
    Prayer extension of L. leg in profile to r.
    Rise — run around Stuart to kneel at his shoulder —
    lift 2X on r —
    into turn & wide 2nd fall

Recover into back bend facing r.
Rise — turn on l.
Run to stage R — kiss

Cave —   Solo I.
Position — on floor — As in "Letter"
    Beats of shoulders —
    use of arms
    rise into Bali attitude on knees
    turn and fall on hip
    Repeat beats of shoulders
    come into 4th & 2nd on knees to Jason —
    Rise — face front —

Warrior stance ⎫ 2X
knee vibrations ⎭
          to front
Back fall on shoulders facing Jason —
come to 4th —
wide turn to rise.
3 Darts to R.
 "   "   " L
⎰Beat r. leg across body
⎱Beat L foot in profile
        3X
        into small turn —
Lifted l. leg in profile
banking upstage to Jason —
Pull skirt in profile
3X to snake
Jump 2X
circle around to face snake
Back shoulder fall
Recover to original position —
Beats of shoulders
Bali attitude
Turn into lean back on both knees —
Sit —
Hip crawls — 11
ending with leg high
crawl thru rocks to touch Jason —

Back away with skirt
4 darts to Jason
Rush downstage hands over eyes
wide falls in 2nd to l.

Bourree across to r —
hands pulsing —
8 Cave turns to L.
2 knee crawls to Jason
Turn to sit on piece
Snake solo —

Bourrees in place while drawing out snake —
Lift over head from side to side with bourrees —
Place across shoulder without bourree
Place around waist
     loop — bourrees —
wide steps beginning to r —
with wide stride holding ends of snake —
Remove snake —
Drop it —
Turn into sit
 "   "   fall forward to pick up snake —
Eating snake — with knee ripples
st. r —
Spit it out with fall to floor
Rise to 4th on knees —
Rise into wide forward fall —
Rise into Bali turns & attitudes
       2X to center —
Spasm-like contraction toward snake —
Long bourree over to snake
sit —
turn — fall forward —
Wrap snake around r. arm
gesture to r — with snake on arm —
Rise into Bali turns to Center
2X —
Thrust of r. leg across body
Beat of l. foot
        2X
accented turn with knee up —
knee vibrations —
Bourrees r — l —

Turn in bourrees — to break-up wrap snake from arm — coil it
on floor —
lift of r arm with flutter of hand
contraction over snake — 3X
pick up — coil in hand — place in dress — contraction
Run to piece — beat r — l — out

The Dark Meadow
of the Soul

The Lady of the Hare.
a dream
   with element of sacrifice
   curious past memories woven into it
      The Priestess
      The Maenad

Hippolytus — Euripides —
"the supernatural power behind the human action is portrayed in the
shape of 2 goddesses embodying contrasting forces felt within the
nature of woman" —   Archetypal P. in Poetry — 170
    Artemis — ideal virginity —
    Aphrodite — "drags virgin youth from its delicate momentary poise
                  into the whirling flux of life and death."
"If the ego arrogates to itself power over the unconscious, the
unconscious responds with a subtle attack."   Jung.
    "provoking" the unconscious as tho' it were a wrathful
    & offended deity.
Phaedra — Euripides —
    like Eve of Milton
    "piteous victim of a Power that makes her its instrument for the
    destruction of man.
    She struggles to resist 'the stroke of the Cyprian.'
    She has moments of longing for the service & comradeship of the
    virgin Artemis — moments when she appears in her own fantasy in
    the likeness of the goddess following the lean hounds to the
    mountain"   Bodkin 172 —

    Ishtar —
Archetypes
    Beatrice (Dante) — Muse (Milton) — Artemis (Hippolytus)
     (soul image — anima — Jung)

"What after all is the secret of Indian greatness? Not a dogma or a book,
but the great open secret that all knowledge & all truth are absolute &
infinite, waiting, not to be created, but to be found; the secret of the
infinite superiority of intuition, the method of direct perception over
intellect, regarded as a mere organ of discrimination."
(Ideals of Indian Art — E.B. Havell)   Coomaraswami

"my work is that of a collective being & it bears
Goethe's name."   Goethe.

"There is no chance;
And what seems hazard in our eyes
Arises from the deepest source."

Schiller (Wallenstein)

Thales
Nature   From Religion to
God   Philosophy
Soul   Cornford — 6

"The All is alive."   Milesian
"The one ultimate stuff."   7.
"limitless thing."

Myth of the Barbarian Stranger — Plutarch ch — 22

"The erotic impression has evidently become mixed in the collective
unconscious with those archaic residues which from primordial time
have held the imprints of vivid impressions of woman's nature; woman
as mother, & woman as desirable maid."   Jung — Psychologic Types
p 277

"Disciplined dreaming" (Eliot)   ⎰ See Jung —
            Visions — Dante   ⎱ 2 Essays on analytical psychology —
                                II — ch. 3 —

"Beatrice is Dante's image of his own profound desire — the image of
that exalted experience which loves its own destiny because it can
understand it."   Bodkin 188.

"The poet who wishes to pass convincingly from love to philosophy
should be a hearty & complete lover"   Santayana

"The Prometheus or Faust figure, passionate for experience, adventure,
knowledge; defiant of human limitations.
Equally, then, with passionate love, we find passionate self-assertion,
ambition, curiosity, concentrated in great figures of legend with perpetual
appeal to human feeling, exiled from Dante's Heaven."   Bodkin 192

Dido — "For thy sake, yet again, my honour is dead and the fair fame of
other days — my sole title to the stars"   Bodkin 196

Brill —
"Mythology, religion, folklore & fairy tales, all of which represent the
dreams of yesterday."   Freud's contribution to Psychiatry   81

"When I question myself, he writes, concerning the love of my neighbor,
my brother, and turn inward upon my own spirit . . .   there comes to

me . . . the suggestion of something . . . utterly unlike all that is commonly meant by loving one's brother . . . not altruism . . . not kindly feeling, nor out-ward looking sympathy . . . but something different from all these . . . something almost awful in its range — yes & in its rage, in its rage & fire in its scope & height & depth . . . something growing up . . . within my separate & isolated lonely being, within the deep dark of my own consciousness . . . flowering in my own heart, my own self . . . so that indeed I could not be myself without this, this strange, mysterious, awful finding of my brother's very life within my own — . . . this terrible blinding discovery of him in me and me in him."   Stanley Mellor (Liberation) Bodkin 197 —

"The man, loyal to a man's code & outlook, discovers within himself woman alive & eloquent, pulsing with her own emotion, looking out on the world with her own vision."   Bodkin 198.

"Aeneas has no such vision (Dante's Beatrice) before him of glorified womanhood; only, for his guide, the austere figure of the sibyl — representing what alone survived in Virgil's age of the ancient magical prestige of woman."   Bodkin 200 —

→ See Legend of Orpheus & Eurydice.
'Lo! once more the cruel fates call me back, & sleep veils my swimming eyes. And now farewell! I am borne away swathed in nights vast pall, stretching toward thee powerless hands — thine, alas, no more! she said; and as a wreath of smoke fades into air, instant she vanished from his sight, left him clutching vainly at shadows, striving to say a thousand things; nor ever saw him more.'   Virgil Georgics — Bodkin 201

"Dante 'descended into the underworld of his own nature, and, more fortunate than Orpheus, released out of the struggling night of impulses an ideal shape, the heavenly Beatrice.' "   Bodkin 204

Masses of undifferentiated Soul-stuff in the fixed stars
          Timaeus   Myths of Plato — 304

The Woman-soul
The Immortal Woman in woman.
"A supernatural action developed in a parallel series with the human action on the stage"   Bodkin 211
"The Paradisal love of earth"   Bodkin 314
Paradise — Hades (life & death.)
man — woman — god — devil.
"The fairy queen was sometimes identified with Herodias."
          Tam Lin — 323

assaults of the spirits.

The Fairy queen is identified in popular tradition with the Gyre-Carline,
Gay Carline, or mother-witch, of the Scottish peasantry.

"The Ghost is the real Hero or Heroine of the Gothic novel"
    (Domination of a place, of people, by a ghost —)
    ghost as ancestor —

Spenser: Faerie Queene.
    (he describes an allegorical dwelling that could perhaps be
    interpreted as representing the abode of earthly lusts & sin.)

"between the acting of a dreadful thing
and the first motion, all the interim is
Like a phantasma, or a hideous dream."   Julius Caesar —

for stage scene — a prism that would turn with different scenes
on each side.

Virginia Woolf —

"Life is not a series of gig-lamps symmetrically arranged; but a luminous
halo, a semi-transparent envelope surrounding us from the beginning of
consciousness to the end. Is it not the task of the novelist to convey this
varying, this unknown & uncircumscribed spirit, whatever aberration or
complexity it may display, with as little mixture of the alien & external
as possible? We are not pleading merely for courage & sincerity; we are
suggesting that the proper stuff of fiction is a little other than custom
would have us believe it."   V.W. (David Daiches)
                                      New Directions book

Joyce is "spiritual; he is concerned at all costs to reveal the flickerings of
the inmost flame which flashes its message thru the brain, & in order
to preserve it he disregards with complete knowledge whatever seems to
him adventitious, whether it be probability, or coherence or any other of
those sign-posts which for generations have served to support the
imagination of a reader when called upon to imagine what he can neither
touch nor see."   Woolf   D.D. 27

———————————————————

art without belief — that is, community belief, is not easy to create.
problem of producing significant art in an individualistic & sceptical
age.   D.D.   39

"To believe that your impressions hold good for others is to be released
from the cramp or confinement of personality."   Common Reader p 328

"The organizing factor is simply the writer's mood, not the pattern of
the story."   D.D. 44

"Such are the visions."   Woolf — Mrs. Dalloway.

about Eliot — 4 quartets. —
"The hero is the Quester, the searcher for the moment in Time which is timeless & always, the visionary of all the possible landscapes, the prototype of Parsifal whose vision of the Grail is the prepared & explicit moment of his salvation. And like Parsifal, the quester in Four Quartets relies upon the children in the tree for direction."   Wallace Fowlie
Accent — Spring 1945 — 168

In the Holy Grail Legend, Parsifal is guided to the grail castle by the voices of children in the tree (as Siegfried the bird)

Burnt Norton — "the leaves were full of children."

The tree of Eden is at the source of the world, & the children who inhabit it are those beings possessed by that immediate kind of love which is innocency, by the deep intuition which accompanies original love & permits a breathless lucidity concerning the purpose & actions of man. The children in the Parsifal legend know the way to the grail castle because they are pure, & the children in Eliot's poems are still waiting for the modern quester to recover sufficient innocency to ask the way.
Ditto —

Destiny —
          Moira
Moirai — daughters of the night
Moira —
    "She represents the apportionment of each God to his province, status, or privilege. It is at once plain why she is above any or all of the gods, & how the limits she sets to their powers can be thought of as moral limits. Hesiod definitely says that the Moirai, the daughters of night, pursue the transgressions, not only of men, but of Gods.
    The original conception of Moira turns out to be spatial rather than temporal. We are to think of a system of provinces, coexisting side by side, with clearly marked boundaries."   17.
Cornford   Religion to Philosophy

Stands for the provincial ordering of the world.

"Moira is a representation of the Necessity & Justice (Must & Ought) of the elemental disposition. That is the whole content of the notion of Destiny."   21 —

"When he has finished his speech, he rises to go away, but is stopped by his . . . Familiar Spirit, & stays to deliver a Recantation of his blasphemous dispraise of Love.

The sanity of the non-lover, on which he had enlarged, is indeed a paltry thing, he now says, as compared with the madness of the lover. Madness is the gift of God. There are four kinds of divine madness: the first is prophetic inspiration . . . the second is religious exaltation — the feeling of . . . the initiated person; the third is poetic genius; and the fourth is the Love by which the immortal Soul is winged for her flight to Heaven."   Phaedrus Myth   306
                        (Myths of Plato — Stewart, J.A.) Macm.

"If a Soul be perfect and keep her wings full of feathers, she flieth high & encompasseth the whole world with her government." Ditto. 309

"For Envy standeth afar from the Heavenly Choir."   311

"The Substance which Verily Is, which hath no color & no shape, & hand cannot touch, is comprehended only by the governor of the Soul, to wit, Reason."   313

. . . "True Knowledge: not that knowledge which is with generation, . . . but the knowledge which standeth in that which Verily Is."   313

_____

". . . and all, greatly travailing, depart uninitiated, not having seen that which is, & turn them to the food of opinion."   315

"but the Soul which hath seen most shall pass into the seed of a man who shall become a Seeker after the True Wisdom, a Seeker after the True Beauty, a Friend of the Muses, a True Lover . . ."   315

"Man must needs understand the Specific Form which proceedeth from the perceiving of many things and is made one by Thought. This is the Recollection of those things which each Soul erewhile saw when she journeyed together with God, despising the things   317
which we now say are, & holding herself up to look at that which Verily Is. Wherefore of right only the Mind of the Lover of Wisdom is winged: for he always cleaveth in memory, so far as he is able, unto those things by cleaving unto which God is verily God. The man who useth these memorials aright & is alway a partaker in the perfect mysteries, he alone becometh verily perfect."   317.

dreaming — Apollonian
frenzy — Dionysian

The curse upon a house.
The House of Atreus —

The Original Sin.
    man's fall from grace.
"Agenbite of inwit."
    incessant gnawing of the rat-toothed remorse.
Shadowy guilt.
"he is a living, aching area of cosmic dissonance, tortured by all the
cuts & twists of guilt & conscience."

"for when a man beholdeth the beauty which is here, & then calleth to
mind the True Beauty, & getteth wings, & desireth with them to fly up,
but is not able, looking up into the sky like a bird, & heeding not the
things beneath — he is accounted as Mad after the manner of the Fourth
Sort of Madness . . . & because he loveth things beautiful with the
spirit of this Madness upon him hath the name of Lover; for, as hath
been said, every Soul which is a man's hath of necessity seen the things
which Verily Are — else would it not have entered into this creature.
. . . Verily few are they which are left having memory present with
them in sufficient measure."   319 —

"Let these words, then, be offered for a thanksgiving to Memory, for
whose sake we, as remembering our joys that are past, have lengthened
this Discourse."   321

"Now, he who hath not lately partaken of the mysteries, or hath been
corrupted, is not quickly carried hence to that other place & to Beauty
itself, when he seeth the things which are called after the name thereof.
Wherefore, looking upon these, he giveth them not reverence, but
delivering himself up to pleasure, after the manner of a beast he leapeth
upon them, desiring to beget offspring according to the flesh . . ."

"The ideas of Reason, Soul, Cosmos & God, if represented at all, must be
represented in Myth."   337

"The Eternal Forms seen by the Soul in its pre-natal life, as 'remembered'
in this life when objects of sense present themselves, are categories."   338

"In the Phaedrus Myth alone . . . we have a complete History of the
Soul — its condition before incarnation, the cause of its incarnation, &
the stages of its life, incarnate and disembodied, till it returns to its
original disembodied state."   338

eschatology

"The Soul falls from her native place in the Highest Heaven, thru the
Heavenly Spheres, to her first incarnation on Earth. By means of a series

of sojourns in Hades and reincarnations on Earth . . . she is purified from the taint of the flesh. Then, at last, she returns to her native place in the Highest Heaven, passing, in the upward flight of her Chariot, thru the Heavenly Spheres, as thru <u>Stations</u> or <u>Doors</u>."   351

. . . The History of the Soul after Death is that of . . . from Earth to Air, from Air to Aether, & thru the Spheres of the Planets to the Spheres of the Fixed Stars."   352

"The non lover is sane, but the madness of the lover is far better than the others sanity. Madness is the source of all that is good & great in human effort. There are 4 kinds of it —
    1. The Prophet's madness
    2. The madness of the initiated
    3. The madness of the Poet
    4. The madness of the True Lover who is the True Philosopher.
It is the transcendental History of the Soul as aspiring after this True Love that is the burden of the Myth."   339

The Eternal Forms —
    Justice Itself
    Temperance Itself
    True Knowledge   **340**
    Beauty Itself.

. . . the fact . . . that man brings a priori principles to bear on his individual experience is explained by an aetiological myth telling how the Soul in its prenatal state goes round, so far as it is not hindered by earthward inclination, with the revolution of the outermost heavenly sphere, from the back, or convex surface of which is seen . . . , where the true food of the mind grows, the eternal truths which grow on this Plain are apprehended by the gods perfectly, by other Souls . . . only in an interrupted & partial view . . ."   341

"In proportion as a human Soul has 'recollection' of these truths while it is in the flesh, in that proportion is it purified"   341

"The Philosopher as conceived by Plato is an ardent lover. He lives all his earthly life in a trembling hope, sees visions, & prophesies."   342

"The apparent death of Aridaeus-Thespesius stands in the myth for the Ceremonial Death which an initiated person suffers, who in simulating actual death by falling into a trance, or allowing himself to be treated as a corpse, dies to sin in order to live henceforth a regenerate life in this world."   377

Mirror & Bowl of Dionysus — Plotinus
"The Bowl, the Oracle of Night & the Moon, at which three Daemons
sit, mixing dreams, is, I think, the Moon, above which the soul of
Aridaeus-Thespesius cannot rise, because the irrational part of it is still
in the body on Earth. . . . Orpheus, when he went to seek Eurydice,
came . . . only as far as the Oracle of Dreams, i.e., the moon."   379

"What is Poetic Truth? . . . 'the feeling of having just now understood
the true significance of things.' "   384

"Minute character drawing, the picturesque portrayal of people as they
strike the eye in their surroundings, dramatic representation of their
doings, & fortunes, & description of the natural world, especially as
scene of man's adventures & musings . . . must be supplied by the
Poet; but they are what I have called the Body of Poetry — they
constitute the material which the Soul of Poetry inspires."   355

"This state of being one with the world is the reflection, in consciousness, of the condition of that unconscious 'Vegetative Soul' in us which
is the foundation of our conscious life . . . that behind the world of
'phenomena which we can never explain' & 'passions of which we have
not yet formed clear & distinct ideas' there is an eternal world — one,
unchangeable good. This is the world which the 'Vegetative Part of the
Soul' puts its trust in; & the other parts, sensitive & rational, follow its
lead . . ."   388

. . . "the essential function of Poetry, as Poetry, is to arouse Transcendental Feeling by inducing lapses into the state of dream-conscious-
ness . . ."   388

"mongst sorrows brides" — Hippolytus —   742–745
    see Chorus — 521–567) (p. 777 —)   p. 783 —

Oscar Wilde —
    "No, I do not seek happiness, but pleasure, which is much more
    tragic."   Aesthetic Adventure 147
                                                     Wm. Gaunt.

Francis Thompson
    "Once step aside from the ways of comfortable men, and you
    cannot regain them. You will live & die under the law of the
    intolerable thing called romance."   Ditto 155

"The head Sublime, the heart Pathos, the genitals Beauty, the hands &
feet Proportion."   Blake — Marriage of Heaven & Hell

"Music never expresses phenomena, but solely the inner being, the essence of phenomena."

"Music . . . expresses the inner being, the essence of phenomena, the will itself, & represents accordingly the metaphysics of all that is physical in the world, the thing per se, which lies behind all appearance."

Schopenhauer — Metaphysics of Music.

"With the doctrine of the fall of the soul from the stars, went, as we have seen, the belief in the indestructible individual soul, persisting through its round of re-incarnation."   From Religion to Philosophy

Cornford — 196

"The soul in its pure state consists of fire, like the divine stars from which it falls; in its impure state, thruout the period of reincarnation, its substance is infected with the baser elements, & weighed down by the gross admixture of the flesh."   ditto — 197 —

"The means of that emotional state of mind had formerly been 'orgiastic' ritual, & especially those dramatic representations of the passion & resurrection of the life-daemon, which point back to the old mimetic dances of magic, & forward to the tragic drama."   ditto 198

"The passionate spectacle (theoria) of the suffering God"   ditto — 200

"The power of darkness, Moira, Lachesis Ananke. Modern critics apparently think of this figure as of a lady whom it is not quite decorous to accommodate with a seat in the center of the earth . . . she is Necessity, on whose knees is the spindle with its turning whorls, in the vision of Er. But she is also Aphrodite, who contrived Eros, first of the gods, & the axis of her spindle passes thru the midst of the Crowns, up to the limits of the world. It is the path of souls who ascend upwards & fall downwards.

> (Plato — a straight pillar of light, stretched all thru the heavens & the earth which is apparently the axis of the cosmos, & the shaft of the spindle of Necessity. The soul's journey to the center of this light, i.e., the center of the earth & of the universe, . . .
> Parmenides path of souls is similar . . .   his Dike is at the center. The Dionysiac path of souls is a circle, from the upper region of light above the earth to the dark region below & back again. Light is also Soul. . . . Fire or Light, is thus the soul-substance, & nearest akin to the substance of God.
> . . . Life which has gone out of God, has come back into Nature. The Goddess, throned in the center, is the Queen of Life, Aphrodite, & of her Eros . . . is born again. The downward fall of life from the heavenly fires is countered by an upward impulse, which sends 'sends the souls back from the seen to the unseen.'   ditto 222

"The flesh is a 'strange garment', not native to the soul." (frag. 126)
cf Xen, Cirop. viii. 7. 17 ff.
Plato — Phaedo — (Varia Socr. 1.33)

The Exile of the Soul.
Empedocles — Frag. 115

"There is an Oracle of Necessity, a decree of the Gods from the old, everlasting, with broad oaths fast sealed, that, whensoever one of the daemons, whose portion is length of days, has sinfully stained his hands with blood, or followed Strife, & sworn a false oath, he must wander thrice 10,000 seasons away from the Blessed, being born thruout the time in all manner of mortal forms, passing from one to another of the painful paths of life.
The power of the Air drives him sea-ward; and the Sea spews him out on the dry land; Earth hurls him into the rays of the blazing Sun, & the sun into the eddies of the Air. One from another receives him & he is loathed of all.
Of these now am I also one, an exile from God & a wanderer, having put my trust in raging Strife."   ditto 228.

✳ "The Soul is conceived as falling from the region of light into the 'roofed-in Cave', the 'dark meadow of Ate' " — frag. 119, 120, 121.
. . .

"The Soul travels the round of the 4 elements: 'For I have been, ere now, a boy & a girl, a bush (earth), a bird (air), & a dumb fish in the sea' ".   frag. 117.   ditto 229.

"The soul is further called, 'an exile from God & a wanderer,' is described as 'following Strife,' 'putting trust in Strife'. At the end of the cycle of births, men may hope to appear among mortals as prophets, song-writers, physicians & princes; & thence they rise up, as Gods exalted in honour, sharing the hearth of the other immortals, & the same table, free from human woes, delivered from destiny & harm".
                                    frag 146, 147.   ditto 229

"The course of the world, as we expect, is modelled on the cyclic movement of the soul . . . It begins in a state of unity, with all the elements mixed in the 'Sphere' by Love. Then, as Love streams out of the mass, & Strife pours in from the outside, there is a process of separation, which terminates at the lowest point of the circle, in complete segregation of the elements into 4 regions. The process is then reversed. Love begins to prevail & draws the elements into fusion again, ending in the complete reunion of the Sphere."   230 —

Coleridge —
   "That willing suspension of disbelief for the moment, which
constitutes poetic faith."   Myths of Plato — 6 —
                                 (referring to Lyrical ballads)

Apulius (Metam, XI — 23) says of the initiation of Lucius into the Isis
mysteries — 'I have reached the confines of death & trodden the
threshold of Proserpina; passing thru all the elements, I have returned.' "
— Jung — Unconscious — note 15   556

"All visible things are emblems" — Carlyle — Intr. Pierre   XXXII

"If our inner awareness is seldom interrupted, it links too logically our
future to the past & thus impedes creation. Only night & sleep bring
metamorphosis; without self-oblivion in the chrysalis, the caterpillar
could not become a butterfly."   Andre Gide — diary
                                             (Paul Klee — ii —)

"The suppressed & the forgotten, in the sense of C.G. Jung, come alive
in the artist like Klee. The essential unity, lost thru overemphasis of
consciousness & one-sided reason, is regained. . . . He simply avails
himself of lost energies in the creation of his world."   ii —

"As great art is to recall primeval darkness of which fragments still
live in the artist (Frobenius) it is also insight into higher spheres
& prophecies."   iii.

. . . "Klee's symbols nothing more than indications of the usually
invisible."   iii

"a little journey into the land of better knowledge"   (Klee)   iv

Klee says
      "The happy symmetry of the first line, then the inhibitions,
      the nerves. Restrained shivers caressing hopeful airs. Before
      the thunder-storm the attack of the gad-flies, the fury, the
      murder."   v.

"God is our own longing to which we pay divine honors"
                                             Unconscious — Jung —
If it were not known how tremendously significant religion was, & is,
this marvelous play with oneself would appear absurd   96

"Man is under the same natural urges as the other species of the earth.
He mates, he fears, he struggles to survive & he expresses himself in
song & in play; he even goes further & acknowledges the progression
of life thru his dream of God"   Talking to the Moon — J.J. Mathews

see — The Quest — Vol — I — II — III — IV — R. Eisler
    Orpheus the Fisher
    The Messianic Fishmeal of the Primitive Church.

Fish — first avatar of Vishnu
    "sacred to the Deities who were supposed to lead men back from
    the shadows of Death to Life."   Eisler
    Lord of the Net (Tammuz — 121 — Weston)

                  389 — Prologomena
Maenad — Mad One
Thyead — Rushing One
Phoibad — Inspired One
Lipsad — Raging One

'she of the ground' —   404
Semele — Mother of Dionysus — The Earth
The god is earth-born —

She who seeks inspiration — the mad one — the inspired one
The prophetess —

The washing of the image —   'Washing Festival' —
                         'to give a shine to'
                         'those who do the sweeping'   116
                         ceremony of expulsion of evil

"The Pharmakos and the Fall"   Revue Archéologique: W.R. Paton

Autumn Festival — Thesmophoria — Women only — sowing

    3 Days —
      1. Downgoing & up-rising
      2. Fasting
      3. Fair-born or Fair-birth

The Rape of Persephone —   Yuriko — Erick — Sasha

Demeter — fasted on the 'Smileless Stone.'   Demeter —
    desolate mother   Persephone

Apollodorus,   127
    The sorrows of Demeter —
    "And first she sat down on the stone that is called after her
    'Smileless' on the side of the 'Well of Fair Dances'."

"Women fast at the Thesmophoria seated on the ground"   128

Winter — Kronos
Summer — Aphrodite
Spring — Persephone

"Pursuit rituals"   129

carrying of the unknown 'sacra.' — a reverent mystery   132
"Aphrodite in the Gardens"

                                        Athene — May?
                                        daubed with white

Demeter — law-giver —

"Hero Feast"   352

"armour of memory"
the soul attains to its high original estate thru memory of it.

the madness of the one who seeks.
madness the gift of God.
4 kinds of Divine madness
    1. Prophetic inspiration
    2. Religious exaltation
    3. Poetic genius
    4. Love
       by which the immortal soul is winged for her flight to heaven.

The ceremonial Death the initiated person suffers.

acts of initiation for the soul
    Seeking
    Ceremonial Death   The acts of the lovers
                         (myth of union)

                         The Guide —
                           (May)
                         The Oracle of Dreams
                           (May)

    the search for poetic truth.
X   What is it?   X
X   'the feeling of just now having understood the true significance   X
X   of things.'   X

The natural world as scene of man's adventures & musings
                    necessity
                    Aphrodite
                    the spindle of necessity

"The dark meadow of Life"

"For I have been ere now a boy, a girl, a bush, a bird, a dumb
fish in the sea"   117
                                    fragment Empedocles —)

The Exile of the Soul.
The Wanderer

✳   "I have reached the confines of death, & trodden the threshold of
      Prosperpina; passing thru all the elements I have returned."
                                          Apulius — (Jung — 556)

                                    'She of the Ground.'
                                    The Smileless One
      The summoning of the condition of vision — To achieve it one
      enters the realms of darkness & fear, and from it is re-born into
      the light.

"The object of these primitive dramas — ensuring the fertility of
      the earth — the freeing of the waters"   Weston

✳   "Riverrun"   (1st word — Finnegan)

      'The Angel of the face'

      "I will come to the fields & spacious palaces of my memory"
                                              St. Augustine

      clasping pillar d. st. L. — kneeling —
                      or
      stretched on rock at d. st. R

The maenads then are the frenzied sanctified women who are devoted
to the worship of Dionysos. But they are something more: they tend
the god as well as suffer his inspiration   Prolog. 401

1) Search — Dream — Ancestral Footstep
   Strings —
2) Initiation   — Birth ⎫
                            ⎬ Descent
3) Loss — Death   ⎭
4) Return — Sacred Marriage

Anamnesis — remembering again —   Plato — 577

Initiation — purgation & emergence of the divine

The Dark Meadow of the Soul / 181

All have rites that tell of things to be & prepare the soul
to meet them 5   581

See note 1 — Page 580

Identification with God
                    The Dark Meadow
She of the ground
He of the   He who guides
They who have found
The Wandering One
The Wanderer   One who seeks

"And following It my spirit demanded to embrace the splendor beheld,
but it found It not as creature & did not succeed in coming out from
among created things, so that it might embrace that uncreated &
uncomprehended splendor. Nevertheless it wandered everywhere &
sought to behold It.
. . .
I lived as one distraught in mind . . .
. . .
and when troubled I sought for It, I realized suddenly that It was in me,
myself, & in the midst of my heart It appeared as the light of a
spherical sun."

                                        Symeon
                                Psychol — Jung 102

"The Soul is conceived as falling from the region of light into the
'roofed-in Cave', 'the dark meadow of Ate' "

                                frag 119 — 120 — 121
                                    Empedocles
                    (Cornford — From Religion To Philosophy)
                                about 229 —
'Smileless Stone' (of Demeter)

Interpreter
messenger —

(see Republic — P. 427 — the choice.)

opening —
    First dance with use of lights
    crossing & darting — silence — like a storm
    seeker — alone   in a cape?

They who have chosen?
One who seeks

He who has chosen?

The Soul wanderers — the flight of the alone to the Alone —
The Path — the landscape of the journey is life — the Dark Meadow —
the place of retribution — Destiny — Karma

    1. Prophecy —
    2. Poetic vision (1st strings)
    3. Anguish
    4.
    5.

1   The arrival (opening)
2   a)   strings 1. choice
      b)   lament
      c)

Vigil

One who seeks & finds by means of love
  Seeks thru
    1 Seeking
    2 Recognition
    3 Losing
    4 Invoking
    5 Praising
    6

"A 1000 yrs after Dante we may hope that his conscientious vision of
the universe, where all is love, magic & symbolism, may charm mankind
exclusively as poetry"   Santayana 104

"The conversion of the soul from her present grief & wretchedness to
a state of grace; & if we consider the anagogical sense (that is the
revelation contained concerning our highest destiny), what is signified is
the passing of the sanctified soul from the bondage of earthly corruption
to the freedom of everlasting glory."
                      letter — Dante — ditto 105

"He had discovered the necessity of saying continually to oneself: Thou
shalt renounce."   119

"For now we see thru a glass darkly but then face to face: now I know
in part; but then I shall know even as also I am known" 1 Cor XIII — 12

The Stone — La Pietra   (Dante —

encantemiento —
    agony
    doubt
    act of sacrifice   One who journeys
    final descent   "   "   seeks

Sarabande
    Vision of peace
    man & woman dancing in concord.
    revelation of love

Paean
    Ecstasy
    Exaltation
                              Sitting on rock at first
                              like Jacob's dream

"Gods, sacrificing, rendered homage to the sacrifice"   Rigveda 10, 90 —
                                                  (Jung — 465)

" 'wise men' unite in sacrificing the primitive being"   Jung 458

Sacrifice of the primitive being within
The world originated thru sacrifice   466
                    — renunciation

"In the same manner that the world originated thru sacrifice, thru the
renunciation of the retrospective mother libido, thus, according to the
teachings of the Upanishads, is produced the new condition of man,
which may be termed immortal"   Jung — unconscious 466

sacrificial horse.
sacrifice of animal nature

```
       1.30 ──⎫
5½     1.35½  ⎬ Prelude
5      1.40   ⎭ Strings (1)      ⎫ The Haunted Castle ──
3      1.43     "     (2)  Soliloquy⎬  dream ── The fears ──
7      1.50(7)  "     (3)          ⎭
2      ────────────────   Interlude
2½     ────────────────   Encantemiento
4      ────────────────   Sarabande
4      ────────────────   Paeon
2½     ────────────────   Postlude
────────
35½
```

The Search
The Quest
The Journey
Crusade

strings ⎧ The Warriors   The red knight
       ⎨ The Drama of Death ── Fear of Death
       ⎩ madness ── escape

Sarabande
  elegiac
  kind of resignation ──
  dignity of acceptance of Fate

Strings
  The Pictures in the Hallway

The Witness   Anna Livia
                             The eternal woman caught up into
                             circumstances ──
                             The resolving of the difficulties
                             The return to the original state.
                             (A Season in Hell)   re-born

A Journey ── Setting out
            adventures
         The Return
            (arrival)

Prelude   Strings ──
   The Quest   Haunted castle
      (question)   fears ──
                                 sense of family ──
                                   Family Re-union

2nd soliloquy
   Erick & Yuriko
   almost like a cradle song of a
   fearful kind.
3rd
   nervous pursuit —
      Errinyes
The Haunted Castles of one's fearful
dreams.
   The Warrior
      The red knight
      his court
   ghost

Interlude —
   waking from dream

encantemiento —
   incantation to summon powers

	Day	Noon	night	
Prelude —	The Hill	A Hill	Strings	The Castle
	The Mountain	Mesa	1 The Hall	
	Elevation		2 The room	(The Secret room)
			3 The Dungeon	Labyrinth

(2)   The secret room —
         of Sorrow
            "Sorrow's brides."
Erick — Yuriko —
The one prone under foot — worked
over — foot on back at times —

Prelude   Strings
                           The Romantic Tale —
                              Gothic tale
   The Hill —   The Haunted Castle
      Promontory   Axel's castle
      Cliff   pictures in the Hallway
                           Inner gallery
                           Interior gallery
   The Castle — Palace   1. ⎰ martial
   Audience room —   ⎱ arrogant
      The Hall —

The inner room
   Secret room   perhaps
   Interior gallery   Charlotte — Maximilian — Juarez —
The stairs (at night)
   The   2. Nostalgic
Pamela figure
Family Re-union

_____

(3) Labyrinth —
     Feverish activity —
     made queen —
     whirled —
     driven
     Eurydice looking for Orpheus
     (The singer)

Strings
     bewitched by the Shi—
     Land of Eternal Youth —
     ″   ″ Death —

The summoning of a condition of Vision — To achieve it one enters the realms of darkness and fear and from it is re-born to the light. It is like a crusade against an enchanted castle to deliver it from the enchantment —

Orpheus & Eurydice
Persephone —
Drama of resurrection —
     Re-birth —
The Enchanted Castle is Death —
Irish Myth
Land of Forgetfulness —

There may be some way to indicate the change of areas — some staging device used
Erick as The Host   Nina
                                    May
                                    Yuriko
                                    Marjory
                                    Pearl
                                    Ethel
                    The Enchanted Castle —
                      The Host — Erick
                      The Guardians — May or Guide

The first arpeggio is as tho' Castle appeared as by magic before her.
It is as tho' there were a curtain or a veil across stage near back —
The first part is her endeavor to pierce the veil with her sight —
It is as tho' curtain came over her, engulfing her for an instant.

————————

Or else everyone has on huge black cape from which they emerge.
They turn to reveal themselves —

————————

Or some delicate skeleton arbor is revealed by cloth falling —

————————

End of strings is a sharp pluck —
like a break —
Interlude parallels opening to a certain point, then diverges & winds
into encantemiento —
A Form of invocation of primal powers.

Prelude —   Strings
   Dawn — 1st part —   Invader
                      conqueror
                 The Invasion —
      Hill —   possibly chorus —
1st { 1 — ceremonial —   3 virgins
half { 2 — Dance —   who go thru it all —
     3 — Entering the specific,
        more human —
        song-like —
         almost rhapsody
       leads into the now —
       { a nostalgia
       { a longing
         which makes her
open the door on arpeggio —

Prelude   Strings
                     1. Exhilaration
It is like being on a pyramid —   intoxication —
A place of ancient ritual —   pursuit of others by the One
Perhaps on the song-like part   2. First sadness —
there could be an intrusion —   fear   — sleep — dream
such as a messenger — perhaps   doubt —
Erick — or Nina or May — or   3. Pursuit of the One by the others
                 Perhaps each woman is dressed like the
                 one woman —

The Poet woman —

                    The Blue-beard myth
                         parallels?
                    The door to the dark
primitive   sophisticate
    in the sense of artist
    priestess
~~~~~~

          Three Ways   Cross Road   Journey
The Hill — A high place   —   Hill
The Castle of Enchantment. — Place of Enchantment
                         Cross Roads
     A Higher Place — Mountain Top
Who are the women who have made the Pilgrimage — The Journey?

                    women.
                    1 Goddess   1. May —
                    2 Doll   2   Nina —
                    3   3   Pearl —
                    4   4   Ethel —
                    5   5   Yuriko —
                    6   6   Marjorie —

There is in this a moment of experience —
What is it?
It is a landscape of the journey of a Soul.
Where does it start from?
What does it encounter?
Where does it arrive at?

It is a legend of temporary enchantment.
What is the power of enchantment?
What is the agent — force?

Who is this woman?   The Barbarian?

There is about her the directness of the primitive — enter the
priestess, the prophetess or the artist.
How can I make her more specific?

At one time she is under the enchantment which colors all the future.
Is the enchantment
     Love
     Death   ?

Is she standing at the Cross-Roads of a Culture?
   (Diana at the Cross-roads —)
Is it like the Pyramids of Mexico —
   The ancient faith
   The Catholic church on top.
   The existence of the primum mobile thruout.

I seem to feel in the first part — the opening — a memory of standing
in the wind on the top of the Mexican pyramid — And then to remember
the descent afterwards — There was an awareness up there of ancient
rites — sacrifices — sufferings — prayers — but enduring through all —
the sun, the wind, the rain —
Perhaps there is some memory of the Orpheus & Eurydice myth —
the Persephone —
Where does a parallel come in the life of the artist —
Who are the more immediate ancestors?
There is something here it seems of the struggle between the Atlantic
and Pacific cultures.
It is the Pacific that emerges stronger — but with a sustained note of
the other under it like a vibration — There is a unity. Almost it seems
there sounds the sacred syllable that is a symbol of that Unity.
How can that be communicated?
What symbols of theatre can I employ to make it evident?

Are the other Women aspects of her?
Who are the Women who have made the Journey — the Pilgrimage —
There must be some way of making this more specific; of narrowing it
down to the scale of understanding, of self-identification —
Or is it meant to be broad & solitary — heroic or epic rather than
individual or lyrical.
It seems that the dress should be a Chinese red,
   perhaps with black
         or
   such dark green as to appear black —

Promontory   dream-like quality of Sarabande —
                                        Sense of fatalism — the way the
                                        jagged dissonances turn into the
                                        Sarabande —

could there be anything of the Dark Madonna in all this?

. . . "the object of these primitive Dramas . . . ensuring the fertility
   of the Earth . . .   the Freeing of the Waters." From Ritual to
   Romance (17)

Perhaps a kind of invoking from within oneself the Powers of the Spirit to bring about a better condition — a health of the land, the World —

>by invocation — evocation — from within —
>by resistance of the Bluebeard —
>>The subjugation
>>The Death

Perhaps a kind of "Fertility Ritual."
>not for rain but for growth on a Waste Land.
>>— after a War —
>The arrival at the Self — the original strength —

Birth — Death — Resurrection (re-birth)
>"Luck of the Year."

"This return . . . was affected by the action of a goddess, the mother, sister or paramour, of Tammuz, who descending into the nether world, induced the youthful deity to return with her to earth."   ditto 35.
"Lament for Tammuz"

"Intermittencies of the Heart"   Proust — Fowlie
>Ritual at Initiation.

muses & maenads —

"Riverrun"   (first word of Finnegan's Wake) —

Mumming Play —

4 Grail Symbols.
>cup — chalice —   female
>lance   male —
>sword
>Pentangle (dish)

Could I make this a drama of resurrection — using idea of old fertility rites, with certain symbols —
>Perhaps Mumming Play — string quartet
>winter — summer — spring —
>Vegetation Ritual.

"Dolorous Stroke"
"Wasting of the Land".
The maimed King — The wounded king — the sick world —
>The healing of the Soul — by the Soul — the Woman —

"The Fish was sacred to these deities who are supposed to lead men back from the shadows of death to life."   Ritual to Romance 120

"Lord of the net" — Tammuz.

"The Burning Bush"

"Once upon a time — "
"Long ago"
"Somewhere, not here"

"The bearer of the mystery is placed in opposition to the multitude of the ignorant".   Unconscious 233

The bond-woman — Hagar —
night journey to the sea — Jung   (see Blue Lagoon
island phantasy   H. de Vere Stacpool
                                                        Paul & Virginia)

Trees —
    Eden — Tree of Life
    Pine tree of Attis

"She flutters like a swallow lamenting around the column which encloses the God sleeping in death".
                                                        — quest of Isis.
Osiris absence — the winter solstice —   Jung 26 —
phallic column placed in temple of Astarte.

Legend —
    all fecundity proceeds from the dead bull of the world, fruits from
    the horns, wine from the blood, grain from the tail, cattle from its
    sperma, leek from its nose — etc.   269

The goddess is
    In morning — the Mother
    at noon   — The sister-wife
    Evening   — The Mother
                        who receives the dying — the Pieta   272 —

The Sleeping Beauty
    Legend — girl is enclosed between the bark & the trunk
            Is freed by youth with his horn.

"The fate of Osiris is explained: he passes into the mother's womb,
the chest, the sea, the tree, the column of Astarte; he is dismembered,
re-formed, & reappears again as his son."   272
. . .
"Osiris lies in the branches of the tree, surrounded by them, as in his
mother's womb. The motive of embracing, and entwining is often found
in the sun-myths, meaning that it is the myth of rebirth."   272

Hera — (beloved of Zeus)
   ritual marriage
   abduction of image — hiding in cave or woods.
   "The disappearance & hiding in the wood, in the cave, on the seashore,
   entwined in a willow tree points to the death of the sun & rebirth.
   . . .

   Pausanius informs us that the argive Hera becomes a maiden again by a
   yearly bath in the spring of Canathos."   274

See magic net with which Hephaestas enfolds Ares & Aphrodite 'in
flagranti' & kept them for the sport of the gods —   note 66 — 531

"The serpent on account of its casting of its skin is an excellent
symbol of re-birth"   276

libido — to wish — Soul — bird —
middle ages — tree addressed with title of honor — "mistress"   278

The Lamias are nightmares
   Lamia enticed Zeus — Hera, jealous, caused her to bring only dead
   children into the world. Lamia as the persecutor of children — kills
   them when she can —   (Hansel & Gretel)
       mother as murderess — devourer of men.   280

Talmudic legend
   "Adam, before Eve, already possessed a demon wife, Lilith, with whom
   he quarreled for mastership. But Lilith raised herself into the air thru
   the magic of the name of God & hid herself in the sea. Adam forced
   her back with the help of 3 angels. Lilith became a nightmare, a Lamia,
   who threatened those with child, & who kidnapped the new-born
   child."   280

Pilkin "Wish fulfillment & Symbolism in Fairy Tales."
Abraham "Dreams & Myths".

   The Sphinx?

Morris "Legends of the Holy Road"   (dispute of Mary & Cross)

Whale-dragon
"dreadful Mother" of the voracious jaws of death, where men are
dismembered & ground up. Whoever vanquishes this monster has gained
a new or eternal youth. For this purpose one must, in spite of all dangers,
descend into the belly of the monster (Journey into hell) & spend some
time there. Imprisonment by night in the sea.   284

abyss of wisdom, book of wisdom — source of phantasie   99 — 534

Rohab.

Isaiah 30 — 7 —
calls Egypt the silent Rohab.
She is the well-known whore of Jericho who later as the wife of
Prince Salma, became the ancestress of Christ.   287

(p 291 —)
. . . "he, himself is the hunter, murderer, sacrificer & sacrificial knife."
328 —

Hercules and Omphale

". . . one more source of the reanimation of the Mother-image. We have
already met it in the discussion of the mother-scene in 'Faust,' that is to
say, the willed intraversion of a creative mind, which retreating before
its own problem & inwardly collecting its forces, dips at least for a
moment into the source of life, in order to wrest a little more strength
from the mother for the completion of its work"   336.

"Poetic rendering is that which allows the echo of the primitive word to
resound thru the form".   Hauptmann   338

Rank — The Myth of the Birth of the Hero.

"I know that I hung on the windswept tree
Nine nights through.
Wounded by a spear, dedicated to Odin
I myself to myself"   (Edda, Havamal)   Jung 295

Grail castle
Castle of Maidens
Castle marvelous
Perilous couch
costly tent
The Host
The Fisherman — Shape — Shifter

man —
    Hospitable Host   Fisherman
    Smith
    cup bearer —
    craftsman
Fairy Folk live under the lake (in the lake) making the bright vessels
of FANd — daughter of Flidias"   Origin of Grail Legend —
                                        Brown — 163 — #109

Grail Legend — (Celtic)

Heroines —   ditto
   "Plain" — land personified   — Macha   (165 —)
   Tear-drop   — Faun
   Splendor of Women   — Lí Ban
   lovely white   — Finnchaem — Einer
   white footprints   Dáirenn.   Rhiannon-Créde.
   Tear of the Sun   Dergreine
   white hair   Etáin
   white woman   Be' Bind
   Beautiful form   Delbchaem
   Fair Head   Cliodna
White or shining — attribute of Feé
Ireland personified — Macha, Scota or Érin (Lug-Bolar story)

Hospitable Hosts.
swift
white
fire of the eyebrow
seal head
slender, crooked hook
best
smooth-speckled
fair haired
many colored

giants
dark
of the heavy blows
shape-shifter
grief-born
red faced
blind
red
    wears red armor

red tower of the dead
   House of Donn rich in hosts, fortress in battle.
   Red-cornered rock of security,
   Royal city on the smooth sea, couch of a boar,
   nest of a griffin of high rank.   (Grail) 169 —

Lita — Proserpina

Descent into the Cave

The Dark Meadow of the Soul / 195

"The parallel for the motive of death & resurrection is the motive of losing & finding. The motive appears in religious rites in exactly the same connection; namely, in spring festivities similar to the Hierosgamos, where the image of the god was hidden & found again"   Jung 377

Attis mysteries —
"On a certain night an image is placed lying down in a litter; there is weeping & lamentations among the people, with beating of the bodies & tears. After a time a light appears; then the priest anoints the throats of all those who are weeping & softly whispers, 'Take courage, O Initiates of the Redeemed Divinity; you shall achieve salvation thru your grief.' "
(Perhaps part of string section)   Firmicus — Jung 379

Divine *that is* = universally human
meaning underlying the church is that of mother's womb
Mass —
magic charm of re-birth —

Longing for re-birth —
Perhaps lamentation ceremonial in midst of strings or else in Sarabande —

Spirit mother
   Hera
   Lilith
"the angel of the face" (that creative will or word)
Brunhilde sleep the enchanted sleep like a Hierosgamos upon a mountain.
(Hecate)
"Bride of Corinth" — (mother of charms & witches — patron of Medea)
     Jung 405

She is confused with Artemis
          "Far-shooting Hecate"
Hecate as nightmare — wild nocturnal huntress
Hecate, orphically, occupies the center of the world as Aphrodite & Gaia, even as the world soul in general   Jung 406

Hecate
   Forked way
   Cross-roads dedicated to her.
   beam on which criminal is scourged.
   Cross-roads — Roman Trivia — forked — Triple Roads

The sacrifice begins at the Point of Crossing
               (title?)   406

The Place of Transformation — The Place of discipline Jung 416

"he heated himself with his own heat." Jung 415
    (Kundaline?)

The Place of transformation is really the place of the uterus
Absorption with one's self (introversion) is an entrance into one's own
uterus, & also at the same time ascetism.
In the philosophy of the Brahman's the world arose from this activity
among the post-Christian Gnostics it produced the revival & spiritual
re-birth of the individual, who was born into a new spiritual world. The
Hindoo philosophy is considerably more daring & logical, & assumes that
creation results from introversion in general, as in the wonderful hymn
of Rigveda, 10, 29 . . .

  "What was hidden in the shell
  Was born thru the power of fiery torments.
  From this first arose love,
  As the germ of knowledge,
  The wise found the roots of existence in non-existence,
  By investigating the heart's impulses." Jung 416

"Hidden in the Shell" (Title?)

The hero is of serpent-nature. 417.
The hero has serpent's eyes.
"The changeful serpent glance guarded the divine mystery of re-birth."
           418.
He is pregnant with the sun — 553 — 124
The fatal charm of the mother, the fear of death. 422
His searching & his finding. His call.

→ Abraham "Dreams & Myths".

Andromeda?

"Rehearsal of own" — Hopkins — Purcell — 41

"Things done" of ritual Prologomena
"Things spoken" of past —

"I will raise myself over this force of my nature, step by step ascending
to Him who has made me. I will come to the fields & spacious palaces of
my memory"
        St. Augustine Bk X ch. 8
        Jung 496

"well of healing" (Grail — 186)
"The power of choice belonging to the Grail is like that exerted by Lia
Fâil, "Stone of Destiny" & by other objects in the Irish ordeals." 186–(29)

The Fisher King
Castle of Maidens
Blanchflor (?)
Ladies looking from the windows — were ghosts — marvelous tent —
(oriental origin?)   191
What is the fateful question to be asked of the Grail?
The Perilous Couch
The Castle marvelous
The mirrors
The shining pillar   195
      (one can see 6 miles about)
Magic mantel (cloak.)

The woman — Orelûse — is the country personified
      (Sovereignty personified, mother earth, goddess)

Dolorous Tower

See ballad — "The Marriage of Gawain."

The hideous hag who turns into a wondrous being when kissed or slept
with — a fee —
      "I am the sovereignty of Ireland."   214.
      "I will tell thee gentle youth;
      With me sleep the High Kings;
      I, the tall slender maiden,
      Am the kingship of Alba & Érin"   215

            (The terrible Mother
            By recognizing the unconscious with its horror & fear & ugly
            strangeness, it can become a source of power — a beauty — it
            can confer sovereignty)

"Perceval's sister, & cousin, & wife, & the grail messenger were one & the
same. It is not incredible that all these personages were originally
different manifestations of one super-natural earth-mother who
controlled the plot."   217 (24)

See "Celtic Myth & Arthurian Romance."   R.S. Loomis — p. 173–281

See G.H. Maynadier "Wife of Bath Tale" —   p. 21–33
            (fees in ugly disguise)
London 1901

See Unpublished dissertation — Harvard Univ. Lib.
G.W. Beach — "The Loathly Lady." (1907)

Journey — Anabasis — ?

See stories of the "hateful fee" —   219.
   "Conn with his 3 druids & his 3 poets was upon the royal rath at
   Tara before sunrise. He stepped upon a stone there that screamed
   under his feet."

                                (Stone of Destiny)
                                Fâl

Harp of Dogda — called "4 angled music"   229 (note.)
Magmon was the land of the dead
By pseudo-historians it was interpreted as Spain.   230 (18)

The music
   The sleep strain
   The mourning strain
   The laughing strain —

summer & winter games.

The Battle and the Wound.   270
The Voyage and the love-making.

Brau sets out on his voyage because of alluring music made by a fairy
branch which is the gift of a fee —
She describes the land to which she invites him as supported by 4 feet.
It contains a tree with singing birds & a music-making stone "Then they
row to the conspicuous stone from which rise a 100 strains. . . ."   271

Plain of white silver
   "   the silver cloud
   "   the sea
   "   of Sports
   "   happiness
   "   Sport
Bountiful Land
Gentle   "
Many colored "   271–272 (note)
"The cat leapt thru him like a fiery arrow, & burnt him to ashes"   273.
cosmic palace — 4 sided Grail castle.
4 fences divided it (island) into 4 parts,
   a fence of gold
       "   silver
       "   brass
       "   crystal   273
another island is a silver column
It has 4 sides & a net hangs from its top.

37th island has a fiery rampart around it.
"And this rampart used to revolve around the island. There was an open doorway in the side of that rampart. Now whenever the doorway would come in its revolution opposite to them, they used to see the whole island & all that was therein & all its indwellers, even human beings, beautiful, abundant, wearing adorned garments & feasting with golden vessels in their hands. And the wanderers heard their ale-music."   275
            (Castle of Maidens — Dolorous Tower)

"The heroes visit many islands."   276
an island was shewn to them with 4 sets of various men therein. They divided the island into 4, to wit a folk sedate, fair-grey, in the (first) place in it; royal lords in the second place; champions in the 3rd place; servants in the 4th place. Beautiful & bright were they all. Play without resting they had."   276

"They of Brian" —   Brian = "divine power"   284 (note)

See — The Black Book — Carmarthen —

Arthur's sister Anna —
In Ireland
    Ana — mother of the 3 gods
          goddess of abundance
          virtually Ireland personified.   317

any Irishman calls any goddess
    "a Brigit"
                3 sisters
a triad   Brigit — goddess of poets
(1 person)   "   — the woman — physician
                  "   — wife of Goebnin —
These 3 Brigits are really 1
They resemble the 3 Fates & the triformed Diana
                              (Diana)   318 —

✳ See — Studies in the Fairy Mythology   Lucy Paton.

Macalister, "Tara"

Medb —
    queen — sovereignty of the land —
    connected with mead — & means   329
        "The intoxicating One."

Earth-goddess & goddess of plenty.
"to the goddesses of anger & of mead"
"Such was the glory of Medb, & such the excellence of her form,
that two-thirds of his valor was quelled in every man on behold-
ing her."   <u>332</u>
The Hag of Baere — winter — the Nun of Baere
Brigit — Spring   — " " " Kildare
    the Hag is a terrible antagonist but may be subdued with the help of
    her daughter.   p. 335 —
The triad —
        The Women in One —
    3 Brigits
    3 Gueneveres
    3 Medb

implacable — fickle — as sovereignty
                            Fortune.   ?
Finnabair — white phantom
Gwenhwyvar — "   "

House of Fame   355
    " " Tidings
Fiery Revolving Rampart — 32nd island   357
"Font of the Shadow"   389

~~~~~~

See — "Folklore in English & Scottish ballads" L.C. Wimborley
Chicago 1928
Fairy folk.

~~~~~~

Dolorous Tower — Dolorous Mountain — Land of Dead.   395

Persephone — Demeter — parallel in Irish   414

"The land was dead & desert . . .
So that they lost the voices of the wells,
And the maidens who were in them."   (Elucidation)   422

The traveler —
    For forthwith there issued, this is my belief,
    Out of the well a maiden;
    They could not ask prettier;
    She carried in her hand a gold cup.

    . . .

    He did violence to one of the maidens
    Against her will he violated her
    And took away from her the gold cup.

The Dark Meadow of the Soul / 201

. . .
The country turned to ruin

. . .
The realm then turned to waste

. . .
No one could ever find
The court of the Rich Fisher   425–6
Who made splendid the country.

. . .

"Woe weeps out her divisions"

                                            Ben Jonson
                                                Sitwell — Planets & —

Linos Song
    mourning for Linos (Homer — Iliad 18 — 570)   Rilke Elegies —
        a dirge for departing summer
        re-awakened by song of Orpheus.

                                            Supernatural Horror in
Cosmic terror   Literature — Lovecraft.
    archaic ballads
    chronicles —
    sacred writings

"The oldest & strongest emotion of mankind is fear, & the oldest &
strongest kind of fear is fear of the unknown" (12)

The terror that stalks in & around us

cosmic panic

ancestral Footstep (Hawthorne)

Incantation of Fear
Domination of Fear
a study of Fear
    walking with strangeness

Perhaps open without music.
Begin everything in silence — alone.
The power of the Footstep to startle us — to send us into
other areas —
Perhaps sitting in an arbor — or standing in some place
or sitting or lying down
It should start with some rhythmic activity —
            If a dancer — exercises —

Spinning
sewing —
writing
until music begins & she is swept into ancient time & ritualistic
dance —
strange shapes — strangely clad — in the semi-darkness —
Fears of unspeakable things —
murder — moments in it —
The death camps in Germany —
The anguish of the mind.
The dark memories of Mexico —
The Indian —
The woman in mantilla —
Someone hands her a fan —
only the presence of the fan —
the giver is not seen —
she is not aware until she has it — and must dance
with it —
or a veil
Veronica's veil
Guadalupe on the serape —
dark shapes bringing gifts —
Two women discovered — fighting —
The attempt to conquer fear —
Encantemiento —

→ See — The Great Return — Arthur Machen (the Grail)
Incredible Adventures — Algernon Blackwood
The centaur
Montague Rhodes James. Ghost stories of an antiquary
warning to the curious
The cup of the Ptolemies — ??

Journey —
In search of an immortal soul —
The Journey of the Soul in search for immortality —

The Enchanted Castle —
Into the land of Death —
Its fears
its beauties   goddess — Fortune
The Hospitable Host —   Sphinx — Chimera
The King —

1 — In the Forest
    at the Fount
    Source
    Day-break
    Dawn —

                                  Lucifer

                                Encantemiento —
             The Castle   The Cave —
Strings —
  The Castle Marvelous
  1

                              The Forest — opening
                              The Palace ⎱
  2 Elegiac   ⎰ strings
                              mountain — incantation
                                             Sarabande
                              garden   — Paean

                            Desert
                            Valley
                            Cave
                            Shrine
                            Temple

The spectral hunt
The Wild Hunstman (Dionysus zagneus) ⎫
(child souls —)   ⎬ Spirit of Vegetation
Spectral army —   ⎪
ecstatic mad women
Phallic Demons of Fertility

The Journey
  Ancestral Footstep (Foot print)
The Sibyl — the prophetess — the prophetic figure — Fate —
                          use of Golden Bough —

Second Section (all strings)
  The Passion

1. Totemic
2. The Passion —   The Descent
3. Sacrifice   (Encantemiento)
4. Prophecy — (Sarabande)   (May)
5.   The Return

Prophetess   — Sibyl of Cumae
                                            Hero — Aeneas
                                               Golden Bough — talisman to
                                               conduct them & safely return them
                                               from underworld
                                                  Thru the cave
                                                     disease
                                                     care
Prophetic figure.   Hunger
Woman — Volcano   war
   Earth-Mother   discord —
      Keeper of fire-heat
         in a box
         in cave
         under skirt
         between legs.

woman — ancient keeper of the fire

                                         Prometheus
                                         Lucifer — bringer of light

conflict $\left\{ \begin{array}{l} \text{Jaguar people} \\ \text{serpent people} \end{array} \right\}$ basic legendary feud that haunts Mexican
                                         mythology —
Phoenix —
   sublimation of fire into light

"On the northwest coast of the American continent between a tempestu-
ous sea & a virgin forest, there arose an art with the profile of a bird of
prey; masks, heraldic columns, torch light dances, myths of the killer-
whale & the thunderbird tell us of a great savage life in which man &
the elements, man & his dream, beast & man mingled in wars & loves
without quarter."
                           Totem Art — Wolfgang Paalen, Dyn 4–5

totem Poles — "true ventrebral columns of the myths & landmarks of
                  social life."   Ibid. 12
               "All objects of Totem Art bear the seal of the same severe
                  & powerful rhythms that ordered the existence of these
                  people"   Ibid. 13 —

"In order to pass from emotion to abstraction, man is obliged, in the
maturation of each individual, to pass through the ancestral stratifications
of thought, analogously to the evolutionary stages of the species that
must be traversed in the maternal womb."   Ibid. 18

Hidden in the Shell
Dark Meadow
Armor of Memory
Ancestral Footstep

Dark Meadow
  "I have been ere now a boy, a girl, a bush, a bird, a dumb fish in the
  sea —"   Empedocles 117

  "I have reached the confines of death & trodden the threshold of
  Prosperpina; passing thru all the elements, I have returned."
                                                     Apulius — Jung 586

I will not be released from this bondage until I have released myself.
No man can do it for me.
There is a cry against Fate when first we see her face. But then after
the terror of recognition passes we can live with her as we are destined
to do — forever —
We can never escape her presence any more — ever —
Then we can cultivate and know Joy because we must or go mad.
For there is no hope — there is only what we do —

Preliminary Studies for Clytemnestra
Canticle for Innocent Comedians

Clytemnestra: photograph by Martha Swope

Clytemnestra
    opens in Hades
            "Why?"
            her question

finishes at beginning before Agamemnon —
    still as ghost —
        with a tragic cry of recognition —
            "The Wheel"

a tracery of gold to fit over face —
        when she is ghost she wears it —
        when she is alive she is without it —

opening & closing with chorus in red —

Helen & Paris
under canopy —

Clytemnestra brooding on throne

same with
    Iphigenia
        sacrifice

"Embattled Garden"
            Honig — Lorca —
            New Directions

"The book of life" — men's writings on "the tablet of the heart" —
    (Ex 32:32 — Ps 69 — 28 — Dan 7:10 — 12:21)
        (changing Concepts of the Bible — 239)

"Man has in his hands the magnet or the magnetic rod to conjure his soul
to the best possible figures, which appear correspondingly in the book of
life that God has in His hands. Psychologically, this magnetic rod is
meditation." —

"Adam is the magnetic man whose task is the configuration of the given
material." —
"Satan or Samuel's function was merely to tempt man for an evil configuration. When he succeeded in this attempt, Satan became the prosecutor
or executioner before the heavenly tribunal. But neither God nor Satan
determines man's actions. Man himself is the creator of himself. The
forces of creation are implanted in his soul"   (240)

The adversary
　　Fallen Angel

Plain of Dawn
Plain of the people of Dawn
("when we leave Thebes in a northerly direction on the road leading to
Livadia . . ."
"Isle of Samothrace
　　island of white dawn
　　Isle of Electra, a goddess of light."
　　　　　　Eranos — Mysteries
　　　　　　　　46 —

Canticle —

　　　　　　　　clown —
　　　　　　　　acrobat of God.
"The clown has had to learn how to banish hope & exist solely
in his performance".
　　　　　　　　Wallace Fowlie —
　　　　　　　　Chimera — Autumn
　　　　　　　　　　(7)　1943

As we create our landscapes (worlds), places for happenings, as we enact
our praises, as we do it in simplicity & joy, we are innocent comedians
on the stage of life —

"They smile in ceaseless manna-fall,
Flutes, & the quills of wings,
Who bear belief, like Coronal,
and tender tokenings . . ." Ben Belitt

Island of the Innocent　　　Job 22 — 30
"He shall deliver the island of the innocent, & it is delivered by the
pureness of thine hands."

"circus of wider pupils"　　　Perse
"Javelins of noon"　　　　　Sea — 188
"Fifes of light"

Dispelling the shadow
　　Day　　— Matt　　　　　comedians —
　　Sun　　— Bert　　　　　David
　　Water　— Helen
　　Earth　— Mary　　　　　1 Carol
　　Moon　— Yuriko　　　　2 Ellen

Fire   — Stuart   3 Akiko
Wind   — Paul   4 Marny
Stars   — Glen & Ethel   5 Lois
Night   — Martha   6 Bette

                                    Helen?
    1 Dawn   — Ethel   (f) Lightning
    2 Sun   — Bert   } (m) cloud (Glenn)
    3 Earth   — Mary —   } Bette
    4 Water   — Helen —
    5 Wind   — Paul — Matt
    6 Fire   — Stuart — Linda
    7 Moon   — Yuriko — Bert   Lightning — Paul
    8 Stars   — Glenn —
    9 Night   — Martha

Scene — structure on stage
1   night within
    Dawn enters —   1″
1   all others enter & break open building
    Night leaves — The pageant of the Day begins
1   Comedians enter — dance ½
2   Sun — 1
1   Comedians ½
2   Earth   1   silence
1   Comedians ½
2   Water   1
1   Comedians ½
2   Fire   1
1   Comedians ½   Jerusalem
2   Wind   1
1   Comedians ½
2   Moon   1   dark lady in duet
1   Comedians ½
2   Stars   1
1   Comedians ½
3   Darkness   1   with sun in duet
2   Dawn — ending

    _____

    Comedians & final scene —

Pageant of a Day & a Night

Mars
Mercury
Venus
Jupiter
Saturn
Moon
Sun

lightning —
2 Eranos — Mysteries
73
214

"Compassionate leave"
  White Goddess — 235

"Spectacles of Earthly things" Philo
  Eranos 2 — Mysteries (234)

"Insubstantial Pageant of our dreams"
  Shakespeare

"From all the things that life offers us we have spun a net, a necessary
cause that chains & enslaves us. But we retain the possibility of undoing
this Penelope's web, for we ourselves have woven it; once we have freed
ourselves from the servitude into which our actions lead us, we find
ourselves at the scene of our great task: possessing neither spirit or soul,
we must achieve a spiritual autonomy.
P) It is almost impossible to encompass the boldness of this venture. It
consists in escaping from our nature by freeing ourselves from the act,
though this act is what we are made of; in regaining our energies from
captivity, & once more putting them to work without succumbing to
egotism; it consists in strictly disciplining our vital functions and
creative genius & so building worlds which do not obstruct the expansion
of self, but on the contrary enrich us with full creative force. If we
succeed we cease to be slaves & achieve full independence by fashioning
it for ourselves."

       2 Eranos — Mysteries — P. 7 —

"Myths & legends are the dreams of nations . . . They are like a pane
of glass thru which the past is visible . . . the eternal struggle between
the powers of darkness . . . Titans . . . & the shining ones, the gods
. . . thru various stories. . . . Imaginary feelings are the
strongest . . ."

       p. 22 — 24 Ritusamhara
       R.S. Pandit

Possible cast for Innocent Comedians —

Helen   Bert
Ethel   Bob
Yuriko (   )   Gene
Matt   Cameron

Hades — Dick
Persephone — Ellen
Hermes — David

3 Furies —
    Carol   1 Restless One
    Ellen G.   2 Avenging "
    Akiko   3 Jealous   "

        She who rests not
        Avenger of murder
        The Jealous one

"Still let me love"
    Title for Heloise-Abelard —

(tho' I may not possess)

Love Story —
    Not only Heloise & Abelard — but "love story" on several levels —

a procession of loves —

Alcestis: photograph by Martha Swope

Place of Shadows —
Dream —
Contemplation of the Inner Image
Place of Images —
Cave of Treasures —   What is to be faced?
Tent   What goes on in the soul?
Trysting Tent   What images are there?
Theatre of the Soul
Theatre of the Dream   What is it one sees?
Drama of the Images   Animals?
    "   "   " Shadows   Colors?
Villa of Mysteries   Shapes?
Circular Desert   supra-human figures?
Temptation in the Desert   Or is it one great Figure?
                                     Like Corn Maiden?
                                     Spider Woman?

The Great Mother —

                             What are the dances to be?
Let something like Picasso   The supreme universal moments — in self
paintings in "Verve" —   realization which are common to all lives —
Shape like that —   (jealousy) Terrible ravening — (Kali)
Color to be cast from   Consecrated — Warrior-like
machine as figures — ?   Magnetic, attractive, beloved —
A tent —   Peaceful — secure —

                             Rope dance —
                                 To give feeling of unity, of common
                                 bond —

Elements
    Death
    fear   Loneliness
    love   Memory of Love
    Vision

Beneath the Sea   Circular
Under the River   Dark king (Death)
Sacred River   Vast Singer (Life)
In the belly of the whale   Keeper of Silences
                                 Lord of the Silence

Contemplation of Inner Image
    She who walks in beauty   Pearl

Day of Doubt   Cave drawings
Contemplation of the Dark   rope dance
Advent of the light

Persephone in Contemplation   Hades
    Seeds of Pomegranate   6 (the number??)
    waiting
    memory   Bride of Death
    emerge
                                       Dark Queen
                                       Hidden Queen

Contemplation
        In Rondo form
Rondo of Contemplation   Circular Desert
Athlete of God

                                   The Trysting Tent

Variations on the fact of Spring —
Drama of recurrence —

"Only the Fireborn understand blue" Sandburg
                            "Rootabaga."

Circular Desert   Villa of mysteries —
    Temptation — solo   Temptation to sorrow — to death
    Promise — group   " anger
    Groupings —   Canaan — Land of Promise
    Dawn —   The Hill
    Mystery   The Mountain
                                        The Valley
                                        The Sacred River
                                        The forest
Trysting tent   The Jungle
Where one speaks with God —   The desert

Bondage —
Egypt — Land of darkness

                            Shadows — Giacometti figures

What of all things do you want to do — to express — now?
~~~~~~
It must almost be like a solo with the others as figures in
a dream — very little contact —

                            The desert
at the cross roads —   The dream — mirage-vision

If I can find the 3 or 4 things I would express —

_____

Aloneness — fear —   —
Twilight   deep dark
meditation — contemplation — prayer   Early dark
Temptation   Deep dark
        (to doubt — to fear)   Storm (at night)
Vision
Groupings
Dawn — hope —   Moon-rise
mystery — exaltation —   Dawn —

                        Light — Early dark — shadows
                                Deep dark —
                                Storm —

                    bestows
One of visions — Pearl — leaves a flower?
        Persephone —

contemplation of the Images —

        Persephone — Spring — Hope — Faith —
        Vast Singer — Hercules — Life —   clown —
        Dark King — Death — (Bob)

gypsy — beautifully sequined — epauleted coat
                        (Orpheus)
                        Figure of Death —
Only the Fireborn —   Enigmatic
    The Ghost —

Storm at night   night
    Solo   Dawn
        girls in white ecstasy   Zenith — Terrible gift of the gaze
        of running, longing —   Sunset

                        Something at Dawn

Landscapes —   who is gypsy?
Peregrination   Figure of Fate
                                        Wisdom
                                        Timelessness
woman as navajo woman —   prophecy
    inner experiences   Dancer
                                        primordial urge
                        all this makes me a symbol again —

Desert — Doubt — aloneness
mountain — contemplation
                    vision
River — deep passionate surge
Valley —   Peace

Woman with Images —

Anabasis —   Desert at Night
          Darkness   The Stone
Storm at night —
   seated on chair — stool —
   arms out as on chair arms.
   When fall comes forward
   it reveals cross painted   Storm at night
   luminously — almost like
   swirling snake symbol.   Psalm — 19
   girls later —   24
                                                   30
           one figure in black or red   42
           who supplies object   62
           always — fan — shell —   67

Time of Darkness — moon-set
   ″   ″ Dawn   — Day rise
   ″   ″ noon   — Zenith —
   ″   ″ Sunset

Read Eve's story

Experience of love
      ″   ″ solitariness

"The eternal presentness of love is the new experience"
                              146 Fowlie — Surrealism

Remembered Valley   El Portal
Pojoaque Valley   Sanctuario
Valley of the Shadow   The wheel
                               The rack
                                  The peach orchard

Contemplation of the mysteries
                               Cave
                               Plateau
                               Juniper tree

The Notebooks of Martha Graham / 220

The complete Song
    Lullaby
    love song   }   woman's song —
    lamentation at death

"The drama of love is played in the mind. It is lyricism of one moment, a flash of time, that is never over, that is anonymous & universal & hence mystical. The mind appears before itself, filled with the image of woman so resplendent in her nudity that she is all degrees of light: angelic & demonic, carnal & spiritual, unique & universal."

Fowlie   Surrealism   150

"The experience of love has finally dominated the experience of solitude, or has made out of the literal experience of solitariness another kind of possession"   146

images of the plain & of madness —
Light is hidden on woman —
"The sky closes her dress in order to break her chains."
This is her myth: she is not dependent on the light of the sky because she has it within her. She is the being who is uniquely free — "   148 —

The fan
The wheel   (on the wrack)
The grass
The road

The mirror of woman (in which he sees himself)
"The mirror where Heradiade saw herself . . . & thru which Orpheus passed in Cocteau's play, & thru which every poet must pass as into the ocean, into the principle of maternity, which may be disguised by the words ocean, sky, stars, cloud, fog."   151

gypsy —   lighter of new fires —

Valley
Plateau
Mountain

Valley
  (Valley of the shadow of Death)
        doubt
        fear
        jealousy   (Kali)

Plateau

The Trysting Tent
The Burning Bush

each holds a tryst —
In a tent on the Desert of Time we have a tryst —
This tent is the tabernacle of our own being —
The Tryst is with the God which is our being —

In a tent on the Desert of Time each keeps a Tryst —
A Tryst with the God of his being —
This Trysting tent is the abode, the dwelling place of God.
This Trysting Tent is all we are —
     Our body, our heart, our imagination, our mind.
     It is the inner chamber of love,
     It is the tabernacle of The Holy One
     Its servants are our thoughts —

What takes place in this Trysting Tent —
Whom do we meet there
       The Discovery of the Self
         Being

The gypsy   night into Dawn
   nomad   Evening & the morning —
   Lighter of new fires

Early

               The Feast
Shore of the Sea

On the Shore of a Sea —

Images from the Dark —   Image from the Deep —
Images for the Dark —

               gypsy
The Storm   Indian
The Heavy Sea   native
Fog

Fear   ⎫
aloneness ⎬ Sunset
―――――
Dream   Moon-Rise   Storm —
―――――   Moon Set   1
Despair   Storm — Deep Dark
―――――

{ Joy —   Dawn
{ Wonder   2 Magic of imagined world
{ Praise

      Ritual meal — Dawn   3

Promontory   Elemental Chorus

Cove   fear

                           joy
Island   love (mating)

Grove   rest —
                  flaming root

Spectral hunt   Tidepool
     image   where the dead of fish,
                    fowl, plant accumulates
                    & floats in suspension —

opening —
     alone —
1)   solitariness.   Day — close
     contemplation   Time of Shadow
     unique song —   Shadows —

       Time of Storm
Evening Storm
         Moon-rise   turbulence
         Moon-set   Cries of the
         Deep dark   Sea wolves
         Dawn   aloneness

                  On the Point of Storm
Evening Storm
Moon-rise
Moon-set
Deep dark   Wolves — inner images
Dawn

Imaginary Landscape —
    1 — Solitariness   Point of Wolves
        aloneness —   Promontory of terror
                       fear
    1 — Sunset Storm —   Fear
       Storm over the Sea   anger
         "   "   " Point —   pacing —
                     devastation —
                     grief

Time of Storm
  end of Day
  Beginning of night

  moon-rise

solo — grief — tearing &
            devastating
men — only —

women —
solo — ritual to moon —

Moon's light

Moon-set

imaginary world of
utter magic — joyous —
aloneness again

Deep Dark
Dawn
Beginning of Day

solo —
contemplation of inner image —

1 Turbulence   (situation at crisis)   25
2 Contemplation of the Image   25
3 Magic of Dawn — (recurrence — fulfillment)   20
                                                                      ――
                                                                       70
                                                                       30
                                              1⅔ hrs. ――――
                                                       100″

1) Drama of Crisis

Evening Storm
Time of Storm

1) Evening Storm

2) Moon-rise
   Moon-set
   Deep-dark

Images of the night
      Love   erotic
      Circe
cult of the Moon —

3) Dawn

Beginning —
shimmer of light on sea

   Point of the Wolves —
A place of danger and great beauty —
   The tent like a lair —
The wolves of one's being — the hungry ones —
They stalk their prey in the night —
Their cries chill the heart

The Cedars of Lebanon —

                    Instant

At a point of crisis it is the Point of the Wolves
(Dante's wolf)

It is an evolution of Wolf into human —
Primordial figures of the far night —
    The race memory —
The Wolves are the creatures of memory —
Ravening —
Predatory

Days End   Mysterious guide —
Early Dark
Nights Fall —   Days Rise
  Storm   Dark fall
                           Dawn Rise
            night cry   Light Rise
   Night Fall — cry at night
             cry in the night
1 — Aloneness   Dark Presences   _Contemplation_
    fear   men   _of the Images._
black envy   lust Circe   _Sarabande_
    jealousy > Kali   or
                         1 man
women protect man by their   several women
hair from her — (shells?)
rope of straw?

---

2 — Moon Rise   Evangels
                    heavenly messengers

   Moon Set

   Deep Dark
red   Incredible quiet   sacrifice — _Dance with_
purple ritual killing —   _Kriss — (fan)_
                         rose _Trance —_

3 — Days Rise — Dawn

1) Early Dark —
     first gesture like cry — lifting arms into shaft of light
     like a sarabande of primordial meaning —
        formal
        nonpersonal   _Sarabande of the images_
        cry in the night   _Pavane —_
     solo beginning   _Hand-restrained_
     (contemplation of images —) _tragic_

2) From Moon-Rise to Moon-Set
      Strange sparkling suprahuman
                  unhuman
   contemplation of the Images —
   Seated — at times
      like Eraskegal — Queen of the Underworld
   Dream of Death
      (like Alcestis)

Deep Dark   (Alcestis story perhaps as allegory?)

   Vast Singer   (life
   Keeper of the Silence —(Death)   Lord of the **Silence**
   Struggle
   all almost in silence —
      Perhaps one instrument — (harp?) guitar?
                          cello like "
   By some terrific effort of will she makes decision —

Dawn
   Revealment of Images —
   (almost like Diversion of Angels —
   Solo part —
      quite simple as against intricacy of group.
      sustained almost unbearable beauty —
        obverse of beginning Sarabande —

The Dreamer —   The gypsy
                       Lighter of new fires.

In first — night Fall — Early dark —
   almost all solo —
      passing, repassing of people —
   Perhaps all solo —
      except for unidentified presences —
              or
      use of tent & cypress tree
           (like dwarfed pine)
        done by unidentified forces —
      change of landscape — as tho by terrors of mind.
      means are unseen —

Second Part
   Moon Rise to Moon Set —   *small daggers —*
   Queen of underworld —   *Kriss —*
      Furious hand dance of men —

Dance of women —
    (with hair — or shells or fans)
    (fall from chair revealing cross?)
       leads into
Third Part
  Deep Dark —
  Struggle between Life & Death for possession of the Dreamer —
  (as Alcestis legend —
    vast Singer
    Keeper of Silences —
  act of decision —
  In this an incredible passivity
              inertness
  tossed — moved like puppet by 2 men figures —
(perhaps against constant dance of women in half shadow — like Hula —
monotonous — never varying —
      suspension —

use of small platform where Dreamer stands & moves — in dream as
tho' directed by 2 figures —

Platform also in beginning —
  indicative of small stage —
    Designated area of conflict —
  like oriental platforms
      or
  gypsies' platform in cafe —
  or like chancel in church where Mass is held —

act of Decision —

Dawn —
  incredible swiftness of figures
  sudden sharp ecstatic attacks by Dreamer with times of suspension
  while group dances —

  Dance with them at end —

? use of duets in each section?
  (almost as in angels)

I first figure of Helen —

                  Mysticism
"self abandonment to the 'saving madness' (Plato) of ecstasy" 32

"That Reality which 'hath no image' "   32

"Pilgrimage to the place of the wise is to find escape from the flame of separation"   32

<pre>
        Soundings —
        Luminous waters
        Deep Dark
        Ocean Floor — (Sea Floor)
        Surface   Sounding —
act of Return   Night and Day
Dawn at Sea   History of a Descent
</pre>

Volcano beneath the Sea }   Sea around us   68
Earthquake "   "   " }

The lost continents beneath the surface of each personal inland sea

A dream in part — (Alcestis)

Alcestis — interlude in "Deep Dark"
    Two men speak —   dialogue
    Vast Singer — laughs?

First part in tent on floor
    slope to small platform so all on floor seen at angle in perspective —

An actress —
    prepares
        for all parts
        performs all parts

Player of Parts

Curtain going up
Curtain Rises

Summer House —
Sarabande with Destiny — Fate — Sybil

Player of Parts —
        Contemplator of the Images of Life & performer of the
        acts of Living —

        actress

She who meets a catastrophe
            a crisis
The Gypsy —

The Itinerant Player —

Like the acrobats
        Circus Clowns

$$\left(\begin{array}{c} \text{Names of States of Feeling} \\ \text{rather than} \\ \text{names of characters from literature} — \end{array}\right)$$

The Play
   The Script is not written — It writes —

(28) — 36

Images
   Aloneness   Farewell
   Memory
   Fear
   Hope
   Decision
   Love   The wife
                          The Mother
                          The Harlot
                          The Beloved
                          The Victim

"The Divine Dark"

"Pasture of Hell"   House of Breath — Goyen
"midnight victory"   "
("we are carriers of lives and
legends — who knows the unseen
frescoes on the private   "
walls of the skull?")

Performer Absolute —
   Separateness — aloneness —
      Women combing hair as chorus of relationship emphasizing the
      One who walked in separateness.

Madness
   There is a supreme lucidity, which is the precisely calculated
   awareness which is called madness.
   A supreme lucidity, a precisely calculated awareness —
   called madness —

Study for a Life

a Rondo —
   a chorus returning in a waltz or any dance form

Love Letter
a letter written   *Many Parts*

Dream in a Desert

The Dream was in the Desert
(I was in the desert in my dream)

"bile & gall of childhood"   House of Breath
"empty purity of memory"   "

"But who comes here, across the pasture
of bitter weeds, wading in thru the   "
shallows, home?"

"O, I am leaf & I am wind & I am
light. Something in the world links   "   45
faces & leaves & rivers & woods &
wind together & makes them a string
of medallions with all our faces
on them, worn forever around our
necks, kin."

"For each time you ascended —   House of Breath
by hard will, by choice, by courage,   47
you had a responsibility to the
vision of descent."

Sarabande at Sunset
      Salutation to night —
      Duet alone

      Late evening
      Early morning

      "Near is
263   and hard to seize the God. But where   Hölderlin
      danger is, there rises the saving one also.
Payne In darkness dwell the eagles . . ."

      "Islands & peninsulas, and
242 Grottos to pray in   Hölderlin
      And a gleaming shield, quick
      Like roses."

246 "It is possible to fall into the heights as well as into the depths"
                                        Hölderlin

Four colors —   Four directions — Four Times
   grey-blue
   white
   yellow
   black   night

To represent seasons of Being —

"and I stood upon the sand of the sea"   Rev — 13 — 1

"I am the Alpha and the Omega, the beginning & the ending, saith the Lord, which is and which was & which is to come, the Almighty."

Rev 1 — 8

I contemplate the existence) solo —
                               } sarabande
I acknowledge the existence) pavane

I evoke the memories   group

I submit to the agony —   Trio

I salute the power
               beauty

The Trysting Tent —

The Tent of the Universe

The Tent of the Gypsy

     The Lighter of new fires —

     The casting of the dice

     The reading of the cards

     The fulfillment of the prophecy

The Tent of Night

                  Schuman's —

Fable —
Once upon a time
Trysting Tent
"We are the carriers of lives & of legends — " etc

                Twilight   — Salutation
Invocation   **Moon light** — Evocation
act of choice — Darkness   — Sacrifice
Revelation   Dawn   — Thanksgiving —

Deep Dark —   The Dream —
                            a large cloak —
                            2 men —
              Silent One — Death — Whisperer
                 Life — Vast Singer

Farewell
Journey by moonlight   — Into moonlight

Sojourn   In darkness

Departure at Evening
Sarabande on Departure
      ″   in memory of Farewell

Sarabande
Rondo with sarabande as recurrence

Farewell, my Fancy.

Rondo
   with Dawn recurrence —

   Dawning — Daybreak — New Day
   First Light —
      clown meets clown

                                   during — mid-during —
"I salute my Love"
   A Contemplation on — music by Bach —

Speaker of lines —

a hammock
      or
slight line in space like my chaise-longue.
woman speaks, lying there —
She stands — speads her arms as in loss —
The tent comes in from top & sides —
      hiding chaise —
      I repeat gesture with arms —
Sarabande follows —

One moment the 2 women kneel facing each other.
They might merge as in kiss at the end —

            3rd
Deep Dark —
      Vast Singer   an allegory
      Keeper of the Silences   Death
      The Woman —   Life
                                The Soul

      Clown

1 Evocation of the Images?
2 Contemplation of the Images
3 Selection　?
4　　　　?

<u>2nd part</u>

Moon —
　　Contemplation of the Images
　　　　　　　　First Love
　　　　　recognition of Love
　　　　　　″　　　　″　the Beloved
　　　　　mating dance
　　　preparation by the women

All as a dream
　　as an imagined garden

"I turn to the South"
　　　　　　　　(the realm of feeling)

"We are the carriers of lives & legends. Who knows the unseen frescoes
on the private walls of the skull?"　　(House of Breath — Goyen)

　　　　　"Midnight Victory"
　　　　　"Pasture in Hell"　　　　(Goyen)

— a contemplation mid-during music —　　———

The moon series —
　　like a wedding ceremony
　　Jambra — (Festival)

　　　　　　　　　　tambourine
　　　　　　　　　　metal plate —
　　　　　　　　　　bag-pipe

cellos used as lute —

Festival
vigil
pilgrimage

Zarabanda
Fandango

"I think, heart of mine, that in my heart I love thee"

The Three Maidens
　　"Three maidens have implanted themselves in the very center
　　of my being . . ."　　(164)

The Trysting Tent / 233

"one is like the full moon, another like the morning star,
The third like a graceful branch of an Egyptian willow.—"

Asha — name of Muhammed's wife
Zohra — Venus, the pagan woman   (Fatima)
Mariem — Marie, the Christian woman

Song at Sunset —

                    like muezzin — prayer

Prayer at Sunset —
Invocation at sunset
Evocation at sunset —
1)   Evocation   music at sunset
     Strings first —   cellos —

2)   Woman's Song   "Pasture in Hell"
                        Song of the Sibyl

3)   Sarabande —   (Harpsichord)
     "I salute my love — "   ?

4)   Festival of the Moon —

＝＝＝＝＝＝＝＝＝＝＝＝＝＝＝＝＝＝＝＝＝＝＝＝＝＝＝＝＝＝

     Schuman music —   note —
3 men — on stage during solo — in presence of angels —"
slowly advancing — pressing in for decision — moving slightly
against her torment of indecision —   (Feb 16 —

What is implicit in that dream, that sterility of moonlight —
    Woman's Song —
    Entrance of the Women — veiled
    Dance of women —   all the women of the world —
                woman —

    perhaps veils placed on dancer so that she wears fantastic garment
    of colors —
       Taken off her as they finish & with it her black sequined gown,
       revealing magenta & gold stripe — or some barbaric dress —

Three memories of Heaven —   (240)
                          (creative Experiment)
Silence — woods — vision   (Sabre Los Angeles)

small platform —
   monotony dance of women?
         or
       of gypsy?

angels — messengers

Morning

"And the evening and the morning."
"The Trysting Tent."

Evening
Sunset   Early Dark
          Point of the Dark

                              Fight with shadows
                                   Giacometti figures
                                   on background

angels — men
Devotees of the night
                    moon

In Deep Dark —
          chair which becomes Burning Bush —
          (a gypsy's fire also?)

Power of the Veil —   ("Angel Teaching of New Test)   (108)

                    Triple aspect of white goddess   (64)
New Moon   white goddess of birth & growth
Full Moon   red goddess of love & battle
Old Moon   black goddess of death & divination

The ghost —
     perhaps — acts as memory of woman — the Dancer
                                        the Gypsy —
     speaks lines from her memory —
        She meets her memory in the twilight —
ghost
     memory of past acts
        "   "   "   experiences —

conflict at times with ghost
ghost dresses woman for various happenings in her memory —

personal memory
race   memory —

Raphael   "God heals" —

                                   helpful
                                   sweet — kind —
                                   merciful —
(angels   )   Big Brother —
(advices of God)

The Trysting Tent / 235

Satan   the accuser
                                         brings against man his
                                         grievances
                                         claims right to tempt Job —

4 Spirits —   4 horses —
                                             black, red, — pie — white
                                             (chestnut)

God advises thru his angels —

cavaliers — angels —

(See 11 Maccabeus — 3 — 24 — 28)

Jesus rejects help of angels in his agony —
It is not the time of angels —

Michael vs Satan — (as long as world)
The certain fall of the Seducer — the loss of his domination —

Hagar — appearance of angel —
Michael — head of celestial army —

Song of the Phoenix

From dust I rise,
and out of nothing now awake,
These brighter regions which salute mine eyes,
    a gift from God, I take.
The Earth, the Seas, The Light, The Day, The Skies,
The Sun, the Stars are mine; if these I prize."
                                  (Traherne — see Man & God 71)

"Bright wings" —   Hopkins
And after all this nature is never spent;
There lives the dearest freshness deep down things;
And though the last lights off the black west went
Oh, morning, at the brown brink eastward, springs —
Because the Holy Ghost over the bent
Would brood with warm breast and with oh!
                              Bright Wings — " Hopkins (80)
                                         Man & God

O, tell us poet, what you do? — I praise.
But those dark, death devastating ways,
how do you bear them, suffer them? I praise.
And then the nameless, beyond guess or gaze,

how can you call it, conjure it? I praise!
And whence your right, in every kind of maze,
in every mask, to remain true? I praise!
And that the mildest & the wildest ways
know you like star & worm? I praise.

Rilke

(Man & God — 89)

quoth a hawk to a nightingale — Hesiod

Gk Reader   112

Helen Laufer
assistant & musical advisor to M.G.

"Island of the Innocent"   Job 22 — 30

"He shall deliver the island of the innocent; & it is delivered by the
pureness of thine hands"

"Canticle for Innocent Comedians"   Ben Belitt

	for		
Praise to	Sun	Bert
Praise to	Earth	Mary
" "	Wind	Bob
" "	Water	Helen
" "	Fire	Stuart
" "	Moon	Yuriko — Bert
" "	Night	Pearl — "

simple
Praise for all accepted forgotten benefits —
neglected

Canticle for Innocent Comedians — Belitt —
"Keep Innocency"

"They smile in ceaseless manna-fall,
Flutes, and the quills of wings,
Who bear belief, like coronal,
And tender tokenings: . . ."

Branches — Mary
Fan
Veil — Pearl

some small object for <u>fire</u>
          balloon?
(give it the girls to hold) — Patsy runs
away with it — etc —

St. Francis —
     "love for all things great & small" —
     gratitude to creator for the manifold beauties of nature
     St. Francis made teachings of Christ a living reality
     opened new path to Christendom —
     "divinity immanent."

"Canticle for Innocent Comedians"

As we create our landscapes — our worlds — places for happenings —
as we enact our praises — as we do it in simplicity and joy — we are
all innocent comedians on the stage of life —

Our Praises —
                    For Sun —
Mary Hinkson — Patricia Birch — Linda Margolies
                    with
               Bertram Ross

               For Earth

     Triumph of St. Joan —

Hers is the triumph over the   whether it be physical death or
oblivion which is death   that oblivion of the soul

_____

Joan still walks the   She has left the world   of
highways of our imagination.   an inheritance   for
                                                                    courage
                                                                    faith
Music
Set   inheritance of memory to be used
Objects   It is the memory of her to be used
Lighting   in diverse ways & places

Joan still walks the highways of
imagination. Hers is a triumph   her allegiance to
over Death —   the voices of her heart
                                                 the
                                                 directive
                                      allegiance to the voices
                                      of the heart —

She is forever the symbol
Her triumph is the transformation of a faith into deathlessness —
Her triumph is the one triumph — the deathlessness of vision —
Joan of Arc still walks the highways of our imagination —

I have tho't of you so many times these two days — (I have been
thinking of you all day) — & of your beautiful eagle eyes which can
gaze unflinching straight into the sun — without fear or any blindness —
with utter acceptance of light —

The triumph of St. Joan
Burned — —
Canonized — —

The Dance

The end of St. Joan <u>should have been</u>:

using lance as stake —
circling it —
falling from it —
hands behind back enfolding it.

Last dance should have been directed to it.

Nov 19 —

A strange day —
So many invitations for this evening —
On this day the line came — I knew I must be about
my Father's business —
I know the teaching must be arranged —
This day I decided.
This day I knew where the values lie —

Four Angels —   Four men in a woman's life —
                                ?   Frontier woman   ?
                                   The warrior
                                    "   gambler
                                    "   Poet
                                    "   Lover

I Salute my Love —
     "Love is a place"
     "Love was not only a place, but a time."
     "Yes, & love was a climate, too"
               "The President's Lady"   Irving Stone.

"Love was a mighty bridge which crosses frozen rivers & frozen
hours; it enabled a man & a woman to walk hand in hand across
a sunlit field when a 1000 miles separated them & the field
was snow-covered under a leaden sky."   (105)

"Our love shall be a fortress"   (211)

gyspy
Dancer   Protagonist

Play within a play   Alcestis

The Bronzeless Net
Additional Studies for Clytemnestra

The Bronzeless Net —
"women veiled in dignities of black"   Libation — 93
outer show of mourning —
"terror, the dream diviner of
this house, belled clear, shuddered the skin,
                    blew wrath
from sleep, a cry in night's obscure watches,"   (94)

"the godless woman" —   "Shame upon the earth"   "
                                     "Net of death"   (68) — 1072
          A man   "Song of sorrow"   (70) — 1114
goes in fear —   "Speech of Terror"   (70) — 1137
                                                                (71)
"Fatal nets" —   (67)   (1047)   1154

"Soliloquy in Hades"
     Clytemnestra as in the net —   (62)
"Daughter of Leda — Ag — 914
The feast of Atreus
the sacrifice of Iphigenia
the Delphic oracle
the persecution by the Erinyu
     (his Mother's avenging spirits)
purification of Apollo
trial for matricide —
     (first evidence of trial by Jury — a tie — the deciding vote
     cast by Athena)

Clytemnestra —
     "We hear before we see her; we see her long before
     she speaks." Thomson — Aeschylus & Athens —   (249)

                    opening of 3 plays

1) Agamemnon opens —
     Watchman's prayer to gods.

2) Libation Bearers
     prayer to Hermes
          (intermediary between living & dead)

3) Delphic Priestess prays to Pallas Athena
                         Saxias (Apollo)
          & other deities —

Tomb of Clytemnestra

1st play
1) When Clytemnestra announces at daybreak that Troy is fallen
    the news will be taken as an idle dream too good to be true —

2nd play —
    She will dream not of victory but retribution

3rd play
    The dreamer will herself become a dream stirring the Furies to
    revenge.

(Helen in Egypt)   (Euripides —)

1 Play —
    The full swinging circle of the past —
Clytem — Herself and Helen   Twins —
    She the dark side of beauty —
        The jealousy — the hatred —
        sacrifice of Iphigenia —

(all this interspersed with the "Mysteries")

"The theme here is the philos-Aphilos or hate-in-love . . ."
                Lattimore 10 —

perhaps reveal tragic history — Iphigenia — as emerging from midst of
chorus — using chorus as a set of actors — mimes — who reveal her
thoughts — which perform them for her —

"We hear her before we see her; we see her long before she speaks.
Each time she appears at the threshold of the palace, the words of the
chorus are designed as an unconscious comment on what is passing
in her mind . . ."
                The Oresteia — Thomson
                Vol I — (11) —

"The Eulogy was followed by a satyr-play, in this case the Proteus, a
light & playful finale which represented the wanderings of Menelaus
as a romantic counterpart to his brother's tragic homecoming."   (12)

"The art of tragedy was the product of democracy".   (11)

    "The characteristic art-form of the landed aristocracy was the
choral-lyric, a combination of dance & song designed to accompany the
traditional worship of noble families"   (11)

form of trilogy — constructed to express —
        offence
        counter-offence
        reconciliation —   (11)

~~~~~~

                  Agamemnon —
The hour — shortly before midnight —   (14)
The season — late autumn
        marked by setting of the Pleiades
        when it became dangerous to cross sea —

~~~~~~

see Shakespeare — 29th Sonnet —
    W. H. Hadow — A Comparison of Poetry & Music —

~~~~~~

"While Orestes is murdering his Mother, the Trojan serving women,
who fondly believe that at last the house has been purified, chant
a hymn, which as will be seen later, is designed to recall the
Mysteries of Eleusis"   (Cho — 941 —4)   (15)

openings of 3 sections
   1 — Agamemnon —
      Watchman prays to the Gods
   2 — Libation Bearers —
      Prayer to Hermes of underworld
   3 — Eumenides — Pythian Priestess prays to Apollo Saxas & the other
      deities ending with Zeus the Highest, the Perfecter —
      It was the Greek custom after supper to offer a grace of
      unmixed wine,

       1) to the Gods of Olympus.
       2) to the spirits of the dead
       3) Zeus the Third   (16)
          also called the Perfecter or Deliverer

"In Agamemnon the chorus relate how, in the happy time
before the war, the girl Iphigenia used to sing the paean
for her father at the performance of this ceremony."

The Prologue — (1–39)

The watchman's task has been imposed upon him by the
sanguine hopes of a woman (10–11) the wife of Agamemnon,
Clytemnestra, who is dreaming of victory. When at daybreak
she announces that Troy has fallen, the news will be dismissed
by many as an idle dream, too good to be true; but, after its

truth has been proved, the deepening conviction that she
is working for another victory will turn the dream into a nightmare   (966–84)

(17) "At the beginning of the 2nd play this woman will dream not of
victory but of retribution (Cho. 928) and finally the dreamer
will herself become a dream stirring the drowsy Furies to
revenge"   (Eum. 116)

(17) "This woman has the will of a man. Her personality is masculine
(?) although she, sometimes ironically, disclaims it — (360,
1661, Cho. 668–9) & she lack the modesty which becomes
her sex (618–19, 847, 931, 1372, Cho 627–8) yet her
feminine charm when she seeks to exercise it, is
irresistible.   (932–4)"

"Unlike his mistress the watchman dare not dream. To keep
awake he sings, but his singing turns into a lament for
the House of Atreus. When he sights the beacon, he hails it
gladly, calls to the Queen to raise the Alleluia & begins
to dance for joy — but breaks off abruptly, arrested
by some obscure misgiving."   (17)
His joy is indeed delusive. Later in the day the inspired
imagination of a prophetess will see the Furies dancing on
the roof where he has danced, & hear their frightful alleluias.
(1105–7) Again & again such premature rejoicing is destined to
pass into brooding premonition. The old men enter with quiet
confidence in the past but before long they are seeking to allay
their fears for the future — Reverting to the past they re-call the
auspicious beginning of the war, but then they remember the
terrible price paid for it, the sacrifice of Iphigenia, so that
when the dawn breaks at last, it seems to herald, not the
deliverance for which the watchman prayed but a worse calamity.
After the Queen's announcement they begin a joyful hymn
of thanksgiving for the punishment of Paris, but the hymn
ends with anxiety for Agamemnon "a hidden fear wrapped in
the night" (466) The herald salutes the rising sun with an
ecstasy of joy but he is soon forced to confess that victory
has already been followed by disaster — The Elders are at
pains to greet Agamemnon in a spirit befitting the occasion
(774–800) but then they have to watch helplessly while he walks
into a trap; & after a final struggle between hope & fear they
surrender themselves in fascinated horror to the inevitable.
So in the 2nd play, the Chorus of serving women, confident

of victory, urge the brother & sister to pray for revenge; but
later losing heart, they can see nothing but disaster. (461–73)
While Orestes is at his task, they rejoice at the deliverance of the
House (934–70); but at the close of the play they are asking
in despair when will its affliction cease. Not until the end
of the trilogy will tribulation issue in true & lasting joy. All
this is latent in the Watchman's speech. Overcome with doubt,
he takes refuge in silence (36–8)

> "These walls, if they had mouths,
> Might tell tales all too plainly."

He disappears into the palace, & then, as if in response, we hear
out of the darkness "alleluia" — Clytemnestra's cry of joy

> (The watchman has summoned her to raise the cry (28) &
> later she tells us that she raised it. (592) The inference
> drawn by J. T. Sheppard (Cambridge Ancient History
> p 122), that a cry was actually heard by the audience at
> this point, is highly probable.)"   (18)

Perhaps —

> after initial chorus in semi-darkness — focusing on Watch-
> man — a light can come — The stage empty — then a cry
> offstage — woman's voice — Clytemnestra appears as in
> the glow of the beacon —

Parados (40–103)
First stasimon (104–269)

"In the parados, & again in the 1st stasimon the poet begins
by taking our minds back 10 yrs to the outbreak of the
war"   (18)

The parados provides a background for the first appearance
of the Queen. The sons of Atreus, in their anger at the rape of
Helen, are likened to 2 eagles robbed of their young. . . . At
this point Clytemnestra comes out of the palace & begins to
sacrifice in silence at the shrines which stand at the gates.
Meanwhile, still thinking of Paris, the Elders declare that the
sinner's sacrifice is vain. . . . Finally they catch sight of Clytemnestra, turn to her, & ask her what is her news (99–103)

Their question is left unanswered. The Queen silently leaves the
stage on her way to the other altars of the city. We expect
to hear her speak but the climax is deferred.

. . .

They sing of a sign which appeared at the departure of the expedition & the prophet's reading of it. . . .

. . .

The storm blows, Agamemnon wavers, the fleet is wasting, until, without questioning the prophet's authority, he is driven by ambition to kill his own child, in the first flower of girlhood, stifling her cries of evil omen.

. . .

During the last words the figure of Clytemnestra reappears on the threshold of the palace, standing against the background of her past   (20)

Perhaps —
    2 dimensions of movement —
        one to show the "Now"
        another to show the "Then"

consider highly theatrical presentation — unreality & beauty of remembered things — Ghosts — highly stylized as a calculated mime or dance — almost like oriental stage — The scenes are enacted for in the theatre of the mind, with Clytemnestra as the spectator. Later, when she becomes a ghost she employs this same movement & manner & dress — & then it is Orestes who sees her —
The Furies Cassandra sees are the same convention —

1) Watchman — (The Beacon light) exit —
2) Bare stage — Alleluia (woman's voice)
3) Chorus of men enter — formal dance groups
4) Clytemnestra enters to shrine —
5) Her vision — Iphigenia — (chorus acts as curtain —
    Helen & her marriage —
6) chorus exit as in fear at her bitterness
7) Clytemnestra's dance of frightful revenge.

    1st Episode 270–366
    2nd Stasimon 367–480

Her language is colored by 10 yrs of brooding over her murdered child.
                                                                    (20)

    2nd Episode 461–685
    3rd Stasimon 686–773

The Elders . . . enquire about Menelaus —

. . .

Menelaus is destined to survive,
Agamemnon is not —

(24) The chorus resume the slow, meditative music we heard in the
first stasimon (170–93). Their theme is Helen, taken from
the middle of the 2nd stasimon . . . The poet is now about
to complete his parallel between Paris & Agamemnon by
drawing another between Helen & Clytemnestra. Just as
✳ Helen tempted Paris, so her sister will tempt Agamemnon.
She was like a lion-cub reared by a herdsman, at first the darling
of old & young, but destined when it grew up to bathe the
house in blood; at first tender & seductive, but in the end (746–8):
    "With the guidance of the stern wrath of Zeus she came as
    a fierce bridal-bewailing Fury."
Her sister is standing at the palace door ready to welcome
Agamemnon —

Perhaps — the dual aspect of the heart as shown by Helen &
    Clytemnestra —
    possibly 2 planes of action going on at the same time —
        Helen & Paris
        Clytemnestra & Agamemnon —

The use of moveable scenery — curtains —a torch — a tent — a litter
— all to be carried on — or contrived from a cape, a coat — a cloak —
of the chorus —

3rd Episode (774–965)

(25) Agamemnon enters in his chariot at the head of a triumphal
procession, followed by another chariot in which is seated the
captive Cassandra.
        "First it is just to greet this land of Argos
        With her presiding Gods, my partners in
        This homecoming, as in the just revenge
        I brought to Priam's city."   (801–4)

With these words Justice, the leading motive of the trilogy, steps
from the orchestra to the stage, & with unconscious irony the
King couples together, as both ordained by heaven, the fall of
Troy & his own return to Argos.
        . . .

(25) Clytemnestra stands silent, waiting her opportunity. Her purpose is to induce him to commit an open act of pride which will symbolize the sin he is about to expiate. That is the significance of the sacred tapestries on which she makes him tread."

He addresses the assembled people, ignoring her. She retorts by doing the same. There has never been love between these two.

. . .

her language becomes richer . . .

. . .

bids them spread out the purple at their master's feet . . .

. . .

The Queen stands behind the gorgeous display of wealth, inviting.

. . .

With frigid formality . . .
"Honour me as a man, not as a God."   (916)
He has refused to be tempted . . .

. . .

Clytemnestra changes her tactics.

. . .

(26) Her arguments are a woman's, illogical but nimble. . . . She
(922) makes a gesture of deference to his authority . . . touches his pride . . . flatters . . .

. . .

After he has gone in, she stays behind to invoke the name of
(27) Zeus who humbles mortal pride.   (964–5)
        "Zeus, Zeus, the Perfecter, perfect thou my prayer,.
        And perfect also that which is in thy care!"

Clytemnestra —
    As a Queen
    as a temptress
    as a Woman —
    as a high priestess about to perform the sacrifice.

        4th Stasimon   (966–1018)
(27)   4th Episode   (1019–55)

The stage is now empty save only the silent figure seated in the chariot — The slow music (170–93, 686–90) begins again, now tense & sinister. The theme of the ode is fear which has routed hope, & it is expressed in the language of prophecy.

. . .

Clytemnestra re-appears at the door of the palace . . .

(27)   She exerts her powers of persuasion.

      . . .

And as she speaks we realize that she is using the language of mystical initiation. With blasphemous audacity, she imagines

(28)   herself as the officiating priest, Cassandra as the candidate for initiation, & the impending murder as a holy mystery.

      . . . Clytemnestra – returns to palace

Kommos   (1056–1176)
5th Episode   (1177–1405)

After a long pause we hear a low moan.
It is Cassandra crying to Apollo.
Then in a delirious flood of prophecy she sings of the children slaughtered long ago; sees the murder that is being done within; hears the Furies chant for joy & sees them dancing on the roof; & finally with poignant grief she mourns her own death & the passing of the House of Priam. In the episode these themes are repeated & developed. To prove her veracity, she interprets the song of the Furies — they are celebrating the sins of Atreus; & she goes on to tell how Apollo inspired her with the art of prophecy (1177–1212). Suddenly the ecstasy returns; the children of Thyestes appear before her eyes — this is the crime for which Aegisthus is now exacting retribution; then she calmly tells the chorus that they are about to witness Agamemnon's death (1213–54) Again the ecstasy returns; predicting her own death & casting off the insignia of Apollo, she foretells the return of the exile "who to avenge his father shall kill his mother" (1280) With a last cry of grief for Priam & his sons (1304) she approaches the door, but recoils sick with horror.

    . . . then, in her last words, her fate & Agamemnon's, captive & captor, slave & king, both confronted by the same death, become a symbol for the tragedy of the whole human race (1326–8)

> "Alas, mortality! when fortunate,
> a painted image; in adversity,
> The sponge's moist touch wipes it all away."

    . . .

    conclusion — (1342–1673)

(29)

"The Elders confer in anxious whispers but do nothing . . . but the artistic purpose of the dialogue is to relax the emotional tension in order that we may respond to the culmination of the play which is still to come.

The dead bodies of Agamemnon & Cassandra are revealed,
laid on the blood-stained purple, while with fearful exultation
Clytemnestra describes how her husband fell, entrapped in
his own wealth."

. . .

   'What of <u>him</u>? Did he not set ruin afoot
   In the house, when he slew
   Iphigenia, the child that I bore him?
   And with long bitter tears have I mourned her.'

"The revelation of Clytemnestra's motive is now complete. In
the course of 10 yrs. her love for her first born has been
corrupted into hatred of the man who wronged her, & the
whole of her passionate nature dedicated to revenge. Yet this
hate was the outcome of love. . . .
For her the murder was a necessary act of purification, a perfect
sacrifice by which the family has been purged of its hereditary
madness. . .
The fate of Agamemnon has been illustrated by the figure
of the hunting net, which was first cast over the city of Troy
& then became a <u>disastrous robe</u>, symbol of his excessive wealth
in which he was trapped & slain. So in the next play Clytemnestra
is figured as a snake, which after strangling the eagle in his
eerie & leaving its nestlings to starve, is itself slain by the
snake to which it has given birth. And in the last play Orestes
becomes a flying fawn with the hell-hounds hot upon his tracks.
Apart from these leading figures, the Agamemnon is characterized by a wealth of incidental imagery. The sun, the
moon, the stars, the interstellar spaces, the sea with its
inexhaustible riches, now sunk in midsummer calm, now lashed
to fury by hail & lightning, the snows of winter in which
the birds drop dead, budding corn, ripening grapes, . . .
the whole pageantry of nature is displayed as a background
to the tragedy of man. In contrast to this the imagery of
Choephorae will be less lavish & more sombre, a withered
(32)   forest oak, meteors, dragons & monsters of the deep. But at
end of the Eumenides the bright colors will return when the
maledictions of the Furies break into sunshine."

Net

Assyrian —   Origins of European tho't —
                                                  372   Onions —

"They have used all kinds of magic
To tie me as with ropes,
To catch me as in a snare,
To bind me as with cords,
To overpower me as in a net,
To strangle me as with a noose,
To tear me as a fabric.
But I by the command of Marduk, lord of charms,
By Marduk, wizard of enchantment,
Both the wizard & the witch
As with ropes I tie,
As in a snare I will catch,
As in a net I will overpower,
As in a noose I will strangle,
As in a fabric I will tear."

Iranian —   Ibid 363
"According to the Iranian Epic Ahriman has a Net. While Tus & Furibur
seize the castle of the Deva Bahman, the mighty Ahriman spreads out
his air-like net.
    "Even the world-destroying lion & the dragon cannot free themselves
    from the net of Fate"

                              . . .

"This is the manner of lofty Fate: in his hands is the diadem & also the
noose; the moment a man sits gaily with the crown, Fate snatches him
from the throne with his noose."   (363)

"As in ancient India, so in Babylonia, disease was often conceived as a
bond attached by a demon. 'They spread out their net; where the anger
of the gods weighs, they fall upon him, envelop him as with a garment,
rush at him, spout poison over him, bind his hands, fetter his feet.' "
                                                              (364)

Settings —
    1) Agamemnon —
            Autumn with its glory & its angers and its ruthless beauty —
                The Bee-Hive tombs —
                The sheets of gold in which the children were wrapped.
                The Implacable Lions —
                "Rage against the dark"
                    Dylan Thomas —

A woman —
    streaked with silver —
    but her bones are gold —
    She is like a majestic tree about to shed its
    leaves —
    to kill her husband that her dream (Iphigenia) be
    avenged & live —

2) Libation Bearers —
    Winter —
    The Stark Tree —
    The appeasement of the gods of Fate —
    The ruthlessness of Youth —
    The tomb of Agamemnon —
    thou Agamemnon —

(32)   "less lavish & more sombre . . . a withered forest oak,
Aeschylus   meteors, dragons, & monsters of the deep"
Thomson
Vol. I.

3) The Eumenides
    The Spring —
    The break of the ice —
    the fear —
    (The snow flurry at Delphi)
    Mt. Parnassus, the home of the Muses, veiled in
    winter —
    The emergence —
    Spring at Olympia —
        The flowers —
         " Day
         " Warmth —
    The return of freedom
            forgiveness of self —

        "at the end of the Eumenides the bright colors will return,
(32)   when the maledictions of the Furies break into sunshine
Thomson   & soft breezes bringing fruitful increase to crops, to
Vol I   cattle & to men."

Clytemnestra —
    in the Underworld
    Hell
    Persephone —
    The endurance of return — of re-birth —

The private hell of a woman who has killed her love because
her love killed her creative instinct —

                                        her child —

Scene as she faces the Fates
Chooses her life — as in Plato — drinks of Lethe —
    only enough — to ensure not too much agony of
    memory —

characters —
    The Underworld —
        Clytemnestra
    /   Persephone
        Pluto —
        Agamemnon
        Cassandra
        Iphigenia —
    chorus of men
        4 voices —
        (The eternal jury —)
        commenting — questioning —

Her reality

Her memory —
    Clytemnestra
    Agamemnon
    / Cassandra
    Iphigenia   ?
    Helen of Troy
    Menelaus
    Paris —

Her dream

The idea of Clytemnestra on trial in the Underworld of her imagina-
ation —
The entrance or revealment like the 7 entrances of Astarte —
shedding her jewels, clothes — etc — until she stands revealed
before her judges —
    Herself — Persephone
    Her Beloved — Pluto —
        (Agamemnon)

The idea of the rape of Persephone —
    as meaning the death of Iphigenia —

The deep struggle is between Clytemnestra & Orestes
                        The old — the new
                        Mother — son —

relinquishment of power
   of new life
   to her son
   " the future
Her devious excuses
her shape shifting —
  Iphigenia
  Aegisthus

Act II —   Play II.
 The Choephorae
   (Libation Bearers)
Prologue 1–21
Parados 22–82
First Episode 83–304

<hr>

(32)

"The interval between the 2 plays is not stated, but it is natural
to suppose that some years have elapsed"
  (Homer: usurpation of Aegisthus — 7 yrs.)
. . .

Standing in the morning twilight at his father's grave he hears
from the palace a sudden cry.

32–33

 . . .

"Orestes has no option: he is the agent of the Gods. . . . We
are thus prepared for the final conflict of the trilogy, in which
the feud between the mother & son will merge into a feud
between the deities of heaven & hell, affecting the welfare
of all mankind."

Orestes has read from Apollo an express command to avenge
(32) his father by killing his mother & her paramour.

"after a prayer to Hermes of the underworld & to his father's
spirit, Orestes lays a lock of hair upon the tomb, & then we
hear a cry, 'heavy, haunting shriek of fear.' (34–5)
Presently he sees a company of women dressed in black, coming
from the palace & stirred by the sight of his sister, walking
among them bowed in grief, he calls upon the name of
Zeus. . . .

(33) The women are beating their breasts & tearing their cheeks
in an oriental dirge. The Queen has had bad dreams, in which
the dead have signified their anger, & she has sent these serving

women with propitiatory offerings to her husband's tomb."

(34)   "they are captives from the sack of Troy".

Orestes recognition by Electra after her scene with chorus & her prayer —

Kommos 305–476
2nd episode 477–582

(36)   "Each of the 3 parts is a little drama in itself — the participants react upon each other . . . the ghost remains invisible; yet, listening to the prayers of brother & sister we feel their Father's spirit slowly entering their hearts. The action is wholly internal, yet for that reason more moving & impressive."

Perhaps
     (scene between Electra, Orestes, ghost of Agamemnon)

(36)   "This is a composition in what musicians call 3-part form. It begins & ends with a lament. But observe the dramatic contrast. At the beginning, Orestes & Electra are lamenting, while the chorus urge them to pray for revenge; at the end, Orestes & Electra are praying for revenge with spontaneous vehemence, but now the Chorus are lamenting — not for the past but for the future. " —

     . . .

This is like a fugue —

     . . .

(39)   "Orestes & Electra remain at the graveside . . . they continue to cry out for vengeance but alone. The curse of Atreus has risen from the tomb & lives again in them."

Clytemnestra's dream of the snake —
                                    lines —   523 —
Perhaps enacted as in a sleep walking scene
At the conclusion of Libation Bearers — Clytemnestra rises from her couch of death as a Fury — a phantom — & walks implacably toward Orestes —
It is her ghost — & in the 3rd scene — Eumenides — she leads the chorus of Furies — as this beautiful, golden, terrifying, winning ghost —
She is as beautiful as he, Orestes, desired she might have been —
     loving
     maternal

beautiful
gentle —
She is the mother as every man desires her — She is the dream of
his first love, his mother —

In "Agamemnon"
   She is the glittering, regal, hate-breathing woman —
      The woman whose creative instinct — her child Iphigenia —
      has been killed by her husband —
            by her need for home,
            (her woman's nature has betrayed her)
            In a sense she is a "career woman" or a woman with
            creative gifts — in that part masculine in her strength
            of will & need to propagate her power —
      passionate
      autumnal woman —
      she kills her womanhood in killing Agamemnon, her husband.
   "nets of ruin" — 1375
   "tangling nets of fury" — 1581

In "Libation Bearers"
   She is insecure
   lonely
   be-set by strange fearful dreams —
   without a husband —
   driven to pander her younger lover —
   aging —
      without love or care —
   afraid —
   Doomed to be killed by her son, rejected by him, because she
   has first rejected him —

   It is for her twin sister — Helen, the eternal woman —for whom the
   Trojan War was fought —
   not for Clytemnestra —
      Helen lived thru men & while they destroyed themselves for her
      phantom, she, herself, never destroyed anyone, or denied herself
      to anyone —
      Helen had no ambition, only the desire to live and love —
      Clytemnestra had ambition & will — lust — no love —

In "Eumenides"
      It is she who must forgive Orestes & herself —
      It is she who must change the Furies into beneficent powers
      (There might be a scene in Hades with Agamemnon which
      enables her to withdraw her venom from Orestes.)

The Net —
    — The Web —
Perhaps first seen in Clytemnestra's vision of the death of Iphigenia
in the first scene – where Iphigenia is caught in a web — a net —
a fisherman's net to guide the ships — & killed —

It may be a glorified one as a cloak in which Agamemnon is caught as
he walks across it & revealed standing, but dead, & then falls —

The net might be used again when Orestes is pursued by the Furies —

There might be a prologue in which the net, the web is woven
      by Clytemnestra & Helen
      under the Guidance of the Fates —
         or
a dance of 4 characters —
      Clytemnestra
      Agamemnon
      Helen
      Paris.   (Menelaus?)
as in a dream —
      perhaps to chorus of lines —
      as the great chorus early in the play reveals the background
      of the action —

      It could be a grave dance but loving also — even joyous
      at times — always ritualistic —
      How the interwoven lives & loves of 4 people weave the net
      which is the instrument of disaster — tragedy —
      It is the same net which catches Helen in its toils —
      laid upon her by Paris —
      The one used to ensnare
      Iphigenia —
      The one used to trap
      Agamemnon —
      The one used to bind
      Clytemnestra —
      The one used to entrap
      Orestes —
      Until some act breaks or disassembles or transforms
      it — it is a weapon of death —
      It is Karma —

Perhaps
      The gods watching the net woven —
            Pallas Athene
            Apollo —
      3 Fates to hold up center
      almost as a maypole —
      (a masque)

"In the seine-net image we can communicate the sense of inexorable
external pressure in the progress of tragedy; the progressive constriction
of the individual's power of choice; the symmetrical narrowing of the
horse-shoe; the illusion of liberty in the meshes, or above the conk-line;
the final hauling of the catastrophic purse to land."
                  (40) — Henn   "Harvest of Tragedy"

"this gleaming snare,
Woman . . ."
            Hippolytus

Fury is a high queen of strength even among the immortal gods and the
undergods, and for humankind their work is accomplished, absolute,
clear: for some singing; for some, life dimmed in tears; theirs the
disposition"   Eumenides — 1. 950

"Fury is a high queen"   Eumenides
Orestes —
      "I have been beaten & been taught"
            X X   X X   276
      It was my Mother of the dark heart who entangled him in subtle
      gyres and cut him down.   459

C.   "A Mother has her curse, child. Are you not afraid?"
            (L Bearers   912
O.   No.
      "It will be you who kill yourself.
            It will not be I."
            L.B. (922)

opening scene —
      The roof-top at night —
      or a back-drop revealing the stars in the heavens —
            The net of the Stars —

A light shatters it —
          Troy has fallen —
perhaps the <u>Narrator</u> catapults the lines — there is a frenzy in the
darkness wrought by the beacon — at the peak of the music & excitement
it breaks into dead silence as
          Clytemnestra enters —
          Dance
          Scene of recollection —
                    1 — with Helen
Perhaps Gods in attendance Apollo — Athene — Aphrodite   sisters but not close —
                    Dominated by the Great Swan —
               duet
          Entrance — as in double bridal
3 men —   Agamemnon
                 Menelaus —   *The God?*
                 The Unknown   (later Paris)

     Dance of 4 or 5
          Clytemnestra — Helen
          Agamemnon — Menelaus —
          — The Unknown —

     Dance of a net —
          either garlands
          ropes
          veils of women's robes

     action leading into abduction —
     all 4 caught laughingly in net made by the dance —

Perhaps   Paris dances in it —
                    or
               Menelaus —

When the 3 are left —
   Dance of 2 men — pledge —
          Agamemnon —
          Menelaus —

Scene of Sacrifice —
          The whips of the priests form a net which holds Iphigenia as the
          sacrifice —
                    or
          Iphigenia chosen from women as sacrifice —

The Bronzeless Net / 261

performed as
"play within play"
highly formalized —

Wild anguished dance of Clytemnestra —
　　　　cradling of daughter in her arms,
　　The seeking to escape —
　　but held in the net —
　　Either whips of priests — or veils of Helen —

At peak of sacrifice scene dissolves to roof top at Mycenae & the
　　beacon —
?　　Ironic dance of Clytemnestra in welcome <u>now</u> or <u>later</u>??

Prologue — Hades —
　　　　Clytemnestra — Helen — Agamemnon — Aegisthus —
　　　　Cassandra　　Iphigenia — Electra — Orestes

The Furies who arise are the
characters involved —

A Jury box — who speak the lines —
shown in part so that 12 are not needed
perhaps only 2 — man & woman —
　　　The Judges in the heart —

Prologue — Hades — or perhaps Act I
　　The question —
　　　　(as in Eumenides — with Orestes at shrine & Furies
　　　　attendant —
　　　　Clytemnestra invokes Furies — who are hooded or
　　　　veiled & when they turn they are the people of the
　　　　drama — her accusers — her conscience —
　　　　The Furies which are her memories —

the dream of Clytemnestra, call "I upon your name."　　　　　　E — 115
　　　　I go dishonored (thus)
among (the rest of) the dead.
　　　I am driven in disgrace
　　　　　　　　I
the dream of Clytemnestra
　　. . . go dishonored . . . among . . . the dead
Because . . . I killed . . .
my bad name among the perished suffers no eclipse.
　　　　　(I am) driven in disgrace

Act I.
    Flash of Beacon —
1) Watchman's dance —
      Brilliant
      wild   David?
      a great cry of joy
      a declamation —
      running about stage
      leaping —
      mad & filled with mad joy.
               Exit.

2) chorus ?
      Formal ritual-like design —
      Something like Primitive Mysteries
        Dividing
      coming together —
        geometric —
      Interior speaking
         in groups
          two's etc.
         groups

3) Clytemnestra
      Enters slowly
      veiled in light veil —
        a hooded woman
          like a falcon
            (or a snake)
      She removes the veil to see
        slowly she tears it   ?
            (chorus leaves?)
      As she paces the stage in a ritual-like pacing perhaps she could
      be re-dressed by ghost-like figures —
        (The Fates?)
      Always one is waiting for her with a garment from the past
        (perhaps her face marked with gold across the brow &
        under the eyes)

Or else this whole scene played with chorus on stage — she weaves
in & out of them regally — at each group in the midst of some
design a new garment is placed on her or removed — & her face
painted — As it is done each time & she appears more strange

increasingly, that particular group exits & as they do 1 remains —
    Helen of Troy
    Agamemnon
    Menelaus (or Paris)

4)   The 4 are involved in a dance — almost like a bridal dance —
    weaving in & out until they have woven a net — either with the
    veils of the 2 women or garlands — or a large net which has been
    left on the floor stage during the dressing —
                or
    as the dance becomes like an ancient bridal by capture — a net
    descends — from the heavens & they are caught & separated in the
    wide crimson meshes —
                or
    The net is woven by the Priests or by something held by the Priests
              or
    By The Fates —
        as Dressing — Tiring Women —
              or
    As she enters she is accompanied by 3 women — seeming
    servants —
    She is helpless as they dress her, pass her from one to the other
    as in a ghostly dream —
    Bring in the others —
    Direct the ghostly dance —

As this whole phantasmagoria proceeds it is like a masque —
    artificial — silent — as a dream —
                      (music or not?)
    or hand-clappings — ?
      crotali — ?
      hand drums — ?
      flute?
      human voice singing dirge like seata —
In the dream the faces painted strangely —

Paris abducts Helen —
There is darkness —
The sound of whips in the darkness —
    whips of the priests —
lights come up on Iphigenia ready for sacrifice —
    She dances a ritual plea —
Clytemnestra is held from action by
                  Priests —
                  Fates —

(This is where music should be like saeta —
                        a dirge of women)
Black again —

(Each time light comes — it is as tho' beacon were re-lighted or another
beacon lighted — Iphigenia disappears — solo of loss, wild grief — only
Agamemnon present?
She falls as in faint —

At the end of the scene — (of dream remembrance)
Clytemnestra stands as she was when she first entered —
It is here she should tear her veil — and dance the solo for
vengeance & victory —
                        and exit

I wish it could be possible to do this scene as tho' the words of the
chorus were speaking the tho'ts of Clytemnestra as she stood there
to behold the beacon —
It might be better if there were 2 Clytemnestras — the one in the
dream — The one who just stands while this all floods over her in
memory —
The act for the dream could be when she veils her face, rather than
when she unveils it —

Clytemnestra   as bride   Patsy
                      " Mother   Yuriko
                      " mistress Linda?

Cassandra speaks
                        — or chants in a wild way — when
Clytemnestra comes to invite her within she does it as a dance — with
some symbol of her meaning which she uses (??)
It is like a priestess preparing to perform some rite of sacrifice —
        The sacrifice — Agamemnon —
A cruel, implacable, beautiful, glittering thing —

Clytemnestra in Hades —
        In remembrance —
        On trial to herself —

Trumpets —
A Voice calling hollowly
        "Clytemnestra"
                (as on trial —)
She is seen as in a wind with her garments blown by the wind in a place
without locality —

The Bronzeless Net / 265

She is summoned for questioning
questions —
Dance of attempted escape
The net descends —
The play Agamemnon begins as in memory —

Scenes —
    Hades   to   Hades —
    Palace
    Shrine at Delphi
          etc —

"The angry ghost"   Harrison — Prolog — 217
"Pointers to Vengeance"   "   219

The trilogy is essentially staged between Clytemnestra & Orestes —
There is much involved — a woman with a grown son. She has a lover &
refuses to grow old — & a son who must grow into manhood —
As such it is a death struggle —

    Red clad Furies act as stage managers
Prologue —

Furies in red as surrounding accusing (?) figures (like Egyptian tomb) red & gold —

    Clytemnestra alone in Hades —
      like an embalmed figure —
      the Tibetan ancients in Gold
      "the angry ghost"

    an incantation-like dance —
    inducing memory —
      why is she dishonored
      among the dead?
    (Furies undress her until she appears as
Act I — human figure in
    Scenes from Libation Bearers —
      Fears —
      dreams —
      appeasements —
her defense of her deeds — offerings —

    Her scenes with Orestes —
    Electra
      while she watches in terror —

Interlude — Beacon —
      Fall of Troy —
    Death of Iphigenia —

Act II
    Arrival of Agamemnon —
    Cassandra —
    The Killings —

Interlude
    Scene with Aegisthus —

Act III
    Orestes
    Her death —
Epilogue
      Terror of awareness —

Furies re-attire her in original costume — She remains in Hades —

"Pythagoreans & Stoics had bro't the dead into more convenient proximity to the living by transferring the site of Hades to the air? "Gks & Irrational" — (111) Re-birth — in/awareness

Iphigenia	—	Yuriko
Electra	—	Helen
Cassandra	—	Matt
Clytemnestra	—	Martha
Agamemnon	—	⎰ Bert
Orestes	?	⎱ Bert
Aegisthus		Bob
Watchman		David
Priest —		Gene
Helen of Troy	?	Ethel

               __or__ ⎰ Clytemnestra & all others —
                    a formal ritualistic inpersonal
△ Prologue — Hades   dance in which she is never
    Clytemnestra alone —   included —
      as her own ghost —   until finally she is left alone
                     on stage —
? Cassandra   Then her question "Why"
     as ghost —   Either Cassandra or Orestes
        her prophecy —   leads her into remembrance —

I Act I
     "Agamemnon"   __love scene__ C & Aegisthus
       (1) The beacon —
perhaps interlude of Helen of Troy   (2) Entrance of Agamemnon
       (3) memory of Iphigenia as she sees him
          (scene of sacrifice —
          C. between 2 lions of gate?

2 scenes as players on a stage —

curtain (net) falls between C & A.
  Iphigenia & priest —
  She throws herself at feet of A. but he does not
  see her because she is only the memory of C —

a drama of re-birth —

1) Clytemnestra alone on stage —   2
   (perhaps pacing stage as bourree in Frontier —)

2) Processional dance   3
   characters draped & veiled as chorus —

3) Clytemnestra   1½
   continues

4) Frieze dance —

5) Clytemnestra
   continues

6) Round dance

7) Clytemnestra
   Incantation
   (a demand to know why she goes without honor among
   the dead)

It seems to me that the only point of writing even a so-called autobiography — & I believe any/every autobiography can only be "so-called" — is to point a way to others who follow —

Purgation is something other than that —

Laughing — making fun of mistakes — is also something other —

The only justification for the pain & embarrassment of self-revealment is to point a way — perhaps to point a way from — rather than a way toward —

Too often it is a glorification of the incident surrounding the personal self & as such a personal appeasement of the Furies —

There is a degree of comfort — complacent — in an identification with another's predicament —

The result is negative — as all such comfort is — its tendency is to lull — rather than stimulate — to justify rather than face — to accept as reality — as causation —

Satan
    Azazel
    adversary
    Satanial
    accuser
    destroyer
    Prince of the power of the air
    Great Tempter

"God created man to be immortal, and made him to be an image of his own eternity. Nevertheless thru envy of the devil came death into the world: and they that do hold of his side do find it"
        Wisdom of Solomon — Man & his Gods — Homer Smith —
        Little Brown

"Movement never lies — "

                                                person   or 5
That was rather strong doctrine for a small (one) of four —

"She carries her head & moves her hands in a strange way"

The small person of 4 or 5 was not listening —
But she was —

The next time the grownup young lady who "carries her head in a strange way" came to call, (the house) the small person of 4 or 5 circled around her, looking, wondering, <u>pondering</u> — imitating — experimenting — grotesquely, lavishly, intensively —
The result in the small assembly was mystification, amusement, gradually discomfort — & ultimately it all ended in being lured to "Lilywhite's Party" — which it took time to fathom meant — "bed" — nothing more —

"Movement never lies — " at 4 or 5 that was an admonition — "Lie" in a Presbyterian household was and still is a clanging word which sets whispering all the little fluttering guilts which seek to become consumed in the flame of one's conscience —

"God . . . who is pure act" — Coomarswami Transf. 11 —

Gestures — "expressions & supports of spiritual resolve"   583
(Phil. of India
Zimmer)

look to thy heart for out of it comes the issues of life — *the bundle of life* —

Holy Ground —
Today is the day of salvation

Education —
                    Myths of Plato —
                              Er —
                    Stewart — 172 —
film of technic —

"The momentary prenatal act of choice which Plato describes in this Myth (Er) is the pattern of like acts which have to be performed in a man's natural life. Great decisions have to be made in life, which, once made, are irrevocable, & dominate the man's whole career & conduct afterwards.

drums — ⎰ like crackling flames —
        ⎱ sacrifice of Iphigenia —
          Voices of priests —
          summons of the winds by priest —

(1st after voice on record ceases) —
also one with inside use —
whole sacrifice in unreal timing — with no realism of sound
or action by dancers —

inside piano — prophecy? (1st one)

High priest — tall thin tight dress — Gene Mc.

Beacon —
Watchman's dance
    exit   stage empty
cry ————➤ ⁓⁓⁓ ◄———— alleluia — Clyt.
    chorus enters —
        dance of wonder — doubt — slow
Clytemnestra enters —
        as with offerings —
All transfixed during drama of mind
Bridal dance ⎰ Helen
             ⎱ Agamemnon
               Clytemnestra (double)
               Menelaus —
               Paris?

opening —
3 Fates on stage
(symbolic dance —
ritual in quality —
strange-beautiful
Between episodes Fates dance lyri-
cally solemnly —
act as tiring women at times
or "property men"
Place things on stage
pick things up if needed
supply anything —

Cassandra
    as focal point —
    instant of prophecy as beginning of drama of revelation —
speech — p. 72 —
        "No longer shall my prophecies like some girl new-married glance
        from under veils, but bright & strong as winds blow into morning
        & the sun's uprise shall wax along the swell like some great wave,
        to burst at last upon the shining of this agony."
                            etc

"Shining of this agony."

— as focus for drama —

"ecstatic in the skills of God"   1209   (73)

"none believed me"   1212   (73)

"storm of things foreseen."   1216   (73)

All takes place during prophecy —

Whole dance drama an outliving of the prophecy —

End — Cassandra goes in to her death —

"We two
must die, yet die not vengeless by the gods. For there shall come
one to avenge us also, born to slay his Mother, & to wreak death for
his father's blood." 1278 (76)

Beginning of "Libation Bearers."

"The day is here & now; I cannot win by flight" 1301 — (76)

The Third Actor   (Cassandra)
{ Cassandra — priestess of Apollo }
{ Orestes   — directed by Apollo }

Kitto — Greek Tragedy — 80 —
"She is slain, but not before she has spread before us a filmy screen on
which we see, as in a phantasmagoria, all the horrors of this House,
past, present, & future. Time & action are suspended; or rather, past &
future action are made to live on the present stage.

For Folly
Notes for dances never choreographed—
Tam Lin
Garden of Eden
Anna Livia Plurabelle

For Folly — see "Achievement of T. S. Eliot" (84) (A Game of Chess)
Beitrage zur Englischen Philologie Herausgegeben von Max Förster

Heft XXX

30–33

R.N.A.

Cox — Introduction to Folklore
MacKenzie   Colour Symbolism — Folklore XXXIII–139
Hart   "Ballad & Epic"

See "Legend of Perseus"   Hartland —

Poetic Origins & the Ballad — Louise Pound

Science of Fairy Tales — E.S. Hartland

{ Secret Commonwealth of
{ Elves, Fauns, Fairies — Robert Kirk

{ Ancient Legends, mystic
{ charms & superstition of Ireland   Lady Wilde

Fairie Faith in Celtic Countries — W. J. Evans Wentz

Elements of Folk Psychology — Wilhelm Wundt

136.4
W 96

822 S5 Hia	The heart of Hamlet's Mystery Karl Werder	Chimera? Sphinx?
294 W48	Tibetan Yoga — W. Y. Evans	

	Haunted Castle — Railo
	After Strange gods — T. S. Eliot
	The Destructive Element — Stephen Spender
821–09 H3–78	The Ballad in Literature Henderson
822.09 B–29	Elizabethan Jig — Baskerville
821–08 C–43C	Ballads — Child
821.08 H18	Ballads & Ballad Plays — Hampden

The maid & the Palmer —
        "Penance I can give thee none,
        But 7 yeere to be a stepping-stone.
        Other 7 a clapper in a bell,
        Other 7 to lead an ape in hell. ◄———
        When thou hast thy penance done,
        Then thoust come a mayden home."

The Magdalen — the woman of Samaria
"The story of the woman of Samaria (John IV) is blended with the
medieval traditions concerning Mary Magdalen, who is assumed to be
the same with the woman 'which was a sinner' in Luke, VII, 37, and
also with Mary, sister of Lazarus."   (Maid & Palmer — 39)

The Lord of Mar's Daughter —
        (The bird-lover)   270 — P. 584

Breaking the bough in the grave of Diana.
                Folk-Lore XVIII — 89–91

"Encyclopedia of Religion & Ethics" (Fairy)
                Vol V — 679

golden bells on the bridles — Tam Lyn
        "The bridles rang"

The dance is accompanied to music of the <u>pipers</u>.

"Childhood of Fiction"   MacCulloch

"Secret Commonwealth" — Andrew Lang

The Ballad in P

291   Myths & Mythmakers — Fiske
F54

809   Evolution of Literature — Mackenzie
M.19

        Studies in Literature — Couch — 25 —
"Undoubtedly ballad comes from the late latin verb <u>ballare</u> 'to dance,'
& should mean a song accompanied by dancing."

Sonnet
    Sonetto — a song accompanied by instrumental music —

Professional minstrels responsible for ballad
                Prof. Ker — 28
"The ballad is an Idea, a poetical Form, which can take up any matter
& does not leave that matter as it was before."

All under the leaves & the <u>leaves of life</u>
I met with virgins seven,
And one of them was Mary mild,
Our Lord's Mother of Heaven.

And what are you seeking, you seven maids
All under the leaves of life?
Come tell, come tell, what seek yon
All under the leaves of life?

"The old ballad was re-adapted to fit a new scandal in high life."

points
    1 — impersonality
    2 — extraordinary rapidity of movement.

Leesome Brand
    Refrain —
        The broom blooms bonnie & sae it is fair —

"They appealed in their day to something young in the national mind."

Fairies — origin
    Fata — Fate
    Arabic — pre-Adamites who rebelled against God.
    native goddesses
    a folk memory of druidesses who have been priestesses
    enchantresses
    beliefs in ghosts
    folk-memory
    W. Y. Evans Wentz.
        has sought to prove that "fairies exist, because in all essentials
        they appear to be the same as the intelligent forces now
        recognized by psychical researchers."
        may have been nature — spirits — divinities

What is Hallow-een?
        coming of winter — death?
    queens — "white women"
    Welsh Ellyllon = Druids
    The Dead — "The furious host"
    "Washer at the Ford"   a revenant
see Chaucer —

Child IV–456
Kittridge — "Sir Orfeo" Am. Journal of Philology — VII–190

Notes for dances never choreographed / 277

bees humming
(violins)
at first of song —
bells?

Tam-Lin —
The holding of the Beloved against all enchantments — the winning of
him back by faith & the strength & courage to hold him against fearful
odds.

The metamorphosis of a being under any spell into beings of
varied natures.
What are some of the ancestral footprints we could and do
make . . . what characteristics show these . . .
The snake —
The lion
The bear
The boar
The Phoenix bird —
Hot iron —
Fire —
The Fire walk perhaps —

What is the central point of focus of the whole — the psychological
kernel?
Is it the man who is bewitched or the woman?
Who fights the battles against the powers of enchantment?
Is it the one who is enchanted?
or another?
Is it that through fighting one's own battles one is cured?
Or is it that through love & faith the fight is won for another?
In either case it is the winning through to the real being in spite of
the battling shadows — the ancestral foot-steps.

The witch?   The Fairy Queen?
The ballad ghost — a singer?   (Susan Reed?)

See —
Cretan tale
Thetis with Peleus (Apollodorus)
Menelaus & Proteus   (Odyssey)
Hercules & Nereus.
The Wife of Bath

See
Campbell —
Popular Tales of the
West Highlands —

382–83–89–91–96
369–376
320–323–345

See p. 198–194–199–285–290–313–314–318
> "Then sounded out throu elphin court,
> With a loud shout & a cry,
> That the pretty maid of Chaster's wood
> That day had caught her prey."

The Power of love —
The affirmation that is union —
Union as the symbol of "the Oneness."
"The Oneness" as the Ocean   The Source — of all —

Sacrifice to the Devil
Tithe to Hell —
    Sacrificial victim
    Druidic rights —

Power of music   (Harp, viol, fiddle, made
    Harping the birds from the trees   from dead girl's body)
    bark from the trees
    dead from the grave —   witch hour

Methods of Enchantment & disenchantment
    Power of music
    physical contact
        kissing
    crying out of the name.

In some way Tam Lin has a quality of the Noh play.
It might be used in its simplicity as a theme — and treated emotionally
as the Noh demands first of all — that very emotionalism creating the
form, dictating the conventions, creating the elegance & the poignancy.

At the cross roads a woman wrestles with the Powers of Darkness — the
demonic powers of Hell — of Death — for the life of her lover —
The transformations — the change into animal characteristics separated
by the Demons — the Fairies — who must pay the tithe to Hell —

Can there be some use made of the Ghost Singer — ?
Perhaps various lines from various ballads could be used — so that in
some sense it was a use of balladry rather than an interpretation of any
one ballad — ?

When the transformations take place is there some way that the two
could be forced into some different shapes?
Or will the two areas have to remain separate?
With the two principals almost sitting & watching the play of forces,
objectifying in some way their inner beings — their thoughts — ?

Notes for dances never choreographed / 279

A sense of stage within a stage — perhaps —
Perhaps there could be some way of the two — man & woman —
sharing the transformations — Sometimes she would hold him, sometimes he, her —
Or is there always some dance by which she dispels the powers of
darkness — ?
   In which case the man will participate in the transformation scenes —
as the center of their revels.

Should I be the woman?
Or should I be Queen of the Underworld?

I think it must be the woman —
Only in that way can it be tragic and heroic in its strength.

It must be that $\left\{ \begin{array}{l} \text{faith} \\ \text{love} \end{array} \right\}$ dispels the shadows — the terrors —

I do not want this to be medieval — except where the superstitions
come into it — the ancient terrors —
The court of Fairyland should be as we know it — or think of it —
medieval in quality — also the fact that superstition should be objectified
by some period.
But the main part of the piece is without time — abstract —

          This might be in musical form of Rondo —

opens with music reminiscent of bag-pipes —
          wild — haunting — strange — tragic
there follows a solo dance
          a summons — a seeking — a calling thing —
          pagan — female — old — eternally woman —
This is shot across by the sound of the ghost voice —
          eerie, haunting —
          It is as though it were midnight — the instant when the
          dead walk —
The ghost singer walks into the light —
The woman backs upstage into the shadows.
          (perhaps until she clasps the hand of the lover — ?)
Either there follows a scene with the elf-King — (Merce)
Or else the Fairy folk appear —
          with them the lover —
          a fantastic swift moving scene — punctuated and accompanied by
          the low sweet ringing laughter (in pitch) of the Ghost Singer —

Second version —
    Opens with a dance between man & woman —
        like bag pipes —
        Dance formal & strange & beautiful — love dance.
    broken by singing voice —
        a chimera comes — a strange creature in
        terrifying aspect — Death
    The Ghost Singer enters —
        moves across in light singing — with words.
        Perhaps dancing, too, in supernatural way.
    The Fairy band enters
        each one like some famous dead person —
        or emotion — some memory —
        Scene shot thru with delicate laughing by the ghost.
    The man springs into a bewitched dance.
    Leaves with the Fairy band.
    Woman's dance of loss — of seeking —

Musical Form
    Theme & Variations —
    Rondo —

Dream of a love —
Legend
Ancestral Footstep —
of a bewitching & a winning
of her true love —

~~~~~~

Perhaps at well?   Perhaps woman with mistletoe?
man appear from it —   Druidic

1.   Unaccompanied singing — no words — a pagan feeling.
                              prophetic
2.   Music like the pipers of Scotland —
        wild & haunting & tragic —
3.   Man & Woman dancing —
        something formal — almost the feeling of a court dance — ?
        Something wilder — more pagan
4.   The Ghostly Singer
        Entrance separates them —
        no words —
        eerie, haunting, pagan —
        crosses stage — pauses —
5.   Chimera
        a strange creature — electric — pagan —
        centers on 2nd part of vocal music —
        dancing —
        Exits —

6 — Ghostly Voice —
    first verse of a ballad —
7 — Elfin Host —
    stage floods with people —   *Witch's Sabbath*
    woman retreats upstage — perhaps walking up a short flight
    of steps backwards facing audience — suspended above
    group — bewitching of man —
8 — Man's dance —
    Like a fantastic jig —
    He is bewitched —
9 —

Perhaps at beginning
    woman could enter bewitched — or rise from bed bewitched or a
    hill —
    The scene could be set with the unaccompanied voice — like a
    Druidic priestess — or perhaps in Gaelic certain words —
    When the faint sound of a horn sounds thru the song the woman
    arises or enters as tho' sleep walking — under a spell —
    A scene forms out of the darkness & she is attired in strange
    garments —
    The music turns to the pipers — savage & strange — as the man
    appears as tho' just becoming visible —
    He dances — a wild dance like a jig.
    They dance together
    The Chimera enters

1)   Unaccompanied Singing —
    Pagan — almost Druidic — a strange — eerie summons —
    The woman enters (or rises) walking as bewitched in a dream,
    when she hears the faint sound of a horn sound thru the song —
                    Perhaps the song has Gaelic or Welsh words.
    Out of the dark things are put on her — she is attired by unseen
    hands — a stage place is built out of the darkness. Like a parade
    of phantoms building a stage —
    She is given a piece of mistletoe with which she dances.
    It is as tho' the singing sent her back into past time —
    or that it is singing heard in a dream —
    The music has been entering — It becomes almost like the savage
    crude sound of bag-pipes —
2)   The man appears dancing something like a fantastic jig. The music
    is hard & wild & strange — & beautiful —
    They dance together —

3) The Ghostly Singer enters — passing between them — singing.
   She crosses stage & waits
4) The Elf-King —
   a creature, the first of the Elfin Host —

1. Unaccompanied singing — *no words at first*
      strange — pagan — clear — *Then perhaps Gaelic*
      or Welsh —

2. Woman enters —
      as tho' asleep or in
      dream — bewitched
      as she dances the stage fills with figure cloaked, only partly
      seen — give her a flower or mistletoe —

3. Man enters — or appears as beside a well supernaturally —
   He dances fantastic hard dance to music like pipes of Scotland —

4. They dance together —

1 Singer
2 Perhaps man should enter first — dance —
3 The woman comes as tho' drawn to him bewitched —
4 The dance together
5 The Singer enters —
6 The Laird of Elfland.
7 The beings of Elfland
      with Fairy Queen —
      man is bewitched & taken away —
      all exit —

========

1. Singer
2. Woman   (Love Rune)
3. Fairy Host
      Transformations —

This should be the story of love which holds the Beloved One against
& thru all charms & enchantments — all the demons of the mind &
heart are overcome by the strength of her love —
      Ancient Pattern
      Ancestral Footstep
      My true love

I think this could be turned to be the woman's voyage as well as
the man's of the ballad.
She could go to Hell for him in the Transformations.
Myth of Hell
      Why pulls thou the rose? —   (Title?)

"They next shaped him into her arms
Like the laidliest worm of Ind;
But she held him fast, let him not go,   345
And cried aye 'Young Tam Lin' "

The call —
        The woman enters as tho' called to her Destiny — awesome —
        fearful —

The sound of ancestral footsteps —
Myth of Hell —
        Where she goes for her love —

Battle with Hecate at the Cross Roads,
The Triumph over fear
                of loss
                of death

Anne Hutchinson —   "Midwinter Spring"
                                                 Eliot —
                Psalm —   (Gidding)

The Heritage   From the hands of the Mother
The Inheritance

        The sinews & bones of joys & sorrows
        The beautiful object for carding wool
                                19th
                                Psalm

        The dress for the bridal
        The dress for the sorrow
        The undergarments of intimacy
                of love —
        The cloak of faith —

"Wine of these grapes"   (E. Millay)

Voices of the children —
Children in the trees —
        innocency guiding the soul to itself —   (Eliot)

"one of the greatest services of poetry lies in its power to 'make us
from time to time a little more aware of the deeper unnamed feelings
which form the substratum of our being, to which we rarely penetrate;
for our lives are mostly a constant evasion of ourselves, & an evasion of
the visible & sensible world.' "
                                Matthiesson — 108

Last books of Eden

The garden of Eden —
    The ejection from it.
    The remembrance of its beauty —
            Sorrow — anguish — contrition —
    The re-birth —
        The return to the garden —
            To faith —
            To innocence
            To first things —
            To reality —

"Bright nature"   "the grace of a bright nature" —   ch. 2 — p. 5 —

"Yet of thy goodness, O, God, do not away with me altogether;
but be favorable to me every time I die, & bring me to life."   ch. 15–4

guest of satan —   ch. LVI

Sphere of fixed Stars   (Plato)

"The flesh is a 'strange garment' not native to the soul"
This strange garment. — Life —

Mirror or Bowl of Dionysus —
        mixing of dreams —

"I will raise myself over this force of my nature,
Step by step ascending to Him who has made me
I will come to the fields & spacious palaces of my memory"
                St. Augustine —   Bk X ch. 8 —   (Jung p 496)

'The artist, I believe, is more primitive, as well as more civilized, than
his contemporaries, his experience is deeper than civilization, & he only
uses the phenomena of civilization in expressing it.'   Eliot
                        (Achievement — 94)
"Eliot knows that no experiment in art is valuable unless it is
psychologically necessary — "   (86)

"The desert in the garden, the garden in the desert"   (120)
Desert of rock

            ". . . The word in the desert
Is most attacked by voices of temptation,
The crying shadow in the funeral dance,
The loud lament of the disconsolate chimera."   Quartets — 8

"at the still point of the turning world"   "   5

Notes for dances never choreographed / 285

"The quester" (like Parsifal) relies on voices of children in the tree
for direction —

"In the Holy Grail legend, Parsifal is guided to the Grail Castle by the
voices of children in the tree (as Siegfried followed the voice of the
bird), & in these new poems of T. S. Eliot, the poet is guided by the
voices of the children & birds hidden in the shrubbery & rose bushes of
a child's garden (Burnt Norton) to the secluded chapel of his mature
faith" (Little Gidding)

> Wallace Fowlie
> Eliot & Tchelitchew   p. 168 —
> Accent — Spring 1945

The rose or the yew tree

Eve — the quester —
>   otherwise she would not have heard the voice of the serpent —

"garden in the desert"
>   Garden of Eden — expulsion —
>   1st step toward maturity —

Tree
"In the medieval tradition the tree can easily be explained on the 4 levels
of interpretation: first, as the literal tree in the setting of Eliot's rose
garden; second as the allegorical tree of the Crucifixion from the top of
which the Voice speaks & directs; third, as the tropological tree whose
life cycle is the moral divisioning of time; and fourth, as the anagogical
tree when, suddenly, at the end of the final poem, it is called the apple
tree & alludes, as does the spitting out of the apple seed to Ash
Wednesday, to the spiritual drama of man's fall and redemption."

> Fowlie — 168

"He shall rise up at the voice of the bird"   Ecclesiastes XII–4
"miraculous messenger"

gospel of Eve —
>   Struggle toward a maturity of being —
>   Struggle to return to that "bright nature" which was lost.
>   Struggle to acquire the "bright nature" of faith —

The Summons to the stage of one's most inner being —
The Summons to appear in the garden before the god —
>   To show the treasures of one's inheritance —

Fan
bridal wreath
veil of sorrow
cloak

an accounting to Eve — Mary — Magdalene — you — of a woman's inheritance

Her care of her treasures that she may achieve the "bright nature" which is hers — her maturity —

Temptation
Ordeal —

From the hands of the Mother   (Eve)   from the tree in the garden —
      Terror — sorrow
      bridal — love — happiness —
Enter into tree — receive dress from within —
      a shrine
      a symbol of Eden —   Yew Tree
some device when she is within —
      ringing of bells —
      darkness —
      fluttering on the strings
          magical — supernatural
          moment of deeply felt terror — beauty —

                    garden in the desert —
                      an oasis of hope — faith
                      symbol of re-birth —
                        continuity of life —

Anna Livia Plurabelle —
    woman —
        Eve   garden
        Magdalene   street   Portrait —
        Mary —   sanctuary   of a
        You —   home   Woman

                      garment for the bridal —   spring
    ancestress   _Eve_   Joy
    Beloved   garment for the sorrow — autumn
    Mother   _Mary_   garment for the sin —   summer
    prostitute _Magdalene_ garment for the faith — winter
                           (guilt)

What would be the Gospel of Eve — ?
    Summoned before the Jury of the World
        she pleads her case
        states her being —
Dark ancestress   (totem animal figure)

Anna Livia Plurabelle is the carrier of the Eternal Yes; she is the
secret of the continuation of the jollification   (— life) Campbell
Skeleton Key —

garments of the soul —
bequeathed by the first to the last of women —

gospel of Eve —
        Summoned in sleep before the Judge of the World
        This is a dream confessional of woman's tragicomic destiny —
        She is the carrier of the Eternal Yes; she is the secret of the
        continuation of the jollification, Life —
        There is a bequeathment from the first to the last woman of
        secret things —
            The sinews & bones of joys & sorrows —

Books of Adam & Eve —
        Apocrypha & Pseudepigrapha of the Old Testament
Vol II.

Vision of Eve of Cain's murder of Abel

    Eve — "O Lord my God, hand over to me his pain,
    for it is I who sinned"

Seth & Eve go to the gates of Paradise for the oil of mercy

Eve wept "Woe is me; if I come to the day of Resurrection all those who
have sinned will curse me saying: Eve hath not kept the commandment
of God!"

"Then the beast cried out & said:
'It is not our concern, Eve, thy greed & thy wailing, but thine own;
for (it is) from thee that the rule of the beasts hath arisen.'

"And Adam saith to Eve: 'Eve what hast thou wrought in us? Thou has
brought upon us great wrath which is death (lording it over all our
race)' "

146
"And instantly he hung himself from the wall of Paradise, & when the
angels ascended to worship God, then Satan appeared in the form
of an angel & sang hymns like the angels. And I bent over the wall &
saw him, like an angel. But he saith to me 'Art thou Eve?' And I said
to him 'I am.' . . . Then the serpent saith to me —

'May God live! but I am grieved on your account because I would not have you ignorant.' "

. . .

"And when he had rec'd the oath from me he went & poured upon the fruit the poison of his wickedness, which is lust, the root & beginning of every sin, & he bent the branch on the earth & I took of the fruit & I ate."
"In that very hour my eyes were opened & forthwith I knew that I was bare of the righteousness with which I had been clothed . . . & I wept & said to him — 'why hast thou done this to me in that thou has deprived me of the glory with which I was clothed?' "

. . .

In that same hour we heard the archangel Michael blowing with his trumpet

                                        Eve's account of her fall —

& calling to the angels & saying: "Thus saith the Lord. Come with me to Paradise & hear the judgement with which I shall judge Adam."   (147)
        curse of God —

Eve —
"Now then, my children, I have shown you the way in which we were deceived; & do ye guard yourselves from transgressing against the Good."

Vision of Eve
    In a dream Eve is
    Summoned to the Judge which is the World —
    to speak of the bequeathment from the first
    to the present — (to the last)
    to show the treasures & the bane of one's inheritance
                                the delights & the sorrows of the
                                        inheritance
                                    bequeathment —

(see Gospel of Eve — a gnostic work describing Eve's seduction by Satan & the birth of Cain & Abel, sons of Satan (the serpent)
Epiphanius, adv. Haerises XXVI. Date uncertain
                        Fabricus, Cod. Pseudigr. Veb. Test. 1.95 (1712)

basic dress of black — ?   purple — red
        bridal —   gladness —
                    sorrow —
                        tattered —
        under —

Eve's penitence —
   Eve rose & went outside & fell on the ground & began to say: "I have sinned, O God, I have sinned, O God of all, I have sinned against Thee. . . . I have sinned before Thee & all sin hath begun thru my doing in the creation"

Eve's Vision —
   Behold the angel of humanity came to her & raised her up —
"& said 'Lift thyself from the earth.' "
"And she gazed steadfastly in to heaven & beheld a chariot of light, borne by 4 bright eagles & it were impossible for any man born of woman to tell the glory of them or to behold their face. . . ."
And the angels fell down & worshipped God crying aloud & saying Jael, Holy One, have pardon for he is thy Image, & the work of thy Holy Hands"   149

This is an affirmation

This is an essentially affirmative dance —

                                        the technic for joy —
It adds up in its parts to that sum of awareness which is   joy.
It might be a dream confessional of any woman
Any woman is Eve —
Her story is the gospel concerning her life —
Eve, the ancestress of the world, stands at the shoulder of each of us —
This is a summons to the stage of her inner being —
There to receive in awareness the bequeathment from the first
to the last —

Dance of acceptance   Ritualistic dance
drama of enactment   fall
      gladness
      sorrow

drama of enactment
      temptation
      fall
      re-birth

stage — a narrow glistening hallway with no place for concealment —
no place to hide —

She enters,
      Summoned in dream to the stage of her inmost being she enters —
      It is reminiscent of the far distant time when "In that same hour we
      heard the archangel Michael blowing with his trumpet and calling
      the angels."

there to receive the bequeathment from the first ancestress
re-enact the events leading to her tragicomic destiny

paean — a thanksgiving — a celebration for the bequeathment of
sinews & bones for sorrow & delight —
She is the carrier of the Eternal Yes —
she is the secret of the continuance of the jollification — Life —

"The glory of Adam & Eve before the Fall, the brightness they lost,
the Resurrection that was promised to Adam, the nature of the
serpent's temptation, the limbs of the serpent, the kind of the
tree of knowledge, the trumpet of Michael the guardian angel of
Eve, the judgement of God coming with his angels, the mutilation
of the serpent"

Holy holy holy is the Lord in the glory of God the Father for to Him
it is meet to give glory, honor & worship, with the eternal life giving
spirit now & always & forever.   Amen

Then the message of the great God fluttered in my breast &
bade me prophesy —   Sibylline book   III — p. 381

Eve

       enters stage as in dream —
       She wears a deep green cloak-like dress wrapped about her.
       It should be like deep emerald velvet — It is not a cape
       or loose flowing but a garment close fitting but apparently
       not made as a dress — It is also reminiscent of a very simple
       elegant negligee.

       In the first she wears this —
       Then for the dance of innocence, of gladness, she removes it as
       in a dream & is dressed in delicate dress with some kind of leaf
       design on it — It is like a young dress — also reminiscent of
       a very formal night gown —

Entrance as tho' summoned —
The soliloquy — an awareness of the tragic state
of her being — her guilt —
               Playing 3 characters in a sense.

The summons
The sense of guilt —
The memory of the bright nature. — Eve
"   "   " "   temptation —   — Magdalene
"   "   " "   sorrow   — Mary.

Notes for dances never choreographed / 291

Summons — Invocation — Evocation

Petition   transformations

cycle of Incarnations   garments of Incarnations
     1 — garment for gladness
     2 —   "   " temptation
     3 —   "   " sorrow

A Dream   A Prophecy —

"Then the message of the great God fluttered in my breast and
bade me prophecy."   Sibylline Books III — p. 381.

I do not want her to be remote
I do not want her to be a goddess, but a woman —

see 396

The Dream —   Dream confessional —
     The entrance to a stage — Summons
     The Petition
     The Confession   (Cycle of Incarnations)
        Re-enactment of the Fall —
     The Penance — The Punishment —
     The Thanksgiving — the Paean

            The Three Mothers —
               of birth
               " life
               " death
            The Three Fates —
               garments of the Fates
                  Past
                  present
                  future

Punishment —
highest tension almost shrill re-iterative sound —
     Perhaps cessation of all activity & stage almost in darkness —
     figure immobile — while music plays —
         (Is it possible hanging by almost invisible rope — by
         bracing feet against something like tree trunk & half
         lying halfway to floor — ?)
Perhaps rope could hang out from Proscenium arch — & a shadow
of a tree could be cast on wall at edge of stage
     (where balcony or box used to be)
Tree like cross —

	Book of Eve —	Gospel of Eve —
Summons	— 1	2
Petition	—	2
Confession	— {1 — 2 / 2 — 3 / 3 — 2}	7
Penance	—	1
Paean	—	2
		‾14‾ ″

Legend of re-birth —

any instant when

"Thus may my divine mission be crowned with success, and may I attain
to the body of glory"   Psychic Energy   391
(little known Tibetan ritual by means of which the yogin seeks to
transcend ego-consciousness & attain to consciousness of the Self.)

Gospel of Eve —

Summons —   Introduction —   Entrance —
Petition —
Re-enactment of the Fall —
Penitance —
          silence or no movement —
Instant of blessing —
Song of Faith — Celebration.

                                        Benedicite —
Dream confessional   Dance of Praise —

          Ejaculation
          Invocation
          Confession —
              Cycle of Incarnations

Examination of Conscience
Act of Contrition
Thanksgiving

Riverrun —

Eve

Tam Lin

"The poet's flight from the conventional world . . . into the dark world
of himself . . . is not so much a flight as it is a search. In every part of
himself & in every dream of his subconscious, Rimbaud is going to seek
& track down his innocence. . . . A poet's flight, then, is always a search
for his original purity. This is the key to Une Saison en Enfer, as well as
Shakespeare's Winter's Tale, to Joyce's Finnegans Wake, to Eliot's Little
Gidding. Art is a retrogression in time, an effort to recapture childhood
and its pure oneness with the universe which Pavel Tchelitchew has
painted in his great work of metamorphosis called 'Cache-Cache.' "

Rimbaud — Fowlie — 87 —

"Is he a clown, a prophet or an angel?"   98
"But who are they?"   Rilke — (5th Elegy)
(Picasso's acrobats)

"Like characters of Pirandello, they are seeking some pattern in which
they can engage their destinies. They perform together but each one is
separate from the others."   Rimbaud — 98

"not angel in the strict Christian sense of the word, but angel in the new
sense created by the contemporary artist — a sense which is transform-
ing the outdated hero of physical action into the new hero of spiritual
action."   99 —
". . . The angel is the new terrible hero who has developed a perfect
consciousness."   99

"image of poet as victim is now heightened by the image of convict
chained to a wall."   89

"The poet's flight from the conventional world into the dark world of
himself is not so much a flight as it is a search. In every part of himself &
in every dream of his subconscious. He calls it first his 'tresor,' which has
to be sheltered in the darkest part of himself; in witchcraft (i.e. poetry),
in poverty (i.e. exile), in hate (i.e. revolt)."   88

"In the first section . . . R. describes himself as being held to his past
by singularly strong and inevitable bonds. . . . He is held by 2 kinds
of past: the distant past of the sacrilegious & pagan Gauls . . . & the
immediate past of 19th C. Bourgeoisism"   88

"It is possible to hide in the world, but in the flames of hell one hides &

one is seen at the same time. As in the children's game of Hide & Seek (Tchelitchew), the victim who is 'it,' that is, the hero, hides his head against the trunk of the tree & blots the universe from his sight. But he is exposed during all the seconds which he counts out. He hides his face but he is seen by all the curious & incurious eyes of the other children.

91 —

the conversation Gide invented between the prodigal son & his mother. When he told her that he hadn't been seeking happiness in his flight, she, unable to comprehend, asks . . . "What were you looking for?" And the answer of the prodigal son, which could be Rimbaud's answer: "I was looking for who I was."   113

Rilke — "Where is the Place?"
"This is the invisible world conceived of by the tumblers who
are angels."   100
          "That invisible place — his own heart perhaps —
          . . . where evenly matched muscles are replaced by evenly-
          matched desires, where action is replaced by being."
                                                                      Fowlie   100

          "a fatality of happiness"   101

                    "Our examination . . . of work in Progress."
"RIVER RUN"
          "The river may be flowing, or he may be wishing to summon up
          the sounds of night or to awaken the emotions that night thoughts
          bring."
                                        book on Joyce —   111 —
                                        Shakespeare Co —

"The stream of consciousness reveals itself, derived from two
sources, (always mainly Dublinesque) of folklore & folksong, of
Celtic bards, of Celtic legends of slim maids with dark hair &
lithe bodies & breasts, of laughter & the continual melancholy
plaint of Celtic whimsy, fatalism, & the erratic shift of mood.
Church music sounds here, & the half remembered refrain of a
sentimental ballad of the '90s breaks in to be itself broken in upon
by a barroom ballad or the ribald refrain of a bawdy house
song. . . ."   112

a time.
act: Dumbshow
closeup,   113
"Poor little brittle magic nation, dim of mind."   114

"It is perhaps necessary to 'trance' oneself into a state of word intoxication, flitting-concept inebriation, to enjoy this work to the fullest. Surely the author himself has written in a state of exaltation, where the mood is witty, comic, or glimmery tragic, according to the passage; but the mood is only indicated rather than stated, defined, & dwellingly insisted upon. Whether Anna Livia is being a lithesome, taunting, wood-nymph of an Irish lass, or a garrulous knotty old washwoman, she is in the process of representing womankind, the femaleness of life; & the old man river as a randy young buck or as a rutty, fibrous, eternally impregnating aged male is representing the masculinities; & the two are composites, not only of humanity, sexes, bi, heter, & what have you, but there is an attempt to suggest thru the ebb & flow of prose the possibilities & relativities inherent in existence."   114–115

. . . the wonder emotions, the religious emotions, that have in their presentiments of death, intonations of fear & despair, or a humour that is mainly Dublin masculine & Dublin teasings.

. . . .

"It seems to me, for instance, to be noteworthy, as marking not a reaction from realism but the carrying on of realism to the point where it breaks of its own volition into fantasy, into the verbal materials of which realism, unknown to realists, partly consisted."   119

"The inferno of modern subjectivity."   123

All those things — objects — creatures — happenings to do with a river & let them in turn suggest the incident — the past —
                              Noah — loaves & fishes
a stone — a fish — a bridge — Tobias & the angel —

"Well, you know or don't you kennet or haven't I told you every telling has a taling and that's the he & the she of it."

Water —
              Tristram & Isolde —   The ship —

                                          Sophoclean tragedy
"a revolution in heroic fortune" —   372
       definition of tragedy — Theophrastus —

Tragic Scheme
Jocasta after she has entered the house and is about to commit suicide —

Her women about her knowing her intention

a kind of elegy —
     a seeing as in retrospect her past —
     a re-enactment of her life — its moods of tenderness, love,
     passion, loss —
         each episode broken by the chorus of women —
        The Rituals of Destiny
The transitions between moods — perhaps Fate or figure of Prophecy
in great cape comes between and breaks the action —

"union of hearts"   Soph. Trag. <u>191</u>
            best marriage
           Odysseus to Nausicaa
             Od, VI — 180–5
"union of hearts makes friendship"   Democritus

"It is hard to fight against anger; for whatsoever it wishes,
it buys at the cost of the soul."   Heraclitus
                            Soph. Trag. <u>194</u>

"In my beginning" — T. S. Eliot — East Coker

              Fenellosa — "Noh"
"Noh has been a purification of the Japanese Soul for 400 years. Kabori
Enshu classified the 15 virtues of Noh, among which he counted mental
& bodily health as one, calling it 'Healing without medicine.'"
"Dancing is especially known by its circulation of the blood, to keep off
the disease of old age."   <u>48</u>
"The Heart is in the Form"   <u>52</u>

              Crime of Jocasta
Chorus on stage — massed —
Jocasta backs in —
Turns to face chorus
Throws arm over face — stands as tho' struck

Dance of women —
Dance of Jocasta
     as though she were a wooden doll —
       Bewildered — deranged — caught in trap —
        (Something of the trapped lion)

1) Women standing silently like granite on stage
   Still for several seconds of music —
2) Jocasta enters —
   Jocasta's gesture —

The Chimera of Desire —
The Mockery of Desire

The intimate scenes —
between the women of a household in a time
when it was hard to be a woman — & very hard to be a great one & wise —
It meant anguish — Chimera?

The embodiment of the sin —
The objectification of the
crime —

The Sphinx
(young girl)
Tragedy of lost youth
Riddle of Sphinx
man —
The quest of woman
after man —
The half woman — half man —

Women like Henry Moore's figures —

Jocasta trapped by agingness
moment of worship at the
feet of the young girl —
the Sphinx — Youth —

The Victim — man — son — lover
Prophet —
Figure of Death —

Something which deals with
metamorphosis —
search for the Soul-stuff —

What subjects —
Jocasta
Judith
The Angel & the Dreamer — (the Fashioner)

What would "Riverrun" hold?
In terms as direct as Finnegan's Wake — from what I could possibly
know specifically & then trace back to the general — the
arch-type —
"In my beginning" —

Fowlie — Rimbaud
"The myth of the voyage is, in each man, the secret desire to leave for
that unrealizable object which barricades him from life."

"The symbol of hell is as closely associated with the work of Rimbaud
as the symbol of the voyage. If the voyage is the myth of man's desire
& of his first impulse, hell represents the place when he stops from time
to time during his voyage."   130

"The dream of man inevitably contains some aspect of the absolute:
absolute of sentiments or actions."   128

"Poetry, like a voyage, is an effort to review life."   128

"But the legend of places is not so indecipherable as the
myth of the heart."   129

Center of the Hurricane
Permit me to try again...

Photograph by Ron Protas

"center of the hurricane"
        (Title?)

Drink not too deeply of the River of Lethe —
        (book)

"One writes to recover a lost innocence"
                Laurence Durrell
                (Mountolive — 104)

"Then touched he their eyes, saying, According to your faith be it unto you, And their eyes were opened — "   Matt. 9 — 29 —

"how the serpent was more subtil than any beast of the field" —

And when the woman saw that the tree was good for food & that it was pleasant to the eyes, & a tree to be desired to make one wise, she took of the fruit thereof, & did eat & gave also unto her husband with her; & he did eat.
And the eyes of them both were opened & they knew
that they were naked — — — — — — — — — — — — — — —

                Gen — 3

And the serpent said unto the woman: Ye shall not surely die:
For God doth know that in the day ye eat there-of then your eyes shall be opened, & ye shall be as Gods, knowing good & evil.
                                See chapter 3 — Gen.
And the Lord God said, Behold the man is become as one of us, to know good & evil — — — — — — — — — — — — — — —

At the beginning —
And where is the that beginning? When we begin as born or when the great over-whelming tide of unconscious memory decides to use us as an instrument for the advancement of life?
When we are re-born —
That is the question —
And then comes the great demand of choice —
"To be, or not to be, that is the question" —

And how did this all begin — perhaps to be a book, or at least, something enclosed in covers, with a jacket —

Vanity, necessity, Lucy Kroll, Hiram Haydn — with their love &
devotion,
or something else — a desire to speak of the lonely terrifying gifts
Life has given me, on the need to affirm a faith —

Miss Ruth — Habukkuk,
"I shall make thy feet like hind's feet —" etc.
The sheep of the desert.

"Christ healeth the crooked woman"   Luke — 13

"In the beginning was the Word, & the Word was with God, & the
Word was God"   John — 1 — 1

When are we born —
    or re-born —
that is the question —
    Van Cliburn — etc —
yesterday — tomorrow —
50 years ago — 5000 years ago —
That is the question —
"To be, or not to be —
That is the question"
necessity — choice — demand —
"Drink not too deeply of the river of Lethe" —
"One writes to recover a lost innocence" Durrell

People say —
How did you begin?
Well — that is the question
And who knows —
Not I —

How does it all begin?
I suppose it never begins, it just continues —
Life —
generations
Dancing —

One takes it up when one arrives with all the richness of blood as one
takes up one's ancestral physical heritage —
Of course, there must be strength of bone & muscle & heart & faith —
but one takes up at the time the necessity of one's heritage & in time it

may become one's "calling," one's "destiny," one's "fame" —
one's "immortality" —

I am a thief — and I am not ashamed. I steal from the best wherever
it happens to me — Plato — Picasso — Bertram Ross — the members
of my company never show me anything — except you expect me to
steal it —

I am a thief —
and I glory in it —
I steal from the present and from the glorious past — and I stand in the
dark of the future as a glorying & joyous thief — There are so many
wonderful things of the imagination to pilfer — so I stand accused —
I am a thief — but with this reservation — I think I know the value of
that I steal & I treasure it for all time — not as a possession but as a
heritage & as legacy —

Shelter Island —
a pirate's lair — (place)
a recluse from the traditional puritan —
It is strange it should begin to be written here — in a pirate's
sanctuary — because I, too, am a thief

A Pirate's Lair —
    It sounds like a mystery story & strangely it is as all
Cinderella stories are —

The curious claw in which the island rests — the gift &
protection from the sea —
not the bravery of Martha's Vineyard — That would be the perfect
place & title — but the hidden slightly illegal thing of Shelter Island
with its illicit trade & its pirates — because I am a pirate —
(I steal, I am a thief, & I enjoy it, because I steal from the
illustrious ancestors of the past —
I am a Pirate —
I bring lovely things from unknown & unknowable places —
Spices — silks — jewels — jades — ivorys —
thoughts & strange images — even additions to the ancient tho'ts —
because I am a 20th century pirate —
I steal what I need for this time in which I live —
This is an ecstatic Voyage — Please do not embark with me unless you
know the destination
an arrivement at a port of call (the self) where the cargo is demanded —

"It is 5 minutes to 12" —
    Tchelicheff —

Tex in a fur coat —
terror of the famous one

"In my end is my beginning"
  Mary, Queen of Scots —

"It is 5 minutes to 12" —
    Tchelicheff —
apartment —   ⎰ fear — ⎱
fur coat —   ⎱ naivite — ⎰
cold apartment
(Charles Henri Ford —)
Ted —
Plato —
Cinderella's midnight
The loss of the Prince if not taken on time —

Lincoln Kirstein —
Naive — "like a fox" —

See —
  "Sign of the Fish"
        Grennell — (18)
  "I am at the end of my nervous resources — "   Baudelaire —
  "the horror of life & an ecstatic awareness of the joys of living,
may be true, of every creative intelligence — and from the resultant
conflict may arise the state of mind that impels an artist towards
aesthetic activity"   (page 18)

I fear it may be a series of "quotes" & yet what else can I do?
⎛ "Gifts of passage" ⎞
⎝ Santha Rau   ⎠

The extraordinary of the suddenly & yet forgotten remembered
(recognizable) instant of experience —
           (M.G.)

The aching muscles —
the remembered glories
the agonies of the future

---

performance

---

the acquisition again of the body, the element of feeling,
of sensation — of life —

Beginning —
Where does anything begin — who knows —
Shelter Island —
a sheltered Island

---

a day when I saw a puppet show in my hotel drawing room — lace
curtains resting on the floor — a green pouf in the center of the room —
the puppets — "Punch & Judy" in a corner — my first amazed awakening to the fact of theatre —

Hokey-Patey Ice Cream
5¢ a package —
The curious slats of light under the "board walk"

The denial —
The atmosphere of choice

---

a letter to Lucy
        to Hiram
        to my ancestors

"This is my letter to the World"

"Yet there are artists who never renounce their genius, or whom
their demon never renounces"   (Quennell 25)

". . . the artist reaches harmony & unity by way of strife &
inward discord"   (p. 26)

Waterways —
why I moved from the cloister of the "Village" to the East River —
a Tide River — I had to be in communication —

What is the beginning?
Perhaps when we seek "wholeness" — when we embark on the journey
toward wholeness —

"In the beginning was the Word —
And the word was God

& the word was with God"
"In the beginning was the Word"
    The act of statement

Beginning —
When did it begin?
50 years ago —
5 yrs ago — 500 years
5000 years ago —
I suppose there is no "beginning"
(find in Dictionary meaning of beginning)

a gold-skinned race —
    blendings
    sun bathings
Clive — Jamaica —

---

west Indian
negro
french
chinese
      ?

"Bliss & bitterness"
(Fanny Bucher) —
Chicago Tribune
(ad — N.Y. Times) —
"Married to Tolstoy"
Cynthia Asquith

Man & Dolphin
John C. Lilly, M.D.
Doubleday —
Concerning the attempts to communicate with other species —
The Dolphin —
Shakespeare — Antony & Cleopatra —
"His delights were dolphin-like —
they showed his back above
The element they liv'd in — "
    Antony & Cleopatra —
        Act V — Sc. 2 —

Gaudy —
"To the public, I failed — permit me to try again."
M.G.

The Island
Gardiners Island
Lion Gardiner — red-headed — 1639 —
descendants still own —
Captain Kidd — etc —
Sarah — spinster —
15th proprietor — died 1955

From an Island
An Island —
Island —
The self —
Isolation
Piracy
Privacy —
The land of the self —
The Place of the Self.

Island —
(surrounded by the unknown, the water, inhabited by the
ancestral fish)

Preliminary Studies for Mary Queen of Scots
Chronique, by St. John Perse

Wrestling with the angel —
    I will not let you go until you give me a name —

Bride in a summer house —
Before wedding —

"At the still point"
    moment of decision — ?

". . . an unexpected presence in the garden, and a miraculous
messenger"
                            (Quartets — re — 14)

"This is the joy of Eden, shattered when the divine light is withdrawn"
                                                                    (13)

"Yet when we came back, late, from the Hyacinth garden . . ."
                    Waste land —

"Heart of light"

                    Dante —   (13)

"The rose-garden is the Garden 'where all loves end' (Ash Wednesday)"
                                                                    12

Family Reunion —   (12)

"I only looked thru the little door"   (12)   Reunion

"Perhaps" —
"Echoes" —
"Even so" —
        could this be like Bernhardt —
        as actress — as woman?

"Sudden vision"   (12)

"Variations on a theme of Mary, Queen of Scots"

"In my end is my beginning"
        embroidered as motto by Mary, Queen of Scots.

Passacaglia —
    Danced "variations on a theme of Mary, Queen of Scots"
    "In my end is my beginning"
    "In my beginning is my end"
    (T.S. Eliot — 4 Quartets)

Drum roll as of execution —
3 beats of staff as in French theatre —

Drum role as of execution —
Light finds figure of woman
extreme stage left —
She speaks —
"What might have been & what has been
Point to one end, which is always present.
Footfalls echo in the memory
Down the passage which we did not take
Towards the door we never opened
Into the rose-garden. . . ."

                . . .

"In my beginning is my end."

                . . .

3 beats of staff —
She walks full length of stage as 'traveler' sweeps
to stage right revealing stage —

Passacaglia —
    Variations in a woman's life —
            on heart —
    an exercise in redemption thru the use of memory
    the awareness it brings —
    (very like Poem by Pasternak) Hunted trapped — escape —
    fulfillment — thru awareness
(Hunted — trapped — liberated —)
                        thru choice
The Casket Letters —
    purported to have been written by Mary to Bothwell — re the
    murder of Darnley —
    8 letters & a set of poems —

    Mary handled her own defense brilliantly —

    Star Chamber

    ---

drums —
    Woman walks from St. L to r —
    and back again —

    ———

    Lines.

    ———

    "In my beginning is my end"

    ———

curtain opens as she walks
    "What might have been & what has been
    Point to one end which is present.
    Footfalls echo in the memory.
    Down the passage which we did not take
    Towards the door we never opened
    Into the rose-garden"

    ———

    Passacaglia —

    ———

final speech — <u>Drum roll</u>

Dowager Queen of France at 18
    1561 — Queen of Scotland
    1542   Born

    ———

     19 —

_____

Young queen
intrigues —
    Elizabeth —
    Darnley
    Bothwell

_____
_____

Time present & time past

    ———

Summer House —
    or garden —
people seated, dancing, rising, separating,
meeting (as in Deaths & Entrances)
"Imaginary gardens with real toads in them"
"The stuff that dreams are made of — "
    Love
    hatred

jealousy
fantasy —
death

Beginning as enormous court dance —
    Frozen at moments for her anguish —

————

    She is center at beginning —

————

    All freeze as she dances — unaware of
her anguish —

————

court dance —
    monstrous courtesies
    falls in second —

————

    men in wide leaps to obsequious demands
of court —

————

    women in back falls
of simulated wonder

————

================

court dance
    men & women —
    dramatization of court behavior —

————

    men in sword play for power

————

    women in play for power —

————

Footfalls of memory —
    a woman at the instant of her execution —
    (death) — (rebirth)

————

"Court Dance"
Passacaglia —
    Court behavior
    Ambition   Love for power
    Intrigue   Desire to be queen —
    Love —

All this is in each life —
the crowning — the love of power — the love of man —
the denouement —

queen —
struggle with ancestral image
        Elizabeth —
affairs of love —

"For woman in tragedy may be either the heart's victim or
its torturer"   (Harvest of Tragedy   106

"Those far-renowned brides of
        ancient song
Peopled the hallow dark, like
        burning stars,
And I heard sounds of insult,
        shame & wrong
And trumpets blown for wars"
                Tennyson "Dream of Fair Women"   (Harvest — 106)

"O God, Why hast Thou made this gleaming snare,
Woman, to dog us on the happy earth?"
Hippolytus — Euripides —   Harvest 120 —
1 Dance of young queens — women
2   "   for "   " courtiers?
2   "   with ancestral image
3   "   for young queen   men?
4   "   with beloved —
5   "   for power — Young Queen
6   "   of judgement — condemnation
7   "   of expiation —

chronique —
   (St. John Perse)
            Ned Rorem —
                music —

---

11 episodes — but connected
11 solo instruments —

Mary Queen of Scots and Chronique / 315

Helen — Bob —

---

speaker of lines —
  a man or myself —

---

a chronicle of hope
        faith
        eternal life

Suggested lines to be read in pauses between musical
parts of score —

"Divine turbulence be ours to its last eddy"   p. (29)

"Fever on the heights & bed of glowing embers. Statute of brides
for a night to all summits washed in gold"   (28)

"Great age behold us. Coolness of evening on the heights,
breath of the open sea on every threshold, and our foreheads bared
for wider spaces"   (27)

"Mendicants of evening"   (30)

"Burning tunic of fable"   (34)

"I shall carry still further the honour of my house"   (39)

"Great age, you reign and the silence for you is number.
And the dream is immense where the dream bathes"   (40)

"And the soul avid for the soul's risk"   (41)

"And let the severity of evening descend with avowal of its tenderness
on the roads of burning stone, roads lit with lavender"   (46)

"For us, already, a song of high adventure. The road traced by a
new hand and fires carried from crest to crest"   (47)

"Great age, behold us.
Take the measure of man's heart"   (48)

"The offering, O night, where to bring it? And the praise
to whom entrust it?
We raise, with arms out-stretched, on the flat of our hands, like a
hatching of nascent wings, this darkened heart of a man where hunger
was and ardour and so much love unrealized. . . ."   (48)

"Listen, O night, in the deserted courtyards and under the solitary
arches, amid the holy ruins, and the crumbling of old termite hills,

hear the great sovereign foot falls of the soul without a lair,
Like a wild beast prowling a pavement of bronze"   (48)

"Irreproachable your chronicle, O Earth, to the censor's eye!
We are herdsmen of the future."   (44)

"O you who led us to all this quick of soul, fortune wandering on the
waters, will you tell us one evening on earth what hand arrays us
in this burning tunic of fable . . ."   (34)

"Wandering, O Earth, we dreamed . . ."   (35)

Great age, behold us. Rendevous accepted, and long ago,
with this hour of deep meaning."   (37)

1
2
3   flute — Helen
4   lullaby — Bob —
5
6   Percussion
7   Cello
8
9
10
11

Folklore Communications
Additional Studies for Saint Joan
Heloise and Abelard

The Triumph of Saint Joan:
photograph by Cris Alexander

The human situation:
common spiritual as well as physical structure

Folklore Fellow communications — (Publication)

. . .

"not an account of Joan of Arc's life, but rather an attempt to
describe the awakening of her supernatural vocation"

Julian Green — Introduction
Péguy Joan of Arc —

a chronicle of the interior drama —

perhaps the years of which she never spoke until later
the year of interior vision
what would she behold —   { as from Péguy

could there be a double image —
        2 people as Joan   ("Letter")
   The conflict in the soul
        To the calling — the dream —
        To the world —
     The 2 within each person —
       The Chosen One
       The One who chooses
making visible the two worlds —
   The cross-roads
   The instant of choice —
   The conflict
   She sees herself as
       woman beloved
       as wife
A   as Mother
       as Sorrowing one —
       That one each of us is as our neighbor is —

B   The possessed one
      The one like —
         Mary Magdalene
         Veronica —
         The one alone —

The conflict in the artist's life —
     How not to be alone in face of what has to be done —

The fear
　　aloneness —
　　The Dark Night of the Soul is not belonging any place
　　to any one —
The Necessity —
　　To do what has to be done —

If the story of Joan of Arc is to be danced then its substance concerns
that which cannot be spoken —
　　It is a conflict each knows in lesser or greater degree —
　　Either one succumbs to the sweetness of the gravity pull
　　with its inevitable death —
　　　　　　　　　or
　　One

There is no nobility in the choice — not even courage —
　　There is only necessity for freedom —
　　freedom
　　　　from what . . .

There is a constant conflict between
　　common sense
　　comfort
　　　　and
　　that which must be done —
　　　　　　The vision

"In the mystics of the West, the highest forms of Divine Union impel
the self to some sort of active, rather than of passive life."
　　　　　　　　　　　　　　　Underhill — Mysticism 172

"Not spiritual marriage but divine fecundity is to be their final state . . .
"You may think, my daughters," says St. Teresa, "that the soul in this
state (of union) should be so absorbed that she can occupy herself with
nothing. You deceive yourselves. She turns with greater ease & ardour
than before to all that which belongs to the service of God, & when
these occupations leave her free again, she remains in the enjoyment of
that companionship."　　　　　　　　　　　(ditto) — 172

"All records of mysticism in the West, then, are records of supreme
human activity. Not only of 'wrestlers in the spirit' but also of great
organizers . . . finally of some immensely virile souls whose participation in the Absolute Life has seemed to force them to a national destiny.
Of this, St Bernard, St. Catherine of Siena & St. Joan of Arc are the
the supreme examples. 'The Soul enamoured of My Truth', said God's
voice to St. Catherine of Siena, 'never ceases to serve the whole world
in general'."　　　　　　　　　　　　　　　Ibid — 173

What she would "vision"
  never the figure of Jesus — but all the legend surrounding
  him —
       The crucifixion
          Thru others —
       The feeding of the multitude
          The mystical meal
       Mary Magdalene —
       Veronica & the handkerchief
       Adoration of the Magi —
          The Coronation of the Dauphin
       The walk to Calvary
       The Roman soldier who pierced the side of Jesus —

The hour of the Angelus —
    morning —

Joan stands still — listens —
  Prayer —
      In the name of Father
      and of the Son
      and of the Holy Ghost
                        <u>Amen</u>
      Our Father who art in Heaven
      Hallowed be thy name;
      Thy kingdom come
      Thy will be done on earth as it is in heaven;
      give us this day our daily bread;
      forgive us our trespasses as we
      forgive those who trespass against us,
      And lead us not into temptation
      but deliver us from evil
                        <u>Amen</u>
      Hail Mary, full of grace, the Lord is with thee;
      blessed art thou amongst women,
      and blessed is the fruit of thy womb
      Jesus.
      Holy Mary Mother of God,
      pray for us sinners now
      And at the hour of our death.
                        <u>Amen</u>

Dance of adoration —

The trial —
   The questions —
      thru a glaze seeing the questioners as men performing a complex,
      formal dance — a pavane — a sarabande — about her — with her
      — increasing in complexity, speed — until her partner is suddenly
      St. Michael —

   The arguments — examinations —
      always the dance of the men —
      her final seclusion with St. Michael — or
      with Catherine or Margaret —

   Then came her answer   to judges

   What happens when no saint appears as
   her partner — ??   The agony

Ladies' Tree   —   Trial — 144
   garlands
   fairies
   witch-craft —
   Fountain
Mandrake   1

Breach of promise suit   148

first command   149
   first voice of saints

"Daughter of God"
"Daughter Great-hearted"   152

Gesture as language
Language as gesture
gesture as communication —
the visibility of the experience —
Warning —
                  bore
(For those) who tire quickly —
   to those
                  discussion
to those who consider the subject of faith — naive —
to those who want to be helped rather than to help
themselves —

to those who do not understand (are not ready to accept the fact) that
dancers are as supreme realists as scientists — as demanding of
results — as tireless in experiment, as arrogant of ideal —
& as modest — of result —
     Do not read —
Gesture is the first (language —)
                 — speech —
Perhaps you argue sound comes first — but movement precedes sound —
& movement is the seed of gesture —

The answer is not control of gesture
first — the technic of outer behavior
but rather the technic of inner behavior — the means (method)
is hard — it means cultivation of the line —
tension for the speech (muscles)
submission to the inevitability of the result — (answer)

The question —
       The tension — the lift
       into listening —
The answer (choice)
       the selection of the line — the choice —
The manifestation —
       The result —
Let us choose a 1,000 as a number)
            good — realized
a 1000 times make — A One — for a dancer
a 1000 tried practise leap
      makes a leap
a 1000 leaps can make one flight
        one dream
         of a leap —
     A One
       never to be forgotten

"The Dance is not only exercise & spectacle but a social function
as well which reveals the spirit of the times."
                       (Dancers thru the ages —4)

a worldly dance
a school for good manners —
a glorified human behavior —
      Its ritual base — court behavior,
          philosophy
          social relationship

Western dance — a direct line from the medieval "court of love" where
the lady of the choice was glorified & man achieved
his glory thru his glorification of her —

It all goes back to one small boring word —

"noble artificiality of Indian dramatic technique"
1 Mirror of Gesture

a clear image of the activity of God.

"The Master has come home" —

I present 3 ideas as suggestions for dance films —
1)   The love of Heloise and Abelard —
2)   The passion of Joan of Arc —
3)   The jealousy of Phaedra —

In each I feel the eye of the camera to be the heart of the
woman involved —

It is, in each instance, less the actual story, but rather the making
visible the inner substance from which the story evolves —

There is the roving of the imagination, the thoughts of the woman —
touching without historical sequence the ports of call on the voyage
which Fate has captained — (charted —)

The commentary — the narration — in each instance is taken
from historical — the known —
1)   The letters of Heloise & Abelard
2)   The documents of the trial of Joan of Arc
3)   The play "Hippolytus" of Euripedes — or the
Phaedra of Racine —

The action is purely imaginary —
expressive in images derived from the text involved —
This action is the flight of the Dream of each human experience
which has made it a legend —
It is universal in its simplicity in each instance —

1)   is derived from love —
human love
2)   is derived from passion —
the dedicated love

3)   is derived from jealousy
                        the distorted love —
In each aspect it touches each of us — & creates or destroys —

1)   In Heloise —
     The action begins as Abelard's body is carried into her convent —
     "The Convent of the Paraclete" —
     The time is historically the early 12th Century in France.
     The characters involved are those mentioned in the letters
     exchanged between Heloise & Abelard after their separation.
     The supreme director of the action is the memory of Heloise —

     The core of the action is the incorruptibility of love — between
     a man & a woman — it becomes part of that light which is never
     extinguished — It is like the sun in its inevitability, its
     beneficence & its terror —
(the play of love   destruction

          exaltation & its despair)
     The windows it opens upon the world
joy & suffering —   or
                        of exaltation & despair

Heloise was the Hypatia of the 12th C.
Abelard was the philosopher, the firebrand, & in time as he learned
to love, the writer of some of the great love songs of the world —
All record of these are gone — but there has been much caught &
sustained in the public memory — what we label "anonymous" — to
make us recognize their power —
Part of "Carmina Burona" is without doubt from Abelard's songs.
These songs were written for Heloise —

Heloise was no unknown — no illiterate woman of the time —
She was called the Hypatia —
She speaks of Abelard's songs in one of her letters to him —
   Page 58 —
"Heloise . . . like Isolde, unites the ages"
                        Mont-Michel — 287 —

(almost a proverb in French)
"where are the snows of yester-year?"   ??
                        Where is the virtuous Heloise,
                        For whom suffered, then turned monk,
                        Pierre Abelard, at Saint Denise?
"The snows of Spring" —   For his love he bore that pain.
                        ____

and Jeanne d'Arc, the good Lorraine,
Whom the English burned at Rouen!
Where are they, Virgin Queen?
But where are the snows of Spring?

Villon —

Adams — 249

". . . the magnet that drew all men thither in the great years when 'Rhinocerus indomitus' lifted up his horn on Mont St. Genevieve & the schools became a bull-ring, where opponent after opponent tosses on the horns of his deadly logic."

Waddell: Wandering Scholars 117

" 'Lucifer hath set' — said Philippe of Harvengt when he died."   117

"In the schools he kept his sword like a dancer:
Goliath they called him with the club of Hercules, another Proteus, flashing from philosophy to poetry, from poetry, to wild jesting: a scholar with the wit of a jongleur & the graces of a grand seigneur"   118

Peter the Venerable was an austere man, a stern disciplinarian of his order: but the tragic splendor of it, the marred beauty of these star-crossed lovers whose violent delight had had so violent an end, triumphs over the ecclesiastic's prejudice. . . . "Him, therefore, O sister most dear, him to whom you once clung in the union of the flesh & now in the stronger, finer bond of the divine affection, with whom & under whom you have long served the Lord, him, I say in your place, or another you, hath Christ taken to his breast to comfort him & there shall keep him until the coming of the Lord, the voice of the archangel & the trump of God descending, He shall restore him to your heart again".

119 —

"Provençal poetry demands no other intellectual background than that of its century — a May morning, the far-off singing of birds, a hawthorne tree in blossom, a Crusade for the Holy Sepulchre — It is the Middle Ages in the medium of a dream."   127

Abelard as trouvere — troubadour — during years of absence?
Dido & Aeneas
Ovid?
Virgil — Georgics
Seneca's Medea
Gods & Goddesses
Plato

. . . "his head was filled with songs & lute accompaniments . . . he must talk with his ancient comrades if only for an hour and breathe again the air of a tavern in le Pet du diable . . ."   George Moore 145

Disguised as a gleeman he sang to Heloise from the street — (borrowed hat & cloak & lute)

"Lovers, Heloise, should think always of each other, & in the courts of love that I visited when I wrote songs for the Comte de Radeboeuf, Queen Elinor decreed that a true lover is enthralled with a perpetual image of his lady-love; it never departs from the mind."

Geo. Moore 151

(The Medieval Satire & Romance Lyric to A.D. 1300
F. BRITTAIN.
Cambridge
At the University Press 1937
". . . Abelard wrote hymns for both seasons & festivals . . ."
his greatest — O quanta qualia — which strictly speaking is not a hymn at all. It is one of the most beautiful & at the same time one of the saddest, of medieval hymns. On the surface it is a meditation on the endless Sabbath calm of the life to come; but the whole pitiful story of Abelard's life, which had known no calm, can be heard in the murmur immediately beneath the surface."   13

Medieval Latin Cynics
    Philip Schuyler Allen
    Univ. of Chicago Press 1931

Twenty-one Medieval Latin Poems
    Edward James Martin   *Sabbath —*
    The Scholartis Press   *Abelard —*
    30 Museum St. London 1931

Quotations   Scholars
                Paulinus   11
"Dye your wool once purple, and what water will cleanse it of that stain?"   St. Jerome
            Scholars xvii

"Mysterium Israelis"
(The mystery of Israel)
"wild goats of Ein Gedi"   (Weiner) P. 46

Scenes from Bible
    "   " mythology
—————————————

The one who questions
The one who participates
The Fate Figure —
    (Judith
    Miriam
    Jezebel
    Esther —
    Sara —

"Israel of the flesh"   (48)

Phaedra —
1) begins as victim of Aphrodite
on bed in spasm of lust —
2) Tormented by vision of Hippolytus & Aphrodite's malicious
playfulness —
3) Her frustration — sleep —
4)? Phaedra as a queen —
(lyric section)
temptation of Hippolytus in her guise as queen —

Should Theseus appear & should her accusation be in form of re-enact-
ment of her desire in which she accuses Hippolytus in front of
Theseus — ?
If so —
Solo for Theseus in form of curse on Hippolytus
with Phaedra as chorus —
observer —
If so —
Hippolytus exits & when he enters he is dead, borne
aloft by men —

_____

On his exit — Theseus & Phaedra sit in hate & anger, waiting — almost
immobile — until procession enters —

_____

Lamentation of Theseus —

_____

Death of Phaedra —

_____

Beginning —
Phaedra on bed
1) On chords —
P. r. knee up sharply
straighten r. leg —
2) On chords
r. knee up
swing leg to back wide
leg straight —
3) Knee lifts again — sit —
r. knee — up — legs fan & close — fan & close — beat body
with hands

4) r. knee up —
       sit — face front.
          r. knee up l. elbow on r. knee —
       strike floor with r. hands 2 X
       Lie back on bed.
5) r. knee up
   straighten
   Twist to back
      ″   front
      ″   back
   straighten leg again
6) Arch back — Phaedra
   Aphrodite opens door
   P. lies down & slowly rises to face front — feet
   on floor — (sitting)
7) Extend —
       l. leg back in profile
          (kind of arabesque)
       body low — crouching —
       Bring legs together
       Repeat arabesque with r. leg extending, facing L.
       Repeat arabesque with l. twice faster —
8.) Spread legs wide facing front — Bring with close together —
   Rise to stand.
   Silence
8) Elbows opening & closing
    hands at temples —
         3 X
9) Side plie with r. leg
   body bending so hand touches inside of ankle,
   rise, walk left kind of interned bourrée —
   (2nd — 4th) moving to st. l.
10) Repeat side plie
   Repeat walk,
11) Turn to shrine for blinding with 2 small turns &
   face front —
12) [deletion by M.G.]
13) Aphrodite on 1st chord
14) Aphrodite blinds P.'s eyes with girdle — (from behind piece)
15) Phaedra sits — drawing legs in
   Aphrodite leaves
   sits in shrine
   Phaedra rises —

16) Elbows again with hands at temples —
17) Aphrodite walks to H door
18) Phaedra does 2 knee crawls after her —
     This has to be done from St. L. & she will have to run *possibly take knee ripples at end*
       into each crawl —
19) Aphrodite snatches girdle off her eyes & knocks at the
       door —
     after Aphrodite strikes
20) on chords door turns or opens
     revealing Hippolytus.
     (4 long measures)
     on shimmering music —
21) back fall from knees
           (muted trumpets)
22) Door begins to close & Hippolytus partly disappears —
23) next music Phaedra opens
     r. leg on floor —
24) rises — goes to door either in knee crawls or
     staggers to door — Hippolytus vanishes —
25) Small dance —
           catch r. leg in arms —
           take circular kick
           catch r. leg in arms
           circular kick
           catch r. leg in arms —
26) Stagger to r in profile, 1 foot
     in front — almost turned
     in position — body crouching
     in contraction —
     Repeat to l.
     Repeat to r.
27) ⎫ 3
28) ⎬ Darts to stage L beyond bed — cave
29) ⎭ Fall wide 2nd —
     Aphrodite dances —
     on 2nd quiet music P. rises —
     3 Elbow arms —   Phaedra rises on 2nd quiet music
       Turn to door
     3 Elbows   Travel stage L. in bourree
       To door —   if necessary for kicks —
                 Go into kicks next page

Additional Studies for Phaedra / 335

Phaedra dances —
Position d. st. L. front of bed.
1 high kick with r. leg in
1) profile toward door —
bourrée facing front
Repeat kick
Finish kicks facing door diagonally

wide 2nd
after kick
between
bed & shrine
Repeat bourrée

2) walks backwards downstage
between bed & shrine
body swaying slightly,
hands behind back moving
as tho' rubbing body — 8 X
9?
3) Face front with bourree
hands at breast —
quick turn to face door —
Repeat bourree facing front
hands at loins —
face door again —
4) lunging run plie on r.
4 X — hold facing back
3 X — hold fall front
in front of shrine
making circle
desperate
5) Spider bourrée wide 2nd to shrine
Turn to front
6) Repeat spider bourree
Turn to front
7) Run to st. r. (darts) 3 X to sit on bed —
sit on edge facing door
go to knees —
8) 3 hip crawls — r — l — r —
hold on silence — to H
9) Touch Hippolytus — 6 times — (back fall)
He thrusts her off
She takes wide 2nd fall —
10) Aphrodite pushes H. & he falls over P.
She clings to him
They rise
He thrusts her away
She takes angry walk to back of Shrine —
(veil)
→ side extension — step draw
" " " "

┌─ on chord
└▶ walk with r. leg accenting
hand claw-like in curse
in front of face — into shrine

        Lyric Section — The Lie —
Phaedra back of Shrine veiled

1)   Theseus crosses to door — 2 phrases
    opens —

2)   P. stops him —
    3 phrases
        step to r on l in profile —
        take Javanese step to front
        holds — moves r arm
                  ″ l ″
        as Theseus back away
        to st. r.
    each phrase the same

3)   Paul —

4)   English Horn —
        High kick profile with
        r. leg — to Theseus
    to wide 2nd facing front
    followed by bourrée toward bed.

5)   Repeat all this —
        She takes veil off her face

6)   Run forward,
        hands at face —

7)   One knee vibration —
    r. leg.
    lift l. knee front & stroke with $^{r?}_{l?}$ hand.

8)   Repeat 7 —

9)   Turn — fall in wide 2nd
    rise
            1 circle

10) Proceed toward bed
    dart on r foot to l.
    Sit
    Paul
            not quite

11) Flute & clarinet — Paul comes
    I rise from his touch to point to door

12) 2 High kick to r.
      knee crawl to Hippolytus
   1 High kick to r.
      knee crawl to Theseus
      gesture to Hippolytus

Phaedra in Shrine with Aphrodite —
Before rape scene —
     "The Lie"
Theseus comes to st. L.
Turns & is about to open door —
Phaedra enters (veiled?) with hand repelling him —
He goes to stage r. to sit —
             (How?)
Phaedra — 3 little phrases
1)   queen step —
      step to r in profile with l. foot —
      turn & take Javanese step to front — r. plie
      r. arm gesture
      L. arm gesture — & turn to back arms high
2)   Repeat
3)   Repeat — end facing back in supplication to Gods
4)   [deletion by M.G.]
5)   High kick circular
      wide 2nd facing front
      bourree moving st. L —
6)   Repeat High kick
      wide 2nd
      bourrée
      Theseus moves
7)   Run forw. to front hands at face. remove veil —
8) A { One knee vibration on silence with r.
       { Strike l. knee on <u>note</u>
   b { Repeat A.
9)   Turn fall in wide 2nd
      rising quickly —
      2 darts — turn — 2 darts turn — 2 darts
10) Darts st. L. around bed
          to sit
       put veil over face in silence
11) [deletion by M.G.]
12) [deletion by M.G.]

13) [deletion by M.G.]

14) A { 2 High kick to Bert —
      { bourrée

    B { 1 high kick
      { Repeat A — *Theseus*

keep crawling to him *Theseus* —
& cover face with hands
                        unveil —
gesture toward door of Hippolytus —
Hippolytus enters —
Solo — Hippolytus

        Enacting the Lie —
        The Perfidy of Phaedra
Duet with Hippolytus

stay for quite a time on my knees by Theseus —
until
One measure after return of theme
crawl on knees (ripple) toward
Hippolytus has a phrase
I crawl to sit on bed —
                (lower r. corner)
Hippolytus comes after me on bed & I crawl up bed by putting
one leg twisting over other — He touches
I run — Then take turn on r. leg.
I run to kneel at Theseus as tho' I threw myself at his knees — I
rise — then go around Theseus —
queen step — 2 phrases —
      { step in profile l.
      { Javanese step with r to plie
  A   { lunge — r hand out to T.
      { Then legs together — walk in profile to H. l. hand
      { out in rejection —
B. Repeat
        (on this H. makes semi salaam)
I walk to doors & stand in front arms outstretched as tho' forbidding
him to enter — He is behind door.
He enters — I bourrée in terror toward Theseus —
He comes & snatches dress.
Encircles P with it & draws her to bed. He stands
on it — also she —
She snatches dagger

He forces her bed — head to st. L.
takes dagger.
She places her foot on his chest —
(arches back)
He forces her down —
Puts his knee over her   2 X
He draws her up to sit facing front —
Makes her hand caress his body —
She lies down — head to St. R.
She rolls off bed —
He follows her —
draws her up —
Takes her in his arms —
Turns —
She forces herself to feet —
He makes her hands touch his face & body — She breaks
away to St. L. wide 2nd.   fall —
                    (front of shrine)

After Hippolytus kicks dagger & leaves —
Phaedra on floor in fall — 2nd
1)   picks up knife — rises —
        dart — dart — turn around bed
                kneel salaam on floor
                    sit in twist
2)   Theseus bringing L. knee up — touch floor with hand —
        rise into beating turn —
        Repeat salaam
        sit & turn beating
3)   [deletion by M.G.]
4)   [deletion by M.G.]
5)   [deletion by M.G.]
6)   3 heel steps to high relevé
        feet close — toward shrine
Aphrodite
            & place knife in shrine
                    stagger 3 times to door —
7)   [deletion by M.G.]
8)   [deletion by M.G.]
9 — Close doors.
10 — wide 2nd draw step
            to bed
        dart — dart —

dart — to shrine
face — open arms as
in supplication to Goddess — kneel —
fall on face to front

After Pasiphae scene —
Veil on head
Take knife from H —

after Pasiphae —
exit of men — cortege
Follow Bob to st. r. with black veil
with knee crawls (3) Bob exits
Turn & drop it (veil) P. point A leg —
$\qquad$ 4 X conversation with P. & A.
shut Goddess in by going around
shrine — 1st & 2nd doors —
accented run to bed (accent on r)
on bed —
action on bed (with   ?   knife)

crawl to veil — St. R.   2 X
run to st. L — turn into veil.
Fall — on 1st chord
Aphrodite opens legs

Choreographic Studies for Clytemnestra and Alcestis

Prologue I

Clytemnestra center stage —
1) Treading   13–14 X —
          progressing d. st.
2) Accented walk to st. l. (bourree)
          2nd to 4th change using arms.
                            ?
3) Knee crawls with cracks 6X
          r — l — r — l — rr (holding dress in r. hand,
                       bend instead of crawl
4) Accented walk to st. L. (bourree)
          Face Helen at piece —
5) Dart — turn to st. r.
          3 sets —
6) Hades opens knees
7) Clytemnestra spins up.st. C.
8) Knee crawls to throne d. st. r.
          2X (with dress)
9) Gesture of arms wide forced 2nd
10) Hades
11) Cave turns st. l. 5X
12) Hades
13) High kick walk with r & small bourree to st. r.
          (4 high kicks — 3 bourrees)
          fall in pitched fall from 4th high kick —
          sit to 4th on floor
          rise (into wide Cave turn) — ?
                Treading & circular kick?
14) Walk backwards with Hades facing — 11 steps beginning
          with l — to st. l.
          Turn from Hades — small contraction
15) Follow Hades with knee crawls
          l — C   1st
          l — center   2nd
          l — down st.   3rd diag. L.
          Turn on knee & fall   4th
16) Hades in arabesque
5th Rise to both knees pushing away from Hades
17) 5 Hip crawls — upst. C.
          beginning on r.

Rise to knees — r in front
Bring l. leg into profile kneel to r —
Rise — semi-profile — r. hand stomach

18) Treading — facing front — diag r.
    On Hades skips turn to watch him go to piece —
    H. gestures to C ←
    Then walk backwards 2X3
    Then turn & go around throne & sit — (15–16 in all)
                                            steps

    (note — This moment is her submission to the sight of the
    Rape of the City — Either she submits to Hades — or else
    she demands that Hades look upon it through her eyes &
    in justification of her cause.)

*wide kick to 2nd
kneel inverted
push up —
walk.*

Prologue II

1) Treading —   D st. R.
                       (at throne)

2) Bourrée   —   to st. L.   Times? 6
      L. arm   moving up — out — down
    ? Times 5   Hand at temple —
                       Bring hands together
                       before 1st dart.

3) Dart — Contraction turn
    3X to d.st. R.

4) Bourrée   — st L.
      arms as before   (4X ?)

5) Dart — turn — Dart — hold
    wide 2nd extension to front
    2 step draws —
    Repeat Dart — hold
            wide 2nd
            2 step draws.

6) Hades

7) Either — or
    (accented run on L to st R.)
                or
    2 knee crawls with cave turn

8) Series of back falls with Hades beating over C.
    3X   fall-rise to front — wide turn
            Repeat fall etc
    Hades walks —

9) Bourrée in place
   st.L.   Gene arms beating
                with branches —
10) Dart — turn with contraction
    Dart — circular kick to wide 2nd — go to knees — pushup
    on Hades last chord
11) Hades
            (Darel's jumps)
                                    commanding gesture to
12) desperately — Hades — walk backward
    1 X 3   sit
    in silence & walk to throne   3 X 3
    l elbow at head, hand thrown back

Clytemnestra Prologue III

(She has done staggering walk to st. L. on Iphigenia exit music)
1) Treading   D. St. L
        ending in Bali attitude
2) { Knee vibrations 2X
    going into Bali turn
    ending in Bali attitude
    Repeat in entirety
    finishing in circular kick
    to wide second on loud music
3) Plunge in kneel in wide 2nd knees in —
   Touch hands to floor in anguished beat & push up
   from floor —
4) Dart turn
   dart turn   D. St. r.
   dart turn
5) Hades enters behind throne
6) Clytemnestra   bourrée-like
        walk 2nd to 4th to D. st. L.
7) Hades takes leaves & follows her (wide 2nd skips?) to D. St. L
8) Both take Dart-turn 3X to throne.
9) She goes on chair l. foot on seat — hand toward sword
10) Hades moves
11) On crash
    Rise to stance on chair
    r. leg over back — head lifted
12) Hades

13) On crash
    she sits on step
14) Hades
15) On Crash
    she rises to face front
    hip sways —
16) She & Hades wrestle for branches — finish at throne

Dance of Vengeance with Sword

A.) Treading on blue
    sword in r. hand high — parallel to floor — pointing L.
    L. arm twisted behind body with hand at r. hip.
    open arm before sit.
1) <u>Loud.</u>
    wide sit in 2nd — sword pointing to ground —
    continue on <u>Lyric</u> into sit on L. hip — feet high —
    L. elbow on floor — sword in profile to r.
2) Loud
    open into wide lean to R toward sword — L. knee bent, foot
    to front —
    Lyric —
    Slide sword to L.
    bow —
    turn to back ripple away — to r.
3) Loud
    switch legs from side to side — facing front on knees
    Lyric
    Bring knees together
    bow in profile to sword
    hands in obeisance,
    to floor — up to face f. on knees
4) Loud
    2 hip crawls to sword
    Lyric —
    sit in lotus
    rise in wide inverted 2nd to knees — coming into
    low crouch to sword on floor.
    Take saraband arabesque to sword — (long phrase
    musically) — recover
5) Loud
    Turn on back — forced arch, sword high, both hands

6) Loud
    Turn flat on face sword held in front — in repeat of high
    arabesque kneel
    Come to both knees, sword in both hands — body crouched
    Turn on back again
    Lyric
        turn to face front with side extension with r. leg to
        r. l. foot in front — body leaning to r.

    Take lotus position
    sword held in front
    Rise to knees wide 2nd
    Bring L. foot forw. sword to L.
7) Tread d. St. sword held in front of body — dedication of net —
   turn to C. st.
8) Loud

A
⎧ High kick with r. forward
⎪ clasp knee in hand — stance
⎪ tread once to r.
⎨ Repeat kick   Repeat
⎪ tread to face back.
⎩ Repeat   A   Repeat
                     Repeat
    Repeat 1 more kick &
    face upstage —

9) <u>On music change</u>

A
⎧ side extension touching sword to floor
⎨ l. knee bent
⎩ step draw facing upstage

B   Repeat side extension with step draw —
                    — step draw
        repeat side-extension
    upstage Turn contraction — sword
            clasped to body —
            catch dress on turn

10)   (piano part — crawls no. 12 —)
       hold dress r. hand across body.
       knee crawls

1
⎧ plie, to r — beat
⎨ sword to floor
⎩ 2 steps forw.

2
⎧ repeat 1
⎪   " 1
⎨ with 2 steps to back
⎩ turn into repeat

```
            of 2 —
            turn into plie l. R.
            2 steps forw. —
            plie to l.
            2 steps to back
            turn into (11) treadings
            (piano part — treading 15)
 11) ⎛ Treading —              St. L. front.
     ⎜   L — r — l — (just the 3 treads)
 A ⎨ Circle kick to wide second
     ⎜ lunge in profile facing r
     ⎜     r. plié — l. straight
     ⎝ spring back to 1st facing front
 B — Repeat A entirely
 12) ⎛ l. leg across r (plie —
     ⎜ (l. leg in Bali position)
 A ⎨ sword in l.
     ⎜ r. arm gestures to throne
     ⎝   little bourrée
 B    Repeat A.
      going into bourrée change to r.
      Repeat Bali position
 13) Cave turn (transfer sword to r.)
      lunge to throne
      take cape for wrapping
 14) Bourrée to l. stage
      wrapping cape over r. arm.
 15) ⎛ Dart to r —-
     ⎜   (step into)
     ⎜ Bali attitude —
 A ⎨    l. leg across r. knee plie —
     ⎜    (step into)
     ⎜ Turn on r —
     ⎝    (step into)
 B.   Repeat A
      ⎛ last turn short & tight —
 3X ⎨ Dart         to throne
      ⎝ attitude
 Paul takes sword — plants it
 She steps to front
 spreads cape in a free exultant gesture —
 Paul picks her up & turns off.
```

Prologue
Dialogue —

Standing at net face Orestes

1) "I — Clytemnestra
    Stark position
    wt on r —
    l knee upturned in
    l. arm overhead
2) "Anguished"
    Lunge to l.
    beat floor r. hand —
    turn tight on r to front
    l. arm flung across body & face —
    feet together —
3) "I . . . call upon your name"
    knee crawls —
        front
        l.
        r.
            ending in kneel
4) "I killed"
    circular kick
    wide Cave turn
5) "I suffered"
    feet together
6) "I suffered not"
    fall wide 2nd —
7) "In fear"
    lean on r side — r. elbow on floor —
    knees drawn up —
    feet off floor
8) "In disgrace"
    l. leg back to rise in 4th
    Then to profile crouch on both knees facing up L. slightly
    Body in contraction
    Turn to bring l. knee up facing r —
9) "Rejoicing I killed" —
    Rise in high contraction
    Kick with r. leg.
    r. hand stomach —
    l. high —
10) Recover to front bringing arms slowly down in bewilderment —

11) "I —   face profile to r —
        l. foot leading
12) Hear me — it is the spoken plea
        knee crawls (1 or 2)
        upstage to behind net —

    As Iphigenia holds on piece —

1) "I — Clytemnestra"
        2 high kicks with l.
            forward
2) "Anguished is my plea"
        Stark position
            on r.
            on l.
3) "Witness he the gods"
        r. knee forced open to r.
        ending wide 2nd plie
        facing front — arms open at elbows —
        Then — snap legs together in parallel — 1st.
4) "I call upon your name"
        circular kick with r
        to wide 2nd stance —
5) Bring legs parallel, facing diag. st. L. knees bent, hands
    on knees, body bent way over —
6) Begin beats to side in 2nd
    arms beating, hands from mouth as in cries —
7) Fall in pitch to st. r —

                Sleep walking Scene
                    Act II
after rise —
1) 9 profile turning walks, feet
    in profile — to r. first.
2) Face front —
    open arms to side (hidden)
    extend L. arm — drop head to L.
    Return arms to side —
3) 4(a) profile turning walks r.
    (b) lift veil over shoulders to face on little rush front
    (c) kneel —
    (d) bring L. arm to face
    (e) Rise —

4)   profile walks to L.
     L. hand partly covering face.
     Turn front. w
5)   Sobbing —   ? 4X
     Lifting of shoulders —
     in pulse —
     Turn to hold robe to body —
6)   Walk slightly upstage (to throne)
     holding robe to body on pulse movement —
     6 times
     open r. arm
     open L arm bring cape over head —
7)   Sobbing walk to bed —
       ⎧stagger as in triplet
  A.) ⎨hold
       ⎩walk 2 steps
  B.) Repeat
  C)   Repeat
          but on last use of step phrase sit & lean on bed.

                    Act II
                Dance of Remorse
(position — on floor — head on pillow — seated on
r. hip, feet to l —)
1)   Lyric
          lift head off pillow
          2 booms
               Go to both knees in crouch body swinging
               to r — to l.
2)   Lyric
          Lift arms — body upright
          on both knees
          2 booms —
               Take off cape —
3)   Lyric —
          Sway body to pick up cape
          2 booms
               Throw cape r — l —
4)   Lyric
          L. knee up — crawl 2X
          2 booms
               rise in Cave turn
               & make gesture to bed.

Clytemnestra and Alcestis / 353

5) Lyric
    Bourrée front to r.
            back ″ r
            front ″ r
    2 booms
        Beat body —
6) Lyric   2X
    dart — turn — dart — dart — turn
    kneel facing ghost
    2 booms —
        Turn on knees
        fall to r. before ghost.
7) Lyric —
    "Letter" beats of L. leg on floor (2 or 3?)
    2 booms
        sit to 4th — L. front
        beat floor
        Rise
8) Lyric
    3 Cave turns st. L.
    2 booms
     catch r. leg in arms across body — facing front —
        beat foot to floor, facing up st.
9) Lyric
    1 Cave turn
    2 booms
        catch r. leg in arm as before.
10) Lyric
    walk 3 high kicks with L. to bed.
    2 booms
        crouch over Aegisthus & back away.
11) Lyric
    walk upstage
        r. st.
        down st.
    2 booms
        side extension
        step draw
            in front of bed
12) Lyric
    Sit on pillow furthest L.
    Stroke Aegisthus
    2 booms
    rise facing front catch & catch r. leg in arm.

13) Lyric
   a)   dart — turn — dart — turn
        2 booms
           Bow to Aegisthus
   b)   Lyric
        dart — turn
        2 booms
           bow to Aegisthus
   c)   Lyric
        dart — turn
        2 booms
           bow to Aegisthus
   d)   Lyric
        dart — turn
        2 booms
           bow to Aegisthus
14) Lyric
    L high kick with step toward bed —
    2 booms
           bow to ghost
    5 high kicks etc. in all.
15) Crash
           Lean over bed.
    Silence
           Rise & prepare to walk
16) Backward walk to ghost
    facing bed —
           13 steps starting L.
           slow face front — hands fall
17) Lyric
    (a) Slow kneel facing ghost
    (b)   crouch to front
    (c)   He rises
    (d)   She Turns & falls to r. hip
18) After walks of the 3 — she rises to face back —
    1 Cave turn
    1 high kick in contraction
    Slow turn to face 3 —
    walk — in circle facing inward
    toward 3 others — 4th to 2nd —
    12 steps —
    arriving at front —
    Take knee crawl to Helen —

Take knee crawl to chair —
Turn on knees & fall —
Ghost steps
Helen strikes
Bert steps on platform —
I rise & take wide 2nd & step draw for walk —
Ghost goes to chair
Bert back stage
Helen & I take darts around each other in small circle —
Helen goes to sit — I scratch at her.
I take wide turn —
Bert advances & puts hand on my shoulder —
I take beats with arms on legs — body contraction —

_____

19) On words — (Mother's curse)
A { 2 circular kicks to front —
    { 2 knee crawls around Bert to front.
B { Repeat A —
C)   Repeat 2 circular kicks to front

_____

Bert has section —
He touches shoulder —
"Redemption I seek" —

_____

Walk around for 3rd time
action with 3 — ending in Helen's position with Bert & ghost —
I take turn & sit on step of throne —
after short phrase —
I lunge to 3 —
Rise —
Two knee crawls under arms of ghost —
2 wide turns (Cave)
They get into position for advance — I fall in front of them
& roll downstage
3 hip crawls to chair — sit on step
        On Mother's curse —

crawl in front of Helen & Bert —
Escape into 3 tilting rims back stage — to bed —

Dance of Vengeance

2nd version —

<u>On blue</u>

1) Treading until off piece —
2) Turn to center —
3) Treading —
4) High Kick with L.
   Tread to face front   1X
   High kick with L.
   Tread to face back   1X
   High kick to fr.
   Tread to face back.
5) Side extension —   ((old version))
   step draw   no. 9
   Repeat 2X
   Then, high kick — & tight turn
6) Treading   (old <u>11</u>)
   Ci. kick
   Repeat —
7) Bali attitude   (as in 12)
        (sword in left)
   small bourree
   Bali attitude
   bourree

   Bourree
   Bali position —

   Cave turn —   (as in 13)
   take cape —
9) Wrapping
   bourree to st. L —
10)   (as in 15)
   A.   Dart
        Bali attitude
        turn on r —
   B.   Repeat all this A.
        Dart.   (as in 15)
        Bali
        Dart
        Bali
        Dart
        bali

Epilogue —

Seated at foot of throne on dais —
Still until —
1) "House of Atreus — "
   kneel on chair —
2) "In Clytemnestra's might"
   r foot resting on top of chair
3) ?
   Stands with back against chair back
4) "Clytemnestra's re-birth"
   crumbles down chair
   to stand on chair step
5) "a seed born in black"
   arms toward Orestes
6) "Clytemnestra's re-birth"
   arms open wide —

   pitches to Orestes —
   He brings her to his knees
   hand covering her face —

   Rebirth kneel & hold his L. hand on her chest —

"Rebirth" —

On last set of "Re-birth" (several)
knee crawls forward & then go to st. L to sit
on Athena's throne —

Return to platform — Take leaves from Hades —
On last chord encircle stage — Black traveler in —
Walk to exit stage r. leaves high & beating —

Clytemnestra
Embattled Garden
Seraphic Dialogue
Night Journey
Acrobats of God
Alcestis
Cave ?
Ardent Song?

Alcestis — Solo
with veil & leaves —

Seated on <u>black</u> side of bed on upright piece — semi-profile —
hands on knees —

1) a) R. hand lifts overhead & returns to
        knees — 2X
    b) lift both on softer music
2)   r. hand under veil
        l   "   "   "
        rise —
3)   On high note walk forward & drop veil —
4)   4 high kicks with r leg using arm between
        to st. r.
            turning to face upstage on answering phrase of
            4th high kick —
5) Walk diag toward wheel
6) Forward fall in 2nd —
    facing front.
7) Sit — look toward Thanatos & slide along
    floor backwards 3 X
8) Lift veil & take side
    ext. position on floor
    knees inverted —
    l — to side
    r — "   "
    l — "   "
9) Bring L. front in inverted 4th & rise —
10) 2 Cave turns with double step draw to wheel
11) Sit on 3rd turn music
    lean in to place leaves in center toward Heracles —
12) On climactic music rise, lift leaves before face
13) Despairing little run to st. r.
14) open leaves — hold — drop.
15) Wrap veil on r   Lament music
    "   "   " l.
    move to throne — sit —

Sequence —

Tympani —
    3 forw.
    3 hold
    3 back to barre
mandolins —
    8 steps forw.
    8 steps to chair

~~~~~~

Entrance of men & girls —
David's phrase
Entrance on shoulders & cross —
Mary's leaps
Entrance of Clive & Helen
     "   " Ethel — crossing
     "   " Dan — crossing
David leaps out
Exit of Helen & Clive
Leaps of girls
Leaps of men
David's phrases on 2 summons —
    He leaps away to st. r. landing on 2nd summons
    in position —

~~~~~~~~~~~~~~~~~~~

pause — I rise —
1st solo —
1)   3 accented steps st. r — hands at hair
      Silence — beat hands face front
2)   3 accented steps st r — beat elbow —
      Silence — beat diamond hands
3)   Deep bow
4)   3 accented steps
      silence — touch shoulders l — r — l.
5)   3 bows backward from mandolins
      silence — diamond
6)   Deep bow —
7)   Repeat 3 bows backward —
      Silence — beat hands to front
8)   Walk in big circle to barre —
9)   Summons
      Touch barre l. hand
      beat 5 brushes

10) Face front (catch train under leg) — weave arms & body
    to kneel while group enters to place girls on barre
11) Summons —
    a)   I walk downstage 4 —
    b)   Hold 6 — while David walks upstage to r. of barre
    c)   walk — to chair.

~~~~~~

    a) { company in plies on barre
       { at end men take girls off on shoulders — let them down &
       { waltz lifts off —
    b)   Helen enters
         David with whip.
         Helen exits over whip —

~~~~~~

    Long note — I rise & walk swiftly to st. r. end of barre
1) Javanese steps forw.
        2 slow
        3 fast
        3 slow
        4 fast.
2) accented walk st. L. & up to l. end of barre, face front —
3) Javanese step
        3 fast
        2 slow
            beat of arm
        2 slow
        2 fast —
4) tipping backwards moving st. r
        3 — hold
        5 — hold
5) face front
        3 twists upstage to barre center
6) Slow Javanese
        6 X
7) Walk to chair 2
        ″   upstage 1   accented?
    (a series of 3)
8) Twisting to center barre 2 X
    face barre
9) David enters —
    places rope on my neck.
    I turn — I am on st r.
            David st l.

10) Javanese step forw —
    2 slow
    3 fast —
11) David crosses me to st. r —
    holding rope.
12) 3 knee crawls to chair —
    D. holding rope —
    I emerge & throw rope st. r.
    I face yellow piece —

    a)   David goes to st. r. picks up whip
    b)   Flying turns from st. r to st. L.
    c)   David takes side skips toward me
    d)   Flute melody — I take 3 step draws toward David — st. r.
    e)   David leaps to yellow piece
    f)   I take 2 draws st. r.
    g)   David jumps & holds on
          summons on 6 counts.
    h)   I walk on next summons
          8 counts to back of yellow —

Bolero   for company
    when David leaves yellow I sit —

In Bolero — warning cue when girls rest on men's feet
David takes leaps on 5 & comes over to yellow piece
While men rise & girls & men to lift there is a trumpet note — & David
& I travel upstage to back of barre — I step on his back & rise to sit
on barre

Bert & Ethel — duet —
when they come to barre for plies — I step on David's knee &
descend & face Bert —
He approaches my face —
I leave & he takes Ethel —
I go front & to sit in chair.

after Ethel & Bert exit —
Minuet.
1)   Dick & Helen begin it.
2)   Akiko & Paul & go out
3)   Linda in back of barre
4)   Bob & Mary —

5) David —
6) Bob & Mary exit in front of yellow —
7) 3 girls (3 little swans)
8) David exits r. in sits —
9) Helen creeps across barre with Dick moving behind to st. r.
   & she lies on barre
   hand on Dick —
10) Linda & Mary from L to r —
    in turning — extension —
11) Dick takes Helen off barre & begins to turn off st. L.
    4 X 3

                    Acrobats —
center at barre facing front —
On 3 tympani —
a)   3 forward (David back)
b)   3 ("   forw.)
c)   3 back to barre
On orchestra —
     walk forward 4 steps
        "   to chair "   "   sit.

~~~~~~

after leaps —
   rise — (cue — David's leap)
             he lands front of mandolins

   hands at hair —
1)   3 little catch steps st. r.
     face front
          beat hands in silence
2)   3 little catch steps st r.
          beat hands in diamond —
3)   Deep bow to floor to r.
     rise —
4)   3 little catch steps
     profile l — r — l. with
     hand touching shoulder   silence
5)   backward bow — traveling
     3 X
      silence — diamond beat
        deep bow to floor

backward bow traveling
3X
   silence — face front — beat hands
6)   large circle back to barre
      facing r — profile —
      On summons l. hand on barre
      5 brushes — with r. foot —
7)   face front —
      side bends with arms
      into kneel —
      rise
8)   Walk forward 4 slow steps
      hold 6 — for entrance of group
      walk to sit — 8 counts

<hr>

II.

Exit of David & Helen as she walks over whip —
On trumpet held note walk swiftly to r. corner of barre.

1)   Javanese steps
      2 slow
      3 fast
      3 slow
      4 fast
2)   walk to st. L.
      ″ ″ barre l. corner.
3)   Javanese steps
      3 fast
      2 slow
      <u>arm</u> stroke
      2 slow
      2 fast.
4)   tilting back step to st. r.
      3 X
      pause
      5 X
      face front
5)   Turning step up to barre
      3 X
6)   Slow Javanese
      6 X?
        <u>Hold</u>

7)   walk st. L.
       " upstage
     Twisting
8)   Turning step upst. to barre
       2 **X** — face barre
9)   David places whip on neck
     I turn to face him
10) Javanese step together
       2 slow
       3 fast
11) David goes to my st. r.
12) 3 knee crawls to st. l.
13) Throw whip st. r —
14) face yellow piece —
         ∿∿∿∿∿∿∿∿

     cue — Flying step —
             David leaps & stops
to st. r — 3 step draws on flute
             David leaps
to st. r — 2 step draws on flute
I wait 6 while David jumps
walk to yellow & stand behind it with David in
front — 8 counts —
    ∿∿∿∿∿∿∿∿

when David leaves I sit
    ∿∿∿∿∿∿∿∿

cue —
1 — 2 — 3 — 4 go —
David at my l.
I come out on long note & force him to back — & step on his
back up to barre
r. hand on David's face.
cue — when Bert & Ethel go to ends of barre I descend
         stepping on David's knee —
         face Bert — he walks to my face — I leave & go forward
         & to chair
cue — Dick takes Helen off barre
as men enter in knee crawls I come out & go swiftly upstage to
center of barre
Bert in front —
1)   Javanese steps
       3 slow
       (Bert 7 fast)

2 slow
(Arm stroke)
2 slow
Bert 3 fast
2) Twist upstage 3X
3) pull whip off Bert
Throw to David —
4) walk around him to barre
5) Bert rolls to me — rises
6) I slip under his arm
7) walk to chair —

～～～～～～

cue
girls fall —
men enter & exit with girls
David sits on floor to r. stage in front of mandolins
faces upstage —

～～～～～～～～～～～～～～～～～～～～～～～～～～～

I rise slowly —
1) 3 small catch steps st. r.
silence beat of hands —
2) Place arm thru rope —
flute solo walk upstage with David
During entrances —
we walk 8 steps from end to end of barre several times —
On 4 tympani — David walks to mandolins
I walk to yellow —
girls & men turn on 1
girls bow & rise on 2–3
men bow & rise 3–4

～～～～～～

On 5th 3 men begin knee crawls
12) On musical change
I go upstage to center barre
Bert is left center with David —

～～～～～～

13) Javanese step as Bert is being bound in whip.
  a) 3X slow
  b) 7X short for Bert
  c) 2X slow
    arm beat
  d) 2X slow —

e)   3 short for Bert
f)   I twist 3X upstage
     (as Bert falls)
e)   I untwist Bert after thrusting David aside & throw
     whip to David (2 phrases)
f)   I encircle Bert on heavier music — again back to barre
                              touch Bert's foot —
g)   Bert falls on barre —
     I duck from under —
     & walk front & to chair — sit.

~~~~~~

Furioso —
1)   Bert climbs to barre while Mary crosses in back.
2)   Dick & Mary
3)   Paul & Akiko —
4)   Pick up Akiko & exit of Paul & Akiko & Mary & Dick —
     Bert comes off barre
5)   Sparkler turn with Ethel Lind & Dan —
6)   Helen enters
                 (David on barre)
7)   Bert & Helen & David
     up to exit of Bert & Helen & David comes to yellow —
8)   Linda & Dan —
     exit —
9)   girls run in & fall
     & rise —
10) men enter to pick them up (8 counts)
     exit —
     David goes to st. r. & faces me —
11) I rise & take 3 accented steps to st. r.
     silence — beat hands —
     go to David — put arm thru whip — we walk upstage to barre —
On flute —
     Bert enters we wait —
David & I traverse barre thruout entrances —
     On last 4 beats for bows we walk to our places —
          I to yellow
          David to mandolins.

~~~~~~

Clytemnestra and Alcestis / 367

Additional Notes for Night Journey

Night Journey: photograph by Martha Swope

Dance I

As girls exit —
High note — l. arm lifted
turn into arabesque on r. knee l. up.

1) Sway back on both knees into back bend —
cross l. in front to kneel & rise with wide extension of
r. leg.
bringing it sharply down.

2) Forward fall in wide 2nd
turn into rise.
1 or 2?

3) Beat with convulsive beats of r. knee

4) Walk to bed in semi-circle r.
back away on music change —

5) Wandering tipping run
3X — r — l— to bed r to chair —
(on 2nd make small change of direction)

6) 2 Dart — turns to st. r.

7) Fall in wide 2nd
rise —

8) knee beats of r. as before
turning to face up-stage

9) Walk sideways to bed facing upstage — r. arm extended to bed —
Turn away with convulsive contraction — to face front —

10) 3 knee vibrations making reverse turn on 3rd
Run to chair — kneel to touch.

11) Rise into contraction
kick & knee crawl 2X to stage r.

12) pulsing of body on small bourrée.
1X plain
2X with hands beating to cover breasts & abdomen with tight
turn after each —

13) Break arms in wild despairing way

14) Bourrée turns
either to r. or in place.

15) To Seer
High contraction kick with l.
knee crawl
2X each —

16) Fall on staff
Seer thrusts her away —

17) Two back falls with rise & into 2 wandering tipping
     runs — st. r & l.
18) Run to bed — fall on it in semi-kneel.

climb onto bed as Seer walks out —
Oedipus enters with girls in leaf dance —
He descends bed —
picks her up & carries her to chair — leaves her —
Oedipus' solo —

Dance II
with branches —
starting at chair
branches open from elbows —
body profile to r.

1)   3 small catch steps in profile taking them after note has sounded
2)   Lift R. arm high over head
      "   L   " out to l. side.
      facing r — take small plie
      almost sitting against L. hip
3)   Straighten & cross branches with elbows locked —
      one branch up & one down.
4)   2 slows darts to r.
      on r. L. up in back.
5)   step back on l & r to face front — bring L. knee across r. knee
      in plie — facing front, branches wide & facing down —
6)   Take bali arabesque to face r on l.
      Repeat L. knee across r. facing front.
7)   Kneel on r facing front
      L. in 4th —
      open almost at once into 2nd
      return to 4th —
      open to 2nd —
      kneel on L & take bali arabesque on floor to face r.
      Recover to 4th front
      slowly rise with branches open downward in silence —
8)   Balinese step forward with r. foot toeing in & opening in 4th.
      Body undulating with lift of L. hip.
      r. branch inscribing circle
      l.   "   hanging downward.
      ～～～

2X
～～～

9) Jubilation step diag. backward veering l.
   r. knee lifted in front
   both branches high.

   ~~~~

   3X

   ~~~~

10) Pass r. leg behind into bali attitude, both knees bent — body
    profile to r.
    Sweep floor with r. branch & bring r. leg in front of body straight
    as in high kicking walk — facing r.
11) Darts to Bert on r leg
          X
    hold
    Take pitch fall to floor on r. & recover to sit
    body facing front
    both knees together
    branch in l. hand to l.
12) open r — knee, passing branch to r.
    2X —
13) Bring l. leg behind in bow, then to front to rise facing front —
14) Turn into profile walk to L.
    step draw
    walk
    step draw
    walk —
15) Sit on chair

End —

Preliminary Notes for Hecuba

Cortege of Eagles: photograph by Martha Swope

Scene I —
Guards before tents —
austere — women not seen, nor Hecuba —
Sense of slavery —
imprisonment —
Doom —

Hecuba —
Tragedy of a Queen —

1) chorus of women as a screen — dance —
    hieratic — using sleeves as screen — dance of sorrow —
    lamentation —
    lateral on stage —
    They never turn their backs.
    When they do, as curtain opening —
        Hecuba, as Queen appears
    They become princesses as a Royal court in memory emerges

Clytemnestra: photograph by Carl van Vechten

Clytemnestra
A Partial Record of Action

Hades — leaves cloak

Prologue

Clytemnestra I
(Position — Center behind net —)
1st Fury

        center

1) Treading in place —
2) Walk to L.U.P. r. knee lifted
    2nd Fury. (from up L)
3) Kneel crawls downstage R —
    use "cracks" in music with gesture
    5 times in all — (3 with "crack")
4) Walk across to D.S.L.
    3rd Fury d.S.L.
5) dart — turn — dart —turn — dart — turn
       into face front — feet close — arms — Javanese
                               in 2nd
                      elbows straight
6) Turn tightly (<u>U.S.L.</u>)
7) Kneel crawls — d. stage r. — 2X
         (hold in same as 5
          Javanese)
8) Cave turns 5× upstage L
         treading walk D.S.R.
           r — l — r over l.   4X
9) Kneeling travel
    4th & 2nd across stage to r —
    (accented knee crawl with arms)
10) Cave turns 3X upstage L. in place
11) Long walk to stage r — 10X
     Dart walk in circle — ending C stage
    Hades — facing Clytemnestra on walk to R.S.
         (Cl. may make Bali turns)
12) Scene with net or robe — with Furies
    (Descent of net)
    walk following Hades —
      with kneel crawls
13) Treading — center stage
14) Tight turn
    March jumps

15) H Dart — turn — dart — dart to chair   (2X ?)
             (walk — contraction —
                      anguish to chair)
16) 5 Bars silence —
             K turns in contraction to chair

                    Prologue
             Clytemnestra II
             Position at chair — D. stage R.
1)   Treading —
2)   Bourree bent knees — r — front to l stage
         6 sets
3)   Dart and turn with contraction
         3 times — downstage r.
4)   Bourrée   to stage L
         4 sets
5)   Dart — turn — dart
6)   Turn into side extension with 2 step draws
7)   One dart —
8)   Side extension in 2nd
      2 step draws
9)   Drop into wide 2nd wt to r —
      with r knee plié
      body bent forward, hands on hips.
10)   Small turn on l to l — into ⟶
11)   2 kneeling crawls
12)   Rise into wide low arabesque turn — Hades rises
      K into back fall
13)   Repeat 9   Hades
              10   beats over K.
              11   8X
              12
14)   Hades 12 walks
             moving about
      K as he does later with Helen
      K rises into wide arabesque turn
15)   Back fall (shoulders) facing H — st. R.
      Hades beats over K 6X
      walks — 7 steps
      around K.   K — rises — wide turn
16)   Repeat back fall — Hades beats 10 over K.
             walks 9
17)   [*deletion by M.G.*]

The Notebooks of Martha Graham / 382

18) K Dart with wide contraction
    turn — Hades stands U S L
        3 sets — to stage R —
    Hades — 2 March jumps —
    K sits in silence — 2 measures

Prologue

Clytemnestra III.
1) Treading —
2) { Stroke into Bali attitude on L.
      2 knee vibrations
      Bali attitude
      Bali turn —
3) Repeat (2)
4) walk to stage L —
    with accent on r. leg demi plié
    body in profile
        ? X
5) Dart and turn
        3 sets to stage r —
6) Repeat walk as in 4
7) Dart — turn into kneel & up into Cave turn
8) Repeat (7)
9) Hades —
    on cries — positions on chair
                with forward fall in 2nd —
                Rise —

Clytemnestra
    Dance of Vengeance (Sword)

    Position — stage L (upper?)

1) Small Ronde jamb — foot on floor — r. ft.
    finishing r. leg straight — crossed behind L — L. plie —
    Sword to L — L. hand gesture over it —
2) Repeat (1)
3) Repeat (1)
    finishing in Bali turn to L on r at end of phrase —
4) Knee crawl to r.
5) rise, face front — gesture to sword
6) Repeat (4)
7) Repeat (1) (2) (3)

8) Repeat (4)
    Rock body slightly —
    1. in 4th across body in kneel
9) Two "Cave" turns
10) Kneel crawl into reclining position
    [*Nos. 11–14 missed by M.G.*]
15) Two "fan" kicks with r —
    facing front
16) "Bali" attitude with r behind into "Bali" turn on R.
17) Kneel crawls   3X to L. stage
18) Dart — turn   3X
                 (with slow suspension)
    d. stage r. —
19) 3 knee vibrations with r. leg into
20) Series of kneel crawls about stage on pattern

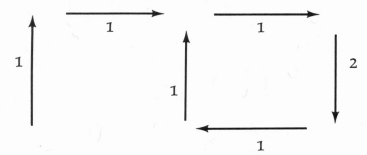

21 Treading —
    up center stage facing front
22) Dart with turns —
    sword held high in L hand by handle — on 4th cry face
    center front (?)   then turns are almost continuous — 4×
23) Lunge to r in plie on r.
    sword in L
    L. leg straight
    Bring sword to touch floor

                                        Exit?

after killing —
Clytemnestra walks thru mesh — faces & watches chariot exit — goes
on platform — sees cloak —

Helen of Troy dances like inner self of Clytemnestra in her instant
of remorse while C. stands —

Helen picks up cloak & bears it off — st. r.
Clytemnestra raises sword — fast exit st. L as Furies enter —

Clytemnestra
        Exultation —
Entrance

            Exultation
        Position D. stage R. at chair —
1)   L leg across r in front with
        L knee bent — r straight —
        L arm flung on top of head
        to touch r shoulder —
                            (Stork)
        4X in all alternating —
            L — R — L — R
2)   Strut position to stage L — semi-profile —
        r. foot at L. knee — L straight
        body inclined over r. knee
        torso front —
3)   "Stork" position — r foot across L knee — r arm over —
        (2 small steps necessary)
4)   Repeat (2) & (3)
        until done 6X in all —
5)   a)   Bourrée (facing front) to r.
                Traveling upstage toward
        b)   step draw facing upstage on L —
                3 sets of a & b
                    (turn on L to r into)
6)   Repeat (2) & (3) ←
7)   Bourrée   a ⎫
        step draw   b ⎭   once.
8)   Repeat   Strut
                    Stork
9)   Repeat Bourree
                step draw
10)   Repeat   Strut
                    Stork
11)   Repeat bourrée
                step draw
12)   Repeat   (1)
            as in (1) — 4X
                    r — l — r — l
13)   Step on L to front —
        Bring r knee sharply up high across body — (foot to L)
14)   Semi-kneel
        L hip thrust forward

15) "Cave" turn
16) "Stork"   2X
        r — L
17) Repeat   (13) (14) (15) (16)
18) Repeat   (17)   faster —
19) "Stork"
        r — L — r — L
20) a)   quick step draw to r
           facing back
     b)   turn to Egyptian bow to r
     c)   Repeat step draw to back
     d)   wide extension in 2nd
           facing front —
     Repeat a — b — c — d —
     Repeat a — b

Meditation
        (on chair)
~~~~~~~~~~~

18 notes

                    ⎧ ping
                    ⎨ gong
                    ⎩ ping
~~~~~~~~~~~~

        10 times accents
           with melodic phrase between
           unequal length —
~~~~~~~~~~~

        Lyrical with accents
           Dance-like phrases   2X

Dance of Remorse — Farewell — ?
     On floor — head on pillow
     seated l — hip — feet to r —

1 lyric phrase
     lift head off pillow
     2 booms — body to r — l — low on both knees
2)   lyric
        lift arms — body upright on both knees
        2 booms — Take off cape

*3 elements in all —
opening walk not
included*

3) lyric
   Sway body to pick up cape
   2 booms
       throw to r — to l.
4) lyric
   l. knee up — crawl 2X to r —
   2 booms —
   Cave turn — gesture to bed —
5) lyric
   Bourree — r front
                back
                front
   2 booms — beat of body —
6) lyric
   dart — turn — dart — dart — turn — kneel
   facing ghost —
   2 booms — turn on knees
               fall to r.
7) lyric
                         Letter beats l. leg & arm
                4–2
   Crawl —   3 X to ghost

       4th   rise
   2 booms touch — rise —

8) lyric
                          catch r. leg up in arms across
       3 Cave turns   body — step — ¼ turn
                          Repeat l Cave turn
9) lyric   Repeat lift of foot in arms
   Booms —
10) lyric   with high kick of L.
   accented walk to bed   3 X
   2 booms
       crouch over Aegisthus
11) lyric
   walk — upstage
   ʺ   right
   ʺ   downstage
   2 booms —
       (1) extension
            step draw —
12) lyric   Sit on front piece
                          on lyric —

stroke him —
plunge away form on booms
ready for dart
then   (hold r. foot in arm)

13) lyric ←
    a)   dart — turn — dart — turn.
        2 booms — bow to Aegisthus
    b)   turn in dart
        ″   ″   ″   (or pulse in body as weeping)

        2 booms — bow to Aegisthus
    c)   Repeat b — 2 X
            (3X in all — b & c)
                step into
14) lyric   High kick with l. to
                bed — bow to throne

15) Crash
    Turn to bed as in farewell
16) Repetition
    13 steps backward to chair
  turn — kneel to ghost
  ¼ turn into 4th facing front
  low crouch —

    Turn on knees — fall to r —
  Family portrait

Meditation —
    Sitting in chair —
1)   Lyric — (hold)
      sit in chair   Paul brings her l. hand to
      accents   face —
        lift hands clasped to mouth
2)   Lyric (hold)
      accents
        bring hands down to lap
3)   Lyric (hold)
      accents
        raise l. knee sharply & bring down — contraction
4)   Lyric (hold)   Paul turns her
      accents
        face front on r hip

5) Lyric — (hold)   Paul rises
    accents
      rise to face upstage
      L. hand at back —

6) Lyric (hold)   Paul turns away
    accents
      kneel on chair
      r. hand on back of chair

7) Lyric (hold)   Paul takes l. hand
    accents   bends her over to
                             touch knife
      lift l. foot bali attitude
      l hand on knife

8) Lyric (hold)
    accents
      sit as at beginning

                              hand at breast — breathing
9) Lyric (hold)   Paul walks away
    accents — rise to bend over knife —

10) Lyric (hold)
    accents
      step off —

11) music change —   a)   Paul — 2nd side
    walk —   b)   ext. on r —
      upstage to Paul   contract on l —
      downstage to chair   c)   turn upst. jump on r
      to sit on front corner —   stand behind chair
    accents
      sit on step r side of chair
      touch knife

12) Lyric (hold) arabesque — Paul
    accents —
      rise to wide 2nd

13) Lyric (hold) Paul foot on chair
    accents   r foot
      rise — face r —
        stand within P. knee

She sits facing Paul
puts her hands on his face
He touches her r. wrist
She bends him over her to kiss her — she lies on chair —
    His head on her breast

He puts her hand on knife
She draws it —
They stand — holding knife high
She turns from him —
He touches knife
She walks away
As she turns he sits with back to audience — face
turned away from her

note — Prologue I
           ending —
walk with Hades, facing him,
following him —
change pattern on knees to include Helen of Troy —
Hades finishes behind piece
Helen walks backwards with Clytemnestra facing her
to sit on chair — C. behind chair —

Prologue —   I
    position   Center stage?
1)   Treading — progress downstage
2)   accented walk St. l.   2nd–4th to piece
3)   knee crawls (5)   r — l — r — l — rr —
      with crack — to d. St. r. diagonal
4)   accented walk — st. L.   2nd & 4th to face Helen
5)   Dart — turn —
      3 sets — d. st. r.
6)   Gesture — Hades opens knees
      facing front — chair — profile
7)   turn — with spin upstage
8)   knee crawls
      2X — d. st. r. to chair
9)   Gesture —
10) Hades phrase —
      K. holds —
11) Cave turns
      5X — up st. L.
12) Hades phrase
    K. holds
13) [*deletion by M.G.*]

*facing piece
2nd–4th
walk in profile r — with r leg beating high
into pitch
Arabesque fall to Hades —
4th sit —
wide turn*

14) Hades phrase (March jump in air from chair
                    forward
15) Walk backwards down st. L
    with Hades — side & back — begin with L
16) Hades walks
    K. answers on her knees   on last one turn
            r to C   1X   on knees fall on back
    l upstage — d. stage — l stage — hold   as H does arabes.

17) Hades move stage L arabesque (plie) over C.
18) C cave crawls upstage to cape — sit to 4th & rise — treading
18) Hades — 2 skips — 2 single M jumps
    Clytem — in Cave turn to pick up cape
                                (6 sets of 3
19) K — crosses in silence to sit

Consider —
    Rape of City.
        Apollo gives helmet to Athena
Good   Perhaps he puts it on high standard which she carries on
 M   her walk among dancers as symbol of War —

Prologue — Klytemnestra II
1)   Treading —
2)   Bourree change to L. stage
        6X ? L. arm extended to L
            5 gestures with r. arm
    beginning at temple — extending up — out — down —
    (Bring both hands together before 1st dart)
3)   Dart — contraction turn
        3X   to d. st. r.
    (Hades goes around throne?)
4)   Bourree change to L. st.
        4X   r. arm moves 4 gestures
5)   Dart-turn — dart-hold —
    side extension facing front
    2 step draws facing back.
6)   Repeat dart-hold
                side ext. in 2nd, face front
                step draws 2 — face back.

Clytemnestra / 391

7) Drop to front
        in 4th knees in ⎫ gesture from Hades
8) tight turn on l.   ⎭
9) 2 knee crawls to Hades —
      or small running — plie on l. r. up
         sharply in profile to Hades
10) 1 Cave turn   back?
    fall to floor on shoulders —
11) Hades walks over with 8 beats
12) Hades walks — 12 walks —
     Clytem — sits to 4 into wide Cave turn
13) Back fall — Hades beats over
               6 counts
    Hades walks 7   "   ½ circle
    K sits to 4th & into wide turn
14) Back fall — Hades 10 beats
    Hades walks — 9 as C. rises to stand
         ??
    Bourree change in place —
    arms front —

    Dart — contraction turn d. st. r.
        4× in place making turns on contractions —
         end facing

Hades — March jumps
C. walks — backwards   4 sets of 3
       (silence)   in all to sit —
         gesture
⎛l. arm with elbow at head.⎞
⎝hand thrown back —   ⎠
?   ?   ?
question
2 or 3 back falls?

    On Iphigenia's exit music walk to stage L — not daring
to look at her —
(Begin treading facing front —)

Clytemnestra — Prologue III

1) Step on L — treading — at st. L.
   face back — front — Bali attitude

2) Knee vibration 2× at st. L.
   into Bali attitude
   &   ″   turn — Repeat

3) Fan kick to 2nd — drop
   to knees — Rise — wide stance

4) Dart — turn — dart — turn
   Dart — turn

5) Hades enters
   Walk — 2–4th st. l —

6) Hades.
   2 wide 2nd jumps to st L.

7) Clytemnestra
   Dart — turn —
   Dart turn — Dart
            turn

8) Hades repeats jumps to chair

9) C —

10) Hades
    March jumps upst. L.

11) C.

12) Hades
    Repeat March jumps

13) [deletion by M.G.]

14) Hades
    Skip to chair l —

15) [deletion by M.G.]
    ~~~~~~~~~

    Hold during girls —
    Sit   ″   Berts —

Sleep walking —
    Position — standing

1) 9 profile turns — feet in profile
   r first —

2) Face front
   open arms to side (hidden)
   drop head L shoulder
   Return arms to side —

(1) go on chair
l. foot on seat
hand toward
sword.

(2) Rise
into Fury
position — r.
knee on back
of chair —

(3) come
off chair —
drop to
crouch,
sitting
on step
on st. r.
facing l.
to sword.

(4) Rise —
face
Hades —
wrestle
with
him —

(5) Turn
& sit as
Orestes
enters

3)   Walk 5 profile turns —
4)   open arms —
     turn to face upstage holding material in back
5)   5 steps upstage
6)   Turn to face front — arms open —
7)   Lifting of shoulders on beats
     like shudder
8)   Hold robe in close to body
     Walk to r — body low
9)   Repeat shudder
10) Repeat walk to r —
     body low — moving from side to side — with accent —
11) Repeat shudder
12) Right hand comes out
     l. covers face
     r. lifts robe over head —
13) walk to bed —
  3 { little catch steps
    { sob
14) on last sob remove robe from head
     kneel — arms wide
     face bed —
     Resume head on pillow

To be considered

New Version ?

Treading
1 wide sit in 2nd
   lotus position —
2 throw swords as
   in disgust, fear —
   rise to knees.
3 turned in —
   weeping ?
   swaying ?
4 hip crawls to
   sword —
   high arabesque on
   floor

Dance of Vengeance with Sword

(Position on blue ground)
facing St. L. profile r ft. front)

Treading — sword in r held slightly to L — with
L. hand near it —

1) <u>Loud</u>
Sit suddenly bring r. leg behind body to l.
sword to r — elbow on floor
movement of hand over sword.

2) <u>Loud</u>
lift to knees in 4th
lyric transition — swaying hips —

3) <u>Loud</u>
slide sword d. st. L. on blue from crouching position
Lyric — both knees — beating arms toward sword.
<u>Loud</u>

4) Two Cave crawls
r. hip — l. hip to pick up sword on lyric

5) <u>Loud</u>
Turn on back —
contraction —
hips off floor

6) sword held point down to body — lift l. leg high
in contraction

7) <u>Loud</u> — rise to hold on blue
hold on blue
lyric — profile — contraction
beat over — sword toward body —
come off blue in dart

8) <u>Loud</u>
Bali turn — sword to back foot.
lyric hold to front — with contraction beats to body

9) } Loud
contraction kick to r.

10) } 2X

11) <u>Loud</u>
Bali turn into profile facing r l. ft. front.
lunge to r. bringing

12) } sword under arm
steps profile to r — l. front

13) } Repeat

14) <u>Loud</u>
     Bali turn
    into
a) quick steps in 2nd facing L. with l. hand on stomach —
    body low sword into body —
b) Turn on r — dart turn to r —
c) High kick L in profile —
    Dart turn on L to L

Repeat entire
Repeat
  into knee crawls —
  7 in all to reach Blue —
Begin extreme stage L

15)

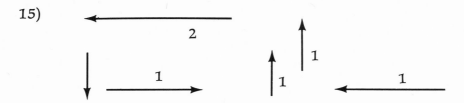

change of music —
16) slow deliberate treading
     using accents to move sword
17) change of music
     Repeat opening.
       sit in wide 2nd
       sword at knees
       sliding of sword on cry
       Cave crawls 2X to sword
       pick up sword
       plunge it in turn on back
       Rise on 4th cry
18) Darts across to chair
    using cries —
    to Paul's knees —
    replace sword
         exit —

(Consider — using knee crawls to go to Paul & pick up transparent
cape from chair on his knees — When music change comes use cape
to wrap sword or use as a bull-fighter — to increase horror or obsession
— Then take darts to throne — & use exit as a walk trailing cape.)

16) Treading — r — l — r
circle kick landing r in 2nd — then profile with plie on r —
facing r stage — walk l — r — l —
turn to face L stage

Treading facing front
circle kick to face upstage
walk upstage L — r — l —
face L in profile —
3 high kicks with L to L
Circular kick —
Cave turn in lunge & take cape —
   change of music.

17) Bourrée to stage L —
Wrapping cape over r. arm —

18) Dart

Prologue —
 Pre-curtain music —
 Clytemnestra — I
 Rape of City (?)
 Clytemnestra II
 Iphigenia sacrifice
 Clytemnestra III
 Recognition.

"Fanfare" open — girls — Electra
"Net" "   "
Entrance — K — 2nd beacon
Fanfare —

Act I
 { Dance of Watchman
 { Beacon
 { Jubilation
Beacon
Clytemnestra
 Visions.
 Meditation
  1) Aegisthus

2) Helen & Paris
3) Iphigenia

    Rehearsal for Vengeance
    Dance of Vengeance
Agamemnon
    Entrance
      Herald
      Electra

Clytemnestra & Agamemnon (spear)
Solo Agamemnon
Agamemnon (cont'd)
    Enticement to walk on carpet
    Exit
Cassandra —
Helen of Troy
Furies —
Exultation —
Duet

Embattled Garden —
. . . "Satan's temptations are chiefly directed toward the Eve in man
The temptations are more complicated, subtle, strenuous than   205
in the garden,"   206
. . .
"man's great temptation to withdraw"
"The fight is not lost in the careless springtime ease of the Garden
of Eden, or won in the unflinching mind of the perfect man, but lost
& won in the mind & heart of the self-ruined hero." —   209

after <u>Recognition Scene</u>
Orestes does not leave —
On piccolo —
    Klytemnestra falls slowly from chair —
On singing —
    Net descends —
On heavy music —
    Furies enter
On "Flesh" — etc —
    K & O approach each other at net — facing —
There is a break for Furies —
in lines
I — Klytemnestra
    (Both standing Center at net – miming of lines) —

I — Orestes
    Orestes mimes —
O & K stand at net for entrance of characters.
Klytemnestra — speaks
    "Cassandra etc"
K. goes to throne —
"I — Cassandra etc"
Down Ramp —
    Then wanders about stage — Orestes at net —
Cassandra exits past throne
touches K. on shoulder —
movement by K —
On monotonous tones —
Orestes exits — perhaps with Furies —
On last crash
    K. falls —

old version

Conversation piece K & O — Prologue

1)   Stark position —
        I — Klytemnestra —
        r foot at knee — r arm over head
2)   "Anguished"
        r foot across l knee
        contraction
3)   I — K —
            call upon your name
    Warrior stance —
    l. knee in l. arm —
  r hand comes slowly down to front with l. foot —
4)   Dance phrase
        weaving of arms & body in bourrée
5)   I — killed
        Fan kick r.
6)   I — suffered
        plunge to both knees
7)   I suffered not —
        rise to wide 2nd
8)   In fear
        little walk to r — l — r —
            profile stance —
9)   In disgrace
        turn to back

10) I am possessed
    little dance bourrée
    repeats
11) Rejoicing I killed
    High contraction kick r.
    ending in 4th stance

Priest —   1   Voice
                                       Music
                                   2   Voice
                                       long music
                                   3   Voice
                                       change of music
                                   4   Voice
                                       into
                                       Clytemnestra
                                       with man's cry
                                       continuing

Clytemnestra — Dialogue —
                Prologue —
1)   "I — Clytemnestra"
        stark position —
2)   "Anguished lunge to r — body low
                    plie on r — l hand
                    r. thigh —
    make complete turn on L small into
3)   "I . . . call upon your name"
        kneel crawls —
            d. st. front
                    turn
        d st L   "
        d. st. R —
            Cave turn

4)   "I killed — "
5)   "I suffered"
        feet together —
6)   "I suffered not"
        split sit —

7 — "In fear"
      turn to back —
      legs parallel
      r. elbow on floor

on L side —
1 contraction —

8) — "In disgrace"
      face back l. knee up — hands behind back —
9) "Rejoicing I killed — "
      Rise to high kick contraction —
                    to r.
      Hold — r. hand stomach — l. high
10) On lyric phrase — drop arms in fear bewildered
11) "I — among the dead — "
      profile position to st r. l. front
      During next lines — alternate profile walk — l — r — l
12) Hold musical phrase
13) "Hear me etc"
      knee crawls upstage to net —

As Iphigenia <u>holds</u> <u>on</u> <u>piece</u>
<u>"I — Clytemnestra"</u>
    2 high kicks with l.
       traveling forward
    Body swing — r — l.
2 high kicks
    Body swing r — l —
    Beat in air with hands
pitch Forward fall on strong music — to Iphigenia
    stay on floor — r hand raised until Cassandra is about to enter —

Traveling d. center

    "Cassandra"
      l. foot in 4th to stand.
      walk upstage
step on "prophetess"   across to st. R.
start down in music
"oh seer in the dark"   down st. r to chair

"Speak"   face Cassandra
"Rejection"   sit —

Judith—*Character Studies*

Judith

Flute solo —

prayer —

1) Circular kick —
2) Circular kick —
3) Darts
4) bow — hands on knees
   wide second —
5) Circular kick
6) Circular kick
7) simple bow
8) rise with arms up high
9) Darts
10) Circular kick
11) Dart pattern
12) 2 Circular kicks —
13) Dart & upstage & walk
    to sit & lie on piece

Judith —

with spear —
1) Take spear —
2) 2 Take lunges to Bert st. L —
   with small back kick to clear dress —
3) wide second — with spear on knees
   Darts to
4) kneel on piece
   circular kick
5) go round & up on piece —
6) red cloth (Helen)
7) pierce Bert
8) come off piece —
9) Dart around to plant spear
10) go to dressing.

stand in cloak during stick dance —
walk around with cloak — place it on piece —
up on top for 1st gazes —

Bert's solo — (I stand st. R.)
Duet with Bert —

Choreographic Indications for
Samson Agonistes

Samson Agonistes: photograph by Martha Swope

On Samson theme — 1st
      Bird in front of curtain —
1)   Wide fall in second with a little crawl on elbows.

2)   Samson theme 2nd
      position on r hip r elbow
      both feet high.
      turn to curtain
      crawl on both knees 2 short phrases beating arms
      { rise in 4th to take high kick with r to r. & bourrée small
        Repeat.

Samson theme 3rd
{ wide 2nd plie —
{ inverted movement to 5th with r. foot.
Repeat —

Turn to face st. L in profile
walk with catch step on r heel — shoulders to audience 6 X — to tent

{ face front
{ high L. kick   to front
{ circular r kick
2 X in all —

         (arrow step?)
{ Back thrust of L leg in profile toward curtain
{ imprecation with r. arm.
  Repeat

  Small back turn to face f.
Eng. horn —
  Profile steps using hand
  down face in weeping —
  facing alternately l. & r

1 long to L	— l. hand		
1 short " r	r "		
1 " " L	l "		
1 long r	r "		
1 short L	l "		
1 short R	r "		

Matt enters (written vertically on left)

down face shoulders front (written diagonally on right)

open arms wide
bring to sides
clasp.

2 knee crawls to Samson —
Matt in doorway —
in silence she walks to men

With spear —
come in with lunge —
cave turn?
lunge —
      wide 2nd —
      back fall — spear up —
      (or fall in 2nd)
(passionate — like Joan of Arc)
All darts low — sinister
First solo — prayer —
Circular kick —
fall — wide 2nd
All darts low & wild —

after dressings —
Think of 3 faces or 2 —
red hair in braids
loose to cover face — ?
(a double faced woman)
Take it off when Helen gives the cloak —

                                (after Paul)
                    Duet (or solo)
Beginning at piece —

      knee crawl   toward Samson st. L.
chord — step back into bird position
2X   wt. on L in profile r. foot at L. ankle, arms
             forced & wide with torso front — to audience

3X   go to wide 2nd plie & turn to r into bird position (chord)

2X   High kick L. step back
          chord position bird —

1X   high kick — into knee crawl
          small walk until chord

2X   bird position (each time step back)
          open to front wide 2nd plie
      on high note
          catch r. foot in l. hand

2X   beats in 5th standing high
        catch step walk st. r.
                         up st.
                         st r
                         up st.
                         st r.
                 to door on st. r.

on violins — Akiko enters — door
small duet to Samson —
Bird with high slow kicks & bird position —
Akiko (turning?)

Take cloak   exit on Bird music

Later Thoughts on Heloise and Abelard

Time of Snow: photograph by Martha Swope

Abelard and Heloise —
    The Cloister —
    Brittany
    Paris
    Paraclete

                ?

opening with Abelard as scholar, teacher —
scene with men —
lifting him on shoulders
"The wolves of Paris"
    (The scholars)
(Wolves — of Paris)
Winter — the scholars who adored & would consume, ravish, eat,
the Philosopher, Abelard

                ?

opening with
    chants from church
    folk songs of love —

    "The Master has come home"

perhaps in silence — but with spoken ecstatic voice —
    "The Master has come home" —
chants of prayer —
        Then
Songs of love —
        then
action —
      or
Heloise alone — hearing the songs of love

Dance of Awakening —
Dance " Spring
   "   " love —

Beginning —
Word with undertone of music — <u>not sung</u>

Beginning — ?
    A Dice Game —
Lucifer — Abelard   (p. 84)

Prince of darkness
Light-bringer —

~~~~~~~~~~~~~~~~

Alberic as Lucifer —
Dice game Lucifer & Abelard

"those that gavest me I have kept, & not one of them is lost, save
the son of perdition."

"I do not imagine that it pleased him to lose Judas" —   (91)   Waddell

"Fornication was the goblin mask they put on the sweetest sin of the
seven. And his sin was not fornication. It was Heloise."   Waddell 105

"Far from my house be thy frenzy, O Goddess" 106   Waddell

"Morning stars"   (109)
"Banner of thy star"   (159)   Waddell
"Torment of malice"   (166)
"The Summer's done"   (192)
"The power of the veil"
Langton — Angel teaching
(108)   New Testament

Something like a wall dividing the stage. It could be veils or
lattice of some kind or ropes —

It could make two areas —
Abelard one side,
Heloise the other —

A Duet — antiphonal perhaps —
of love, grief, despair —

It is as tho' they each walked their separate ways in the garden at
night — never touching, but always their thoughts touching —

Perhaps there could be a vision of what they had been & meant to
each other.

It might be reminiscent of the night Fulbert discovered them —
and when Fulbert had a vision like Bosch —
        "Torment of Malice"

Heloise in battle with the Madonna as Astarte images fading from
Madonna to Astarte in and out —

Austerity — anguish of hopelessness —

The Notebooks of Martha Graham / 416

consider words in whispers —
        man & woman — recitative
Two gardens — or cloisters —
        music — of love songs —
Heloise in one
Abelard in one —
never touching but tho'ts touch.

        running thru are
Duet images of themselves as lovers —
letter from Heloise to Abelard
    ″   ″   Abelard to Heloise —
She as abbess   Hopeless love
He as monk
giving a sense of distance
                absence
                anguish —
sometimes only visible in pools of light — never visible to each other —
At end of scene only Heloise is visible. Then there is an entrance
of the bier of Abelard being carried in by men — distraught Abbess
"The Master has come home"
Scene becomes a chapel with bier — chant for the dead —
The Abbess kneeling —
Ritual dance of nuns —
alone — Heloise as abbess
a moment of cry — a great anguish —
"I would rather be your whore" etc —
        Go into memory of past — Song like love
                or
The wolves of Paris —   Fulbert
        Young students with Abelard & Lucifer
at dice —
men's dance as they carry him on shoulders & about —
1)   men with Abelard
2)   Abelard & Fulbert
                as Lucifer
        or
else a double image of Abelard & his alter ego — Lucifer —
        in dice game —
duet
        Heloise
        Fulbert
          (uncle — father)
          lover

like sarabande —
     then
Heloise alone as Abelard sees her for the first time.

~~~~~~

Then the love scenes

~~~~~~

Then Fulbert as he discovers them — He stands at foot of bed
& the
     Torment of Malice —
     Bosch scenes of obscenity —
Violence of attack —
on Abelard —
He dances as a castrate perhaps in front of Heloise as Madonna

Abelard — as Lucifer —
"Lucifer, tho't Gilles, but not the light bringer tonight.
The Prince of Darkness."
                                Waddell 84

1)   Separate Gardens —
        Heloise —
        Abelard —

        pacing —
        shot thru with images of their youth —
        and ecstasy —

        Letters —
        perhaps words whispered — from letters —
        If the memory of youth comes they seem to tread on Heloise —
        on Abelard in anguish of memory
Perhaps Abelard as on a cross a little tilted —
Perhaps his fellow monks hold platform like cross —
Stations of the Cross —

1)   Gardens (duet in Isolation)
     ~~~~~~~~~~~~~~~~~~~~~~~

2)   Master has come home
     entrance of cortege
3)   Dance of the nuns —
      (stations of the Cross)
4)   stripping of Abbess of her robes & she becomes the Magdalene
       (Florence —
       Bellini ??)

It is what she desires
"I would rather be thy whore" —
5)   He is a shining man — almost naked

At <u>end</u> —
—

Castrate
Madonna —
whip —
She is his soul
his conscience
She beats him —
        ?   ?

when they meet
there could be a dance of now.
the whole scene could shift into <u>Now</u>

scene with
Fulbert (ghost)
Abbess — with whip —

            Heloise —

Walk forward 9 steps (mus cue)
turn &
walk to thorns
retreat
little catch walks
        forw.
        St. L
        forw
        st. r.   to bench —
(Bert sits)
(she sits)
Bert rises —
        falls backw. on bench —
She rises
        faltering catch steps L
          "   "   "   r
turn, fall wide 2nd —
Rise —

hands scratching at face
    r —
    l
    r
    l.
Darts making small circle to bench —
sit —
   Nolmi enters
   Long scene —
         Bob & Nolmi
·Bert rises
        & falls

Martha
    On knee slide — l. knee up
    3 X to Center —
switches on knees 4X
    r — l — r — l
beat hands to floor
push up
catch r. leg in arms
walk quickly to back chair — sit —

~~~~~~~~~~~~~~~~

Bert takes off robe
scene of crucifixion
Bert exits
Bob picks up Nolmi
exits —
4 girls enter
       &
with Martha walk front ritualistically as in prayer.
girls circle —
fall —
as a choir singing —
girls exit
Martha walks after them to chair & stands facing back — hands
over chair —

~~~~~~~~~~~~~~~~

students entrance —
scene with Nolmi — Bert
Bob —
Bob exits —
Bert pushes bed over as Nolmi goes onto it.

Martha encircles chair & kneels behind it during love scene —
At interruption by Bob
Bert lifts bed — Martha rises goes around to sit —
Game —   Bob exits —
M. watches —
when Bert lifts Nolmi over bed —
Martha rises — staggers front —
strange knee kicks with r. knee —
beats of l. foot — 4 times
Darts around
fall wide 2nd —
girls enter & cover with cape —
Castration scene —
after Bob chases Nolmi off —
Martha rises —
Cortege enters —

"Lady of the Labyrinth" —
"Goddess of the Seal"
"The consort of the bull — "   (42)
Occidental Mythology —   (Jos. Campbell)
"Goddess of the World Mountain"   (45)
Goddess with 2 lions
"To the Lady of the Labyrinth,
A jar of honey"   (47)
"The Serpent's Bride"   (9)
"Infinity"
"Tidal Seasaw"   (4)
"unidentified gods with no settled abode who have to be propitiated"
                        (The Other Mind.)   (68)

"Theatre as a material fact or spiritual concept"   (20)

"For the word had power in those days & a word mispronounced
might bring an earthquake" —

"The story told in the Natya Sastra is that Indra, the Lord of the
Immortals, entreated Brahma to devise a pastime accessible to
all castes . . ."   (20)

". . . and put a spell upon the dancers, freezing them into Immobility,
til Indra hurled his banner & put them into flight. And so the
first theatre was built . . ."   (21)

"to present a true reflection of the world, to imitate its movement" . . .
"to hold as were the mirror up to nature, to show virtue her own
feature, scan her own image and the very age & body of the time his
form & pressure"
"But the mirror which reflects this image is gesture . . ."   (21)
"The noble artificiality of Indian technique"   (Mirror of Gesture (1))

A queen
        One who is supported
The leg lifts
        men supports
she sits —
        men seat her —
She loves
        men attend her
(Mirror of Gesture)
"noble artificiality of technique"
                        (Title)

"Tidal season of exchanges
East & West, west to east, east to west, & west to east again . . ."
                        (Occidental Mythology — Campbell — ④)

6 perf — in October
Mon & Tues — last 3 wks of the month —
Salome
Ballet (with 3 characters of opera or 4) —
opera — 1 hr. 10" (or 20")
Ballet — 30" or (20")
my people — choreograph here —
spoke of music commission
yes — "strange" combination
"so popular today" of instruments
sub-conscious of characters in opera —
she returns Monday & will call here —

Did not speak of set
                lighting
        or money   costumes
                composer
She would like me to do Herodias (possible?)

Lester told me
Boosey & Hawkes ✒
Vocal score of Salomé

~~~~~~

Low G to D sharp above middle C —
Lester told me of man's voice — told Norman
Ming Cho Lee —
        3:30 Monday

Nautilis —
self evolving as a creature in a shell
evolved by that microcosm of life
for living a life —
where does it begin?
In its urge for a place for life, a habitat for the eternal
manifested as a soul in a body frame — shell man — what?

Nautilis —
    sound —
    poet — seeker —
    strange voice
        Oracle —

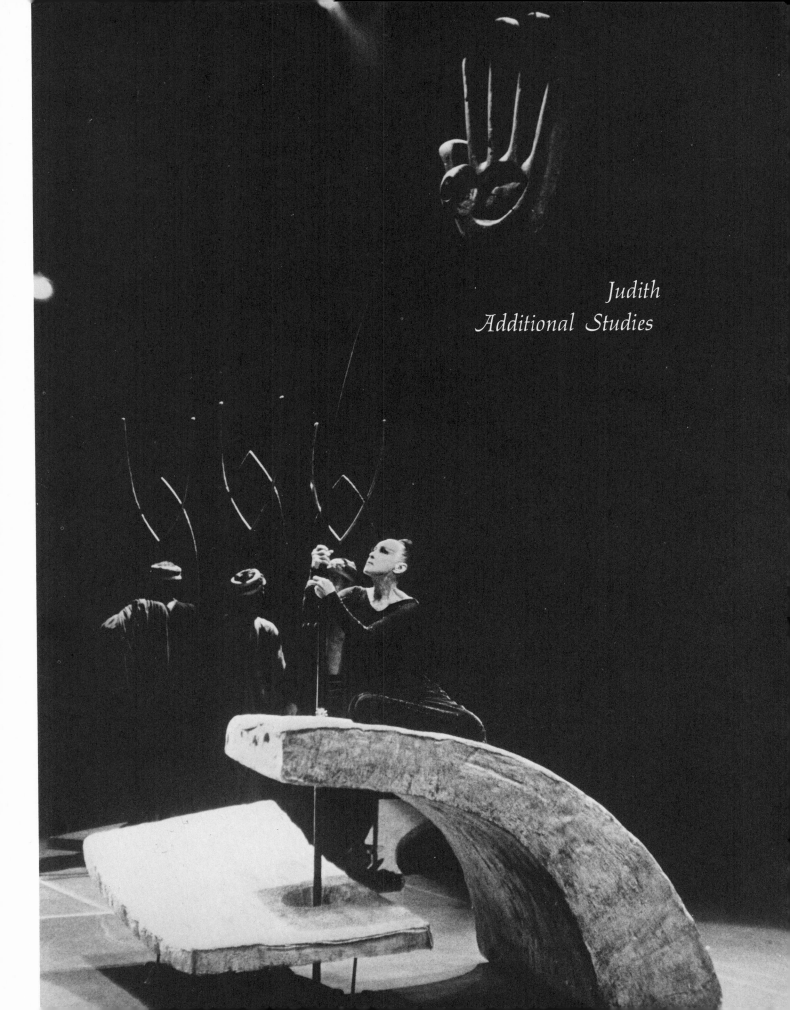

Judith
Additional Studies

after descent from Piece
Angels bow
Judith bows
Angels bow
opens arms to front — 2 meas.

Judith —
Flute solo —

1)   2 circular kicks
2)   Darts
3)   bow in wide second, hands on knees —
4)   2 circular kicks
5)   archaic straight bow from waist
6)   arms lift in 2nd
7)   Darts
8)   2 circular kicks
9)   Darts
        open section
10)   fall in wide second —
        Turn & crawl to bed & lie down —
11)   Darts to lie on piece

Cortege —

Angry Dance
stagger forward
fall wide second
rise —
catch steps r
  ″   ″ L
  ″   ″ r
lunging runs to r
beating body
r foot in hand
Silence —
figure 8 walk

wandering steps
    r
    l
    r
2 high kicks to r
wide 2nd facing fr
2 darts r —
sit —
Mary enters
walk to her
upstage
Then gesture to her
go upstage

                    Cortege
entrance —
    high kick
    weaving downst.
        "   up   "
    high kick
    step draw
    wide 2nd
    walk forward
    Turn in place
    kick to r
    little circle
    kick to r
    little circle
    kick
    circle
    face back & sit

Episodes: Part I: photograph by Martha Swope

In My End Is My Beginning
Studies for Mary Queen of Scots

Prologue —
      Song — David Riccio
         a sacred song —

James VI — Scotland
James I — England
her son

Bothwell died as an insane man in a Danish prison —

"In my end is my beginning"
a passacaglia on a theme of Mary, Queen of Scots —
                              (or the theme of a Queen)

The Queen
The Four Marys
Bothwell
Elizabeth   (as spectator?)
The executioner
      The axe when reversed is the standard of the Queen —

Riccio —
      deformed —
      mountebank —

      If one of the Webern songs might do it could
      precede Passacaglia —
            Riccio — in mime —

Scene —
      Scaffolding indicative of a throne

Perhaps it could be on top of an arched door way — a grille — thru
which the Queen makes her initial entrance directly to the audience —
alone — Then turns to ascend her final throne — someone at side
could bear her train & see that it curves the stage & finally forms
a path descending the steps along which she steps when she enters her
"rose-garden" with her "footfalls of memory"

Elizabeth   as spectator
                              (chorus in classic sense)
                        fear
                        anguish
                        hate —
                        compassion —

whole as play for Elizabeth
in box at theatre?
use of box frame for her

Plastique in frame of theatre box

{ fear

anguish

hate

Rivalry of 2 women —

Pageant for Elizabeth
        ″   ″ a Queen
        ″   ″ Power

opening —
    a terrible wild song —
        (no music)
    by Riccio —
        (the cripple)

Drum Roll (consider court dance to drum only preceding & closing.)
    curtains open
    Elizabeth revealed *in box*
3 staff beats
    Elizabeth makes gesture
Drum Roll —
    Herald moves forward with standard —
music — 8 measures
    Mary revealed in arch
<u>or</u>
    Herald moves

The final ten minutes of her life —
Her final act as a queen — when she is crowned by death —

If drum roll is used at beginning & end like elaborate court dance
no need for other music & no need to use company
in frame-work of music —

Platform is high enough for canopy — or else seats where company
sits to view the show facing front —
It is like monstrous chorus —
ceremonial of the drums —
(perhaps exclude Elizabeth) but if there on throne —
the viewing is ironic —

Drums
Blows of staff — taps of Elizabeth's fan — music

1) 8 measures —
    no action

2) 8 measures
    queen walks forward —

3) 8
    across to steps

4) 8
    ascends —
        company makes slow fall
            ? second or arabesque ?

5) ⎫ 8
   ⎬   company —
6) ⎮ 8   40 measures —
7) ⎬ 8   lament — anguish
8) ⎮ 8   ? perhaps 4 Marys?
9) ⎭ 8

    (suggestive of "veil of temple" rent)
    company veil faces & do not see her descend

10) ⎫ 8 — Queen descends
11) ⎬ 8   ? front or back ?
12) ⎭ 8

Section II

"her servants who sat around the bed for the last time thot she slept
not, albeit her eyes were closed, & her face tranquil, & she seemed
to be laughing with the angels. . . ."   (302)

"The sheriff entered with his white staff in his hand" . . .

. . . "Melville took from the altar the ivory crucifix & gave it to Hannibal
Stouvant to carry before her ere she passed the threshold" . . .

. . . "and taking the Crucifix from Hannibal, the Queen bade farewell
to her servants & they took leave of her with cries & lamentations,
kissing her hands, some her feet, some her dress"

"Weep not, for you shall shortly see Mary Stuart at the end of all her sorrows. You shall report that I died true & constant in my religion & firm in my love for Scotland & France"

"Since she could not leave Scotland, she had established a Little France for herself in Holyrood, a tiny corner of the world where, withdrawn from inquisitive eyes, she could follow her most heartfelt inclinations. It was her Trianon. In the round tower of Holyrood she had her rooms equipped after the French model, with Gobelins brought from Paris, Turkey carpets, ornate beds & other furnishings, pictures in gilt frames, her finely bound books — Erasmus, Rabelais, Ariosto, Ronsard. Here they talked French & lived French. In the evening, by the light of the flickering candles, music was performed, verses were read aloud, and madrigals were sung. For the first time at this miniature court, were staged on the western side of the North Sea & the Channel those masques which were subsequently to attain their highest blessing in the English theatre. Dancing would continue till long after midnight. In one of the masques, 'The Purpose', Mary appeared as a young man, wearing black silk breeches, while Chastelard wore a woman's gown — a sight which would certainly have aroused the fury of John Knox"   (Zweig — (65)

??(a masque before an episode)?
Episode with Chastelard — 68 —
"His death was like a ballad"

Miniature of a Queen —

～～～～～～～～～～～～～～～～～～～～～～～～～～～～～～～～～～～～～

. . .

Holbein's "Alphabet of the Dance of Death"
"They trailed along in the wake of the black & bony drummer; step by step, year after year, monarchs & regents, earls & other men of birth & station, priests & warriors, striplings & elders, all sacrificing themselves for her who, tho' innocent, was yet guilty of their drear fate and had to atone for it with hers. Seldom has it been decreed that one woman should have so many deaths woven into the tapestry of her life. Like some dark magnet, she lured the men who came into contact with her to enter the spellbound circle of her personal doom. He who crossed her path, whether as friend or foe, was condemned to mischance, & to violent death. No luck ever blessed him who hated Mary Stuart, & those who loved her were consigned to an even more terrible end"   (70–71)

Tattoo —
    Elizabeth & Mary
        in duel

or
4 Marys & 4 lovers —
        or
group in slow motion dance around the 2 Queens.

Executioner's tattoo —
    men —   ?   women
            Darnley   4 Marys —
            Riccio
            Bothwell

~~~~~~

Those who died for her & in her sphere of magnetism —
        ~~~~~~

            or
Elizabeth & Mary in duel —

"Mary Stuart as woman was wholly woman, first, last & for
always . . ."   (77)

(tattoo — game of tennis between 2 Queens —
            Mary — a priest
            Elizabeth — a minister —

When the queens missed the ball — the priest & minister took the
thrust —
            or
The Queens
        & the courtiers —

"Mary Stuart never gave anything creative to the land of her birth
except the saga of her life"   (81)

"Mary Stuart was Mary Stuart, & nothing more; whereas Elizabeth was
Elizabeth plus Cecil, plus Leicester, plus Walsingham, plus the superla-
tive energies of her subjects — "   (81)

"Mary Stuart wanted to be resplendent here & now; Elizabeth Tudor,
the thrifty & far-sighted, devoted her best powers to the future of her
nation" —   (82)

In My End Is My Beginning / 435

"Elizabeth, the realist, the conquered in the realm of history; whereas Mary, the romanticist, has conquered in the realm of poetry & legend"

(83)

"The story of the duel between Elizabeth Tudor & Mary Stuart . . . was always malice confronting malice & never courage confronting courage" —

(83)

(Court tennis is believed to have originated (about the 14 Century) in medieval France. . . . it was patronized by both French & English royalty . . . & it is often called tennis royal —)   Col. Encyclo. (470)

End of tennis — ball seems to go wild — or else Mary turns to see a man (Darnley — Bothwell?)

Perhaps night dress could be reminiscent of her first bridal dress —

(Baring — 5)

Her wedding day — Apr. 24 —
Saint for the day —
        The Penitent Thief —

"Pageant & Triumphs"   Baring (7)

"And there were horses upon which Princes were mounted, made of wicker & covered with gold & silver trappings; & unicorns & ships with silver masts & sails of gauze, which sailed in mimic voyage round the hall."
                                                                            Baring (7)

See Ronsard on Mary —
"In this period of dule the queen, who was dressed all in white, & was more beautiful than she has ever been before or since, for her whiteness which was extreme became her, wavered for a time between two desires: the desire to pass from the life of the Courts & the desire to rule. And it was the latter which prevailed"   Baring — 11

Riccio —
Darnley
Bothwell   24 yrs
M. d'Anville — a "braggart of false pretense" —

". . . at Shrove-tide, there was the grandest feast which had ever been seen in Scotland. . . . The Queen still wore her dule-robes of black & white, & she was attended by her gentlewomen & her maidens, apparelled, as were the four Maries, in black & white . . ."   Baring 30

"The two armies remained standing in order one before the other from eleven o'clock in the morning until five o'clock in the evening. And on the Queens standard there was a lion, & on that of the Lord's was a white ensign on which was pictured a dead man near a tree, who was the late King; & a child, representing the Prince, holding a small scroll on which was written: Judge & Revenge my Cause, O Lord."   Baring 64

The curiosity & courtesy of legend are so beguiling & so great —

Visual image as imagined —

Two platforms — small r. & l.
in Tennis game — Elizabeth on one, Mary on the other, dance between —

At the end. Elizabeth alone in a fury of simulated grief with the Mary platform vacant.   see — Zweig — (354)

"The Dance of Death that had begun with Chastelard had now drawn to a close. No one else, except Mary herself, would perish on behalf of her dream of power & greatness"   Zweig (321)

". . . the invisible presence of England's queen . . ."

"as a great princess she wished to die a great death; —   Zweig 345
& with the immaculate sense of style which had always characterized her, with her native artistry & her inborn talent for seemly behavior on solemn occasions, Mary prepared for her exit from life, as one prepared for a festival, a triumph, a grand ceremony."   345

". . . the prisoner had a gold & jewelled ciborium containing a conse-crated wafer sent her by the pope, with a unique dispensation to administer the Eucharist to herself if denied the attendance of a priest" . . .   Zweig 346

For final robing see p. 346 Zweig

Description of hall & scaffold —   (349)

"With unmoved countenance Mary entered the hall. A Queen since she was but a few days old, she had learned to demean herself royally, & this exalted art did not forsake her in the supreme moment. Head erect, she mounted the two steps to the scaffold. Thus, proudly, when a girl of 15, she had ascended the throne of France;"

unrobing —   352

"on no one (however much the books & reports may lie about the matter) can the execution of a human being produce a romantic & touching impression. Always death by the executioner's axe must be a horrible spectacle of slaughter — "   352

In My End Is My Beginning / 437

<u>A</u>

Hold 8
walk 8 front — turning on 8th
walk 8 diag. to steps — hold 8th
ascend steps —

<u>B</u>

Descent — 8 steps —
    (catch to front)
High kick
circular kick
    into tight turn   Touch
                                   platform
Bourrees to st. r.   st. L. in profile
    hands & arms locked — /   arabesque — dress.
                           /
High kick front   come erect — turn to
    waltz turn   platform — hands back.

3 times to dress on platform —
    Bowing head to platform in profile
                        on st. r. of dress
spin to center — left arms to throne

                    ↓

<u>C</u>   Mary's first solo —
        Section II.

Center entrance at back where she first enters —
Kerchief around r. wrist holding l. hand. (same as the eye-binding piece)

1)   Knee crawl forward   hands at abdomen holding dress
      face upstage   then elbows come sharply together
      knee crawl forward
      face upstage
      knee crawl forward
                    face upstage
                        then
      quick spinning turn d. st. L.
2)   Slow fall in wide 2nd — use arms on floor
3)   Bourree st. r. using arms.
4)

      Cave turn
      step draw
      side extension

step draw
cave turn
step draw
side extension
step draw
      into 2 knee crawls upstage
         kneel in front of dress
         hands on platform

1 diag. — to st. L —
facing upstage —
2nd to kneel
at platform
at dress

D

Duet

Variation
    Entrance of Marys for dressing
    3 X 4
    plus 2

Development
    Dance of Marys — 8 X 4
    plateau —
      6 X 4
        Mary the Queen

Variation
    5 X 4   —   men —
    3 Strokes of doom — 3 X 4
            plus 1 — 2
      dwindling away —
    until everyone leaves —
    The Queen —
      6 X 4
      6 X 4
      plus 1 hold 2 —
    percussion

E
Break thru after dressing as girls take back fall.

Coda — F
Strokes of doom — hold
1)   2X   1{High kick 1 — circular kick.

gesture — wide 2nd & recover to 1st
    into

    ↓

2)   forward fall in wide 2nd
       & rise —   (2) rise —
       (6 counts)   measures —

3)   Walk of room in farewell
       ending st. r.
       4 X 4

4)   3 cave turns   *between each but only 1 after 3 turn*

2 step draws facing upstage
slow walk upstage to dress
               low bow
— face front   (sarabande)
               on high note
   kneel   rise
               quick walks
  crossing   to scaffold
               st. r & up st.
rise — hand to mouth
final gesture of hand.
        as a kiss —

In silence —   Heralds enter at back
            Executioner mounts to top —
            Mary — gesture with hands — ?

G Executioner — 8 steps to top
Six pieces —

                  I
1)   *Executioner descends* chair turns — Elizabeth revealed
       Mary faces Elizabeth
       Mary in high kick walk
       alternating to st. r. platform
       4 times — twist r into bourree
                 " L " high kick
        mount small platform
       Stand on platform wide stance
       semi plié —

2) Harp — Elizabeth's gesture
    E. rises on end of 1st piece

〜〜〜〜〜〜〜〜〜〜〜〜〜〜〜〜〜〜〜〜〜〜〜〜〜〜〜

Executioner descends — 8 steps

〜〜〜〜〜〜〜〜〜〜〜〜〜〜〜〜〜〜〜〜〜〜〜〜〜〜〜

? ?

1) Ex enters center with racquets
strides out on percussion

II

Executioner
descends with Elizabeth
touching his shoulder

Elizabeth descends
Elizabeth's dance.
   4 alternating high kicks to st. L —
   wide Cave turn
   bourree to st. R.
Darts to L.   stance
   (with Mary) Ex.

2) Ex. jumps & turns
into kneel — 2X

H

   stance —
      2 Queens face

Executioner enters & presents racquets —
Enter from wings   queens?
? 4 men walk forward
   as Executioner walks to Center with 4 men jumping
   Heralds extend net — queens?

                        I   Game

                  III
Entrance of 4 Marys —
Court dance

                     girls in lean on men
End of III —
   Executioner walks to Elizabeth in silence
   holds

                  IV
girls in lean on men
                     Elizabeth —
On 1st gong   — 1st stroke

In My End Is My Beginning / 441

                                    Mary
         2nd gong   2nd stroke
    or bells continue play —

    As girls come off men's shoulders & tip, Executioner walks with
    Elizabeth's racquet to st. r. & takes Marys & exits

    Executioner's entrance with racquets
  ?   (air turns with walk between to front)   ?
         ?spins?   same progressing back —
    Entrance of Heralds — fondé low — each side

In IV
    Perhaps men could lift Elizabeth after wide seconds by men — or
    part way thru them so that she towers over Mary
    All this before her turns — perhaps these taken diag. back from
    Mary to st. L. & then walk to her platform
             Mary falls wide 2nd

End of III
    Executioner standing behind net jumps 4X in silence —
    Exits on percussion —

                              IV
                                   Elizabeth's turns

        ⎧ 1 kick l.   As men make beats
        ⎪ 1 circular kick r.   in wide second
   4X   ⎨ facing front   Elizabeth crosses
        ⎪ after each kick   from st. L to St. R
    as men take beats   with high kicking
    in wide second —   walks —
    Then bourree change
    in walking tempo   During this Mary
    to center before   stands defiantly
    exit
        Turns —
        walks on 6th   Snares —
        measure to   Exit of
        platform St. L.   all men with
                                   standard bearers.
    As Heralds go upstage
    & men jumping forw
    in 2nd Ex exits |
                                             |
                                             |
                                             ↓

The Notebooks of Martha Graham / 442

1) On quiet measure
   Mary covers face with hands
2) knee crawls to st. L.
   "   "   " st. R & kneel on platform
3) On mounting chords arms slowly make full circle to prayer
   bend to touch platform & pushing into a rise —
   On continuous chords
   Back fall — rise to knees facing front & stand —
                kiss —

3 high kick walks upstage
center on tympany —
final gesture of hand —
Ex. mounts to first level —

V

             first 2 notes still —
men & women enter on 1 of 1st 3
         small ecstatic turns d. st. 6 X 3
Mary walks slowly to front
          (7 counts)
On bourrees of girls she spins upstage center —

On 5 counts — ? or kneel on platform st. r.
?   high kicking walk forward
     with knee crawl —1 high kick
                       1 circular
                       1 high
                       1 knee crawl
men go around her   (to rise
She walks between lines touching their hands —

mounts to first level at end of piece —
(Executioner mounts in silence 8?)
Elizabeth crosses to st. R.

VI

men & women in despairing fall & bow —
Elizabeth walks thru to Mary's platform
girls knee ripple
men falls in 2nd following them.
Ex on heels — turns standard —
Mary sits on throne
Executioner kisses her hand —

In My End Is My Beginning / 443

She rises
He tips chair
She kneels —

Group in turns — girls high —
Elizabeth weeping d. st. L.

Between 6 pieces —

Before 1st   from 1st level
    Executioner mounts to throne to stand beside chair —
8 steps   Turns it on music
        stands behind chair
Before 2nd
    Heralds face platform & lift standards —

8 counts Elizabeth descends with Ex. & dances —
    as she descends standards lowered & men face her as she makes
    high kicks — on wide turn they face front —

End of 2nd   8 counts
    men jump
    heralds stretch net
    queens walk to sides —
    with racquets —

End of 3rd
    where girls are leaning —
    Ex. walks to Elizabeth along stretched net
    (kneels? — stands ?)

End of 2nd
    Executioner enters on music & presents racquets
    men jump —

Before 3rd
8 steps Executioner exits
    net is stretched

End of 4th
    Exit on snares of
    Elizabeth   down stage L
    Heralds
    4 men —
        (Mary d. st. R.)

Before 5th
    Executioner mounts to first level

Before 6th
    Executioner to top

In 4th when men put girls down ex. walks across to take
Mary's racquet —
        4 X 4

End of 4th
    Ex. mounts to top —

End of 5th
    Elizabeth crosses to st. r.

Staff 3X
4 jumps facing front — men with 4 strokes of racket
Mary misses
    Mary 1
    Eliz 2
    Mary 3
    Eliz 4
            (Mary misses)   back fall?
4 jumps upstage facing — men —

1st drum roll
    Elizabeth walks high to st. r
        alternating kicks with catch step between
        4X — to touch foot to platform
    (Mary turns off upstage)

Girls enter

"A novel in a sigh"
  6 Bagatelles —
 1 Duet
 2 woman
 3 man
 4 woman
 5 man
 6 Duet

small enragements

meeting & parting
or
quarrel
&
making up again
reconciliation

6 Pieces —

Elegies —

or
Invocation of the inner angel

Notes on The Witch of Endor and Circe

The Witch of Endor: photograph by Martha Swope

Suggestions for the characterization for Judith —

Possible use of back of dress as head covering — to be removed before the swoop.

The bow — of acceptance —

Going to tree & wind dress tight like sarong —

In flute solo use eye as shield —

Stay at tree during wedding

release dress & stagger thru arches to be caught in spears —

Wind dress again —

There are 3 aspects — the widow, the warrior, the courtezan

after Battle —
    men go to thrones
    David waits —
    men approach him —
    He faces them
    They join him & follow or carry him off as king —
    Saul watches them go
    Then turns to his throne
    He is utterly alone except for the Witch —
    He may fall —
    On Samuel's music she makes gesture to comfort him —
    Duet —
      Saul — Witch —
    Tender — compassionate on Witch's part
    Bewildered, grief-stricken on Saul's part
    Occasional bursts of majesty & anger —

Last section — Witch —
    after men go to thrones Saul & David step apart —
    The break is irrevocable —
    David turns his back on Saul & looks at men (his)
    Then turns & appears to walk thru Saul —
    His men follow & they exit st. L.
    Saul faces his men —
    They defect —
    It is disorganized like a rout & they exit —

Single flute note — <u>alone</u>
Saul, looks about alone
(Witch upstage with her head on her knee — sitting —
Saul little wandering
Saul comes upstage to witch on solo cello — kneels —
Witch rises — Witch moves d. st. center —
Saul goes near throne
Shivers — falls —
?   Witch circled him?

          Witch of Endor —

Witch
King Saul
King David
Evil One — Tempter

Soldiers —

Saul's men	David's men
1 Bill Luther	1 Clive
2	2 Gene M.
3	3

2 girls —
    Nolmi — Juliette

∼∼∼∼∼∼∼∼∼∼∼∼∼∼∼∼∼∼∼∼∼∼∼∼∼∼∼∼∼∼∼∼∼∼

Scene opens —
    Saul & David on thrones — St. r.
    men grouped behind — 3 on Saul's 1 — three on David's r.

    Witch center —
    all rather dim except on Saul as he begins —

Saul's solo —
    despair — doubt — anguish —
      (Saul rolls to his throne)
    Witch thrusts her hand thru veil
    shows red leg —
    rises —
    Witch advances forward
    unveils face —
    advances to Saul
      with accented walk r. knee up & down sharply — 5 X
    Covers Saul with veil

.   (sits on edge of throne)
                on low tone
        goes around throne wrapping
        Saul in veil   silence
high kick? 3 high kicks (low tone) st. <u>L.</u>
            2 X twitches to St. L. (foot out & in) Torn between?
            (Saul following wrapped in veil — crawling)
            2 X more twitches to center
Witch moves St. L.

        Saul rolls to throne with veil — rises on it
        Witch 3 kicks in place
        high note Saul on throne — throws veil to Evil —
        Witch gestures to Saul
        Saul comes to St. L. 2 pitch falls
        <u>M</u>. bourree place —
        M. to wall — (on another note)
        on high note — goes to wall — Saul comes
        W. moves down st C — She throws Saul back —
2 circle kicks —
        back to seat on high melody —
        sits in her place

K. David's solo —
        sits on his throne turns his back as Evil Spirit enters —
"The Evil spirit was upon him"
pushes Saul
rides Saul
stands on Saul
Evil spirit gestures to girls & returns to throne area
girls in dance to David
pitched fall —
        girls touch K. David's leg —
David rises — passes leg thru —
girls rise & go around <u>David</u>
                etc —
circular kicks around etc
pitch fall forward & turn on back —
K. David's solo —
girls repeat dance —
run to Saul
David sits
pitch fall girls —

Saul crosses — takes cape
solo —
Then Duet with Witch —
She kicks his hand away 2X
moves forward as tho
Turns, goes to her piece
Bert turns her —
struggle —
She spins him into D. St. r.
when he returns to her he falls at
her feet — During this she rocks forw &
    back side to side as in
    beginning of "possession"
On high note she gives into prophecy —
on rumbling struggles, takes up & puts on her cloak of prophecy —
She becomes witch.

beckons to Saul —
He comes —
She turns Saul
 " " swooping turns to wall with gesture to Saul.
grabbing at spikes in wall — turns — does shiver — cape caught in
hands — 4 hieratic walks to Saul — Covers him — sits
Wall rises — she faces front —
Anger of Witch —
turns to wall —
throws cloak over l. arm
  " " " r. arm
brings it up to frame face —
turns front
moves across to S. r. with cloak at temples —
low steps — swaying in 2nd — agitating cape.
5X to D. st. R.
walks —
 front
 r.
 back
 L.
 front —
Turns — opens cape goes to Saul in low stride
arrives in time for fanfare
unmasks Saul — throws cape on high climax to Evil spirit D. st. L.
He catches — tosses it into wings —

She beats Saul with her cape.
Walk center — go up on platform

Try to find place for dance of summons or conjuring before wall
descends — as tho' she made wall descend.

<u>(This is final version)</u> (<u>so far</u>)
opening — at wall on platform
In silence walk front
          "   r
          "   behind Saul's throne
Music on Saul's arch of back
He is aware of her — or has tho't of her.
Continue to walk thru most of Saul's dance —
She sits

As Saul sits on throne she thrusts hand thru veil
in rejection — warning
Unveils leg as if in warning — rises — walks to front
          3 diagonals
Unveils —   (or circular kicks?)

Advances to Saul as in warning or rejection — as tho' spirit quickening
                                  within to accept power.
5 accented walks — r. knee up sharply — (between ¼ turn to fr.)
Goes to Saul —
Rises on throne behind him —
He senses her presence —
uses r. arm to bar her passage,
      long note in silence
She advances to St. L 3 high kicks with L. like signal to begin
2 accented walks
2 high kicks
accented walks around Saul who has crawled after her.
Witch — 3 high kicks in place — at stool
Saul rolls to throne — rises
She advances to him —
2 pitched falls to her St. L.
She is at stool do. St. L.
She goes to wall —
Rises on ramp —
Saul approaches her —

She throws him back
She goes to front — 2 circle kicks
She walks back — up on piece

~~~~~~

David's solo
       she faces wall — in meditation —

~~~~~~~~~~~~~~~~~~~

Evil spirit
Temptor
      with action to Saul & David

~~~~~~

2 girls to David I go around Saul 3×

~~~~~~

David's second solo
David sits —
girls at his throne I go around Saul
I go to back & stand on piece girls 3×

~~~~~~

Long solo — Saul —
hand out — Saul seizes it — she rises
she crosses cape   hair pull — ?
She kicks his hand away 2×
walking front —
re-Turns to piece — at upper back level
Saul turns her —
She throws him off ??
Spins him to St. r.

~~~~~~

He has solo — returns to her, falls at her knees —
Throws him away & he spins —
      he comes on knees —

~~~~~~~~~~~~~~~

on high note she raises her hand in despair & accepts burden of
prophecy —
She picks up Cape —
      on boom
turns to front — goes d. St st. r.

as tho seeing 2 Kings on thrones

~~~~~~~~~~~~~   4 swooping turns to l.
(Think of place here for witch)

call Saul
grabs spikes   turn him to wall
    4 bending turns to wall
Turn to shiver front

4 Hieratic walks to Saul who is at stool —
She turns him to face wall — (She might have dance here)
                by removing cape to cover Saul
seats herself and covers Saul with cape —
He unveils himself under her cape.

~~~~~~

      Wall descends &

Samuel —   She encircles st.
                      when David takes sword

Saul
                      she goes to stool — diagonally
David   1st stab —
W. divination of stool —   2nd stab — cloak on thrones —

~~~~~~

                    as he rolls down she crosses to
                    cover him
Wall rises —   she goes to wall
Anger of Witch —   pushing it up.
dress on arms — 3 chords —

~~~~~~

She makes 5 turns St. R.
with cape at temples —
agitated — (Open cape)
moves in low crouching run
to Saul — after walk r — up — L — front

On Fanfare —
     She unmasks Saul
Throws disguise to Evil Spirit

Beats Saul with her Cape —
on drum role up st. to
goes up on platform
        (David & Saul center)

stay during battle music
Episode with Evil spirit, Saul-David
Wait 3 chords — walk between 2 kings —
Turn in front   (David turns away from Saul in silence.)
Go back to my throne

The Witch of Endor and Circe / 455

men
     again —
Exit K. David with men
Saul's men in rout —
She is turned upstage
Saul falls at her feet
cello music — she touches Saul
He touches her face —
Saul goes to st. r. shivers —
Soldier walks —
She is sitting — on stool —

Light goes on —
He reaches for it —
        in compassion
She thrusts him back —
He goes to run around —
When he goes to throne she takes his face, leads him to C.
Walk together for walk together d. C. 5 X —
separate —
she stands on stool —
Saul runs around — Fanfare
He kneels at her feet
After men off —
              3 turns —
Then seeking to keep him from throne — 4 touches —
Drape throne —
his run —
3 great chords to kneel

     Witch of Endor —
opening — standing on piece, perhaps facing audience —

Walk in silence to front
        " st. r.
        around Saul's throne
           Music and Saul's opening —
Walk around stage all during Saul's solo, keeping to edges —
Saul sits on throne
She Sits —
    hand out
    reveal knee
    walk forward

Unveiling —
Turn to Saul —
Small accented steps to Saul — 5 X
Rise in back of him on throne.
Descend to front —
Saul tries to touch

3 high kicks to st. l. (r. leg.)
2 accented steps
2 high kicks St. L —
Go around Saul who has followed her — & then rolls to throne —
Witch following —
Saul follows with 2 pitched Rolls
She goes up to the wall.
She thrusts him away

walk to wall
front circular kick
then back to wall

She stands facing back
David's solo — (1st)

Also Evil spirit — on this (Ward's solo) she stands with r. l up on
spike —
When girls come to Saul she descends & encircles Saul
seated on stool st. L.
On David's 2nd solo, she stands again on piece —

When girls move she again circles Saul St. L.
going back to sit on David's 2nd solo —
Saul takes disguise —
She sits or stands at wall —

He comes to her —
hand again —   hair —
    she goes   walks front with kicking
    back to wall   away Saul's hand
    He reaches for her & I turn — throw him back — sits —
                        He does shoulder walk —
Finally falls at her feet —
                        He puts hands on knee
            she repels him & he spins st. r.
High note she lifts arm & accepts the prophecy —

Puts on cloak —
3 slow chords to r.
goes to st. r —

The Witch of Endor and Circe / 457

4 bending turns to St. L — calls him.
I turn him to wall — & do 4 bending turns to wall
goes to wall — clutches spikes —
shiver facing front
hieratic walks to Saul — 4X

she sits — covers him
Wall descends —
Vision —   sits — then sits on
                                                  Saul's throne —
She sits on stool —   Wall starts up
Then 3 men — string quartet — David's walk to his throne
Vision —
When wall rises she goes to wall as tho' pushing it.

                        3 chords —
Cape across her arms — turns with hands at temples — agitated 5X
angry —
        fr. St.
Walks r S
        up. S
        L. S
        d. S.
Releases Cape — in low walk to Saul —
On fanfare she unmasks him
throws it to Evil One —
Beats Saul with Cape —
Drum roll — go upstage —
David & Saul — move to center
men's entrance
when they finish —   ⎧ hold
She walks thru them   ⎨ walk fr?
                        ⎩ walk up
On silence David faces men
David & men exit
Sauls men rout.
I am up on wall —
Stay there
Let Saul come to her —
He goes down piece
cello — she turns — & touches him —
        He touches her face —

She moves to d. st. l. sit on stool

Saul dances
until light on Samuel
She moves center to stop him —
struggle at wall —
He rolls —
I stay at wall
He does soldier walk —
struggle — 3X —
he runs
      near   She takes his face
Face — raise him
walk to center

Processional to fr. 5X
We separate
I go to stool — stand on it
Fanfare —
Saul clasping her knees
all exit —
I shield him from throne
3 touches — turn
1 touch —
go to throne — cover it
Then he runs — opens cape
falls, she goes to him
covers him —

Entrance of Ulysses —
as tho' calling his men — (4X)
Entrance of animals —   deer?
                                 goat?

Harp — flute — etc —
Trumpet Ulysses (strings —
Harp — flute — etc —
       (glockenspiel)   snake
                   — Ulysses
        flute & oboe (strings)
strings first — then trumpet —

                       Snake — Bob P.
                       Snake — Dick

                              Goat? — Bob
                              deer? — Bob
                              elephant
                              A Man — Clive
                              Lion — Clive?

                              Man — Cohan?

Anguish of Ulysses
creatures who were men creep about him —

transition — entrance of Circe — (no strings)
                              all winds
Aria (with celeste)
     love for suffering of man & release as they become animals.
     relationship to creatures
     (Perhaps Ulysses not visible)

Section 3   animals
                       & Circe
              ? ⎧ Circe   ?
     trio   ⎨ lion
              ⎩ deer

Perhaps in Section IV
it is the man who makes Ulysses remember
~~~~~~

First Performances of Dances Discussed in the Notebooks

Beggar Prophet

> not choreographed

Errand into the Maze

> *Errand into the Maze*
> Music by Gian Carlo Menotti
> Settings by Isamu Noguchi
> First performance February 28, 1947

Imaginary Gardens

> *Embattled Garden*
> Music by Carlos Surinach
> Settings by Isamu Noguchi
> First performance April 3, 1958

> *One Other Gaudy Night*
> Music by Halim El-Dabh
> Settings by Jean Rosenthal
> First Performance   April 20, 1961

Techniques of Ecstasy

> not choreographed

Pocahontas

> not choreographed

The Eye of Anguish

> *Alcestis*
> Music by Vivian Fine
> Settings by Isamu Noguchi
> First performance April 29, 1960

> *The Scarlet Letter*
> not choreographed

> *Eye of Anguish*
> Music by Vincent Persichetti
> Settings by Henry Kurth
> Costumes by Fred Cunning
> First performance January 22, 1950

Voices of Desire

> *Phaedra*
> Music by Robert Starer
> Settings by Isamu Noguchi
> First performance March 4, 1962

Observations on Deaths and Entrances

> *Deaths and Entrances*
> Music by Hunter Johnson
> Settings by Arch Lauterer
> Costumes by Edythe Gilfond
> First performance July 18, 1943

I Salute My Love

Ardent Song
Music by Alan Hovhaness
First performance March 18, 1954

Notes on Voyage

Voyage
Music by William Schuman
Settings by Isamu Noguchi
Costumes by Edythe Gilfond
First performance May 17, 1953

Fragments for Solo Dances

Deaths and Entrances
see page 461

Appalachian Spring
Music by Aaron Copland
Settings by Isamu Noguchi
Costumes by Edythe Gilfond
First performance October 30, 1944

Night Journey
Music by William Schuman
Settings by Isamu Noguchi
First performance May 3, 1947

Cave of the Heart (Serpent Heart)
Music by Samuel Barber
Settings by Isamu Noguchi
Costumes by Edythe Gilfond
First performance May 10, 1946

The Dark Meadow of the Soul

Dark Meadow
Music by Carlos Chávez
Settings by Isamu Noguchi
Costumes by Edythe Gilfond
First performance January 23, 1946

Preliminary Studies for Clytemnestra
Canticle for Innocent Comedians

Clytemnestra
Music by Halim El-Dabh
Settings by Isamu Noguchi
First performance April 1, 1958

Canticle for Innocent Comedians
Music by Thomas Ribbink
Settings by Frederick Kiesler
First performance April 22, 1952

The Trysting Tent

Ardent Song
see above

Canticle for Innocent Comedians
see above

The Triumph of Saint Joan
Music by Norman Dello Joio
Settings by Frederick Kiesler
First performance December 5, 1951

Alcestis
see page 461

Seraphic Dialogue
Music by Norman Dello Joio
Settings by Isamu Noguchi
First performance May 8, 1955

The Bronzeless Net

Clytemnestra
see above

For Folly

Tam Lin
not choreographed

Garden of Eden
not choreographed

Anna Livia Plurabelle
not choreographed

Center of the Hurricane

not choreographed

Preliminary Studies for Mary Queen of Scots
Chronique, by St. John Perse

Episodes: Part I
Music by Anton von Webern
Settings by David Hays
Costumes by Karinska
First performance May 14, 1959

Mendicants of Evening
Music by David Walker
Setting by Fangor
First performance May 2, 1973

Folklore Communications —
Additional Studies for Saint Joan
Heloise and Abelard

The Triumph of Saint Joan
see page 462

Seraphic Dialogue
see page 462

Time of Snow
Music by Norman Dello Joio
Settings by Rouben Ter-Arutunian
First performance May 24, 1968

Additional Studies for Phaedra

Phaedra
see page 461

Choreographic Studies for Clytemnestra and Alcestis

Clytemnestra
see page 462

Alcestis
see page 461

Additional Notes for Night Journey

Night Journey
see page 462

Preliminary Notes for Hecuba

Cortege of Eagles
Music by Eugene Lester
Settings by Isamu Noguchi
First performance February 21, 1967

Clytemnestra
A Partial Record of Action

Clytemnestra
see page 462

First Performances / 463

Judith — Character Studies

Judith
Music by William Schuman
Settings by Charles Hyman,
    William Sherman, and
    Isamu Noguchi
First performance January 4, 1950

Legend of Judith
Music by Mordecai Seter
Settings by Dani Karavan
First performance October 25, 1962

Choreographic Indications for Samson Agonistes

Samson Agonistes
(Visionary Recital)
Music by Robert Starer
Settings by Rouben Ter-Arutunian
First performance March 6, 1962

Later Thoughts on Heloise and Abelard

Time of Snow
see page 463

Judith — Additional Studies

Judith
see above

Legend of Judith
see above

In My End Is My Beginning
Studies for Mary Queen of Scots

Episodes: Part I
see page 463

Notes on The Witch of Endor and Circe

The Witch of Endor
Music by William Schuman
Settings by Ming Cho Lee
First performance November 2, 1965

Circe
Music by Alan Hovhaness
Settings by Isamu Noguchi
First performance September 6, 1963

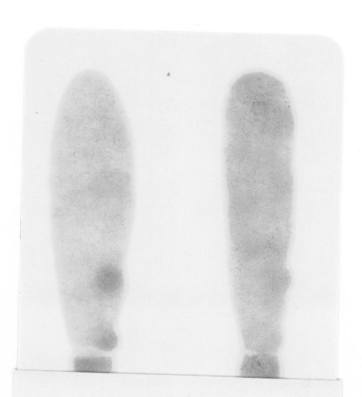

Once upon a time —

there was a lady, who (for her cruel
ways) was imded an enchanted moat
by the master of the dark forest in
which she was hopelessly lost—

She was bewitched into being a
sort of serpent princess,
condemned to wear a terrifying
& painful crown until she found
some means by which to break
the spell—

Lost & desperate she devised
small dances in memory of
the hidden & lost Sun — & in
time her small prayerful
dances reached the Sun & he
penetrated the forest breaking
the spell of darkness & &
freeing her from the painful
enchantment —

The place of action is the phantom arena
of a woman's being the time, the duration
of one night — the characters, herself
peopled by two women, those of day
who speak & those of night who are
silent a part of the shadowy
mystery of night itself —

The time of the action is the duration
of one night — night-fall
                      moon rise
                         "   high
                         "   set
                    deep dark
                    dawn
                         (a morning without clocks)

The action takes place on 2 levels
of experience —
There is a supper scene — in a
courtyard or on a balcony or
in some cool remote room

in an unnamed country
of a tropical nature—
there are 3 men & one woman—
The men speak — they are living
are few but they are philosoph-
yzing about the great images
by which we live—

A sentence — a word — releases
the silent woman into the scene
of the night — her inner woman—
never leaving the room yet she
leaves it — & the gate is opened
by a keeper of the gate — &
she enters a phantom arena
peopled by 3 maladows & finally
creatures of
silent — & even they
memories —

x